Gender and the Politics of Rights and Democracy
in Latin America

Also by Nikki Craske:

WOMEN AND POLITICS IN LATIN AMERICA
DISMANTLING THE MEXICAN STATE? (*co-edited with Rob Aitken, Gareth Jones and David Stansfield*)
MEXICO AND THE NAFTA: WHO WILL BENEFIT? (*co-edited with Victor Bulmer-Thomas and Mónica Serrano*)

Also by Maxine Molyneux:

WOMEN'S MOVEMENTS IN INTERNATIONAL PERSPECTIVE: LATIN AMERICA AND BEYOND
HIDDEN HISTORIES OF GENDER AND THE STATE IN LATIN AMERICA (*co-edited with Elizabeth Dore*)

Gender and the Politics of Rights and Democracy in Latin America

Edited by

Nikki Craske

and

Maxine Molyneux

Women's Studies
at York

First published 2002 by
PALGRAVE
Houndmills, Basingstoke, Hampshire RG21 6XS and
175 Fifth Avenue, New York, N. Y. 10010
Companies and representatives throughout the world

PALGRAVE is the new global academic imprint of
St. Martin's Press LLC Scholarly and Reference Division and
Palgrave Publishers Ltd (formerly Macmillan Press Ltd).

ISBN 0–333–94948–X

This book is printed on paper suitable for recycling and
made from fully managed and sustained forest sources.

A catalogue record for this book is available from the British Library.

Library of Congress Cataloging-in-Publication Data

Gender and the politics of rights and democracy in Latin
America / edited by Nikki Craske and Maxine Molyneux.
        p.cm.
    "This edited volume emerged out of a conference organized
by the editors...held at the Institute of Latin American Studies
of the University of London" – Acknowledgements.
    Includes bibliographical references and index.
    ISBN 0–333–94948–X (cloth)
    1. Women's rights – Latin America – Congresses. 2. Women's
rights – Latin America – Case studies. I. Craske, Nikki. II. Molyneux, Maxine.

HQ1236.5.L37 G455 2001
305.42'098–dc21
                                                              2001036886

10   9   8   7   6   5   4   3   2   1
11   10   09   08   07   06   05   04   03   02

Printed and bound in Great Britain by
Antony Rowe Ltd, Chippenham, Wiltshire

Contents

List of Tables

List of Abbreviations

ACOMUC	Asociación de Cooperación con la Mujer/Peruvian Association for Cooperation with Peasant Women
AL	Alianza Liberal/Liberal Alliance (Nicaragua)
AMNLAE	Asociación de Mujeres Nicaragüenses Luisa Amanda Espinoza/Luisa Amanda Espinoza Association of Nicaraguan Women
ANR	Asociación Nacional Republicana/National Republican Association (Paraguay)
ARENA	Alianza Republicana Nacional/National Republican Alliance (El Salvador)
CCP	Confederación Campesina del Perú/Peruvian Peasant Confederation
CEDAW	Convention on the Elimination of all forms of Discrimination Against Women
CEPAL/ECLAC	Comisión Económica para América Latina y el Caribe/Economic Commission for Latin America and the Caribbean
CFEMEA	Centro Feminista de Estudos e Assessoria/Feminist Research and Advisory Centre (Brazil)
CHR	Commission for Human Rights
CIDEM	Centros de Información de los Derechos de la Mujer/Information Centres for Women's Rights (Chile)
CIM	Comisión Interamericana de Mujeres/InterAmerican Commission for Women
CLADEM	Comité de América Latina y el Caribe para la Defensa de los Derechos de la Mujer/Latin American and Caribbean Committee for the Defence of Women's Rights
CLT	Consolidação das Leis Trabalhistas/Consolidated Labour Law (Brazil)
CNA	Confederación Nacional Agraria/National Agrarian Confederation (Peru)
CNMD	Concertación Nacional de Mujeres por la Democracia/National Coalition of Women for Democracy (Chile)

COFEAPRE	Comisión Femenina Asesora de la Presidencia/Presidential Women's Advisory Commission (Venezuela)
CONAIE	La Confederación de Nacionalidades Indígenas del Ecuador/Confederation of Indigenous Nationalities of Ecuador
CONAMU	Consejo Nacional de Mujeres/National Council of Women (Uruguay)
CONAMUP	Comisión Nacional sobre Mujeres Peruanas/National Commission on Peruvian Woman
CONAPRO	Concertación Nacional Programática/National Consensus-Building Forum (Uruguay)
CONFENAIE	Confederación de Nacionalidades Indígenas de la Amazonia Ecuatoriana/The Confederation of Nationalities Indigenous to the Ecuadorian Amazonia
CONG	Coordinadora de Organizaciones No-Gubernamentales de Mujeres/Coordinating Committee of Women's Nongovernmental Organisations (Venezuela)
CSW	Commission on the Status of Women (UN)
CTV	Confederación de Trabajadores Venezolanos/Confederation of Venezuelan Workers
DINAMU	Dirección Nacional de la Mujer/National Women's Directorate (Ecuador)
ECOSOC	Commission for Economic and Social Rights
ECUARUNARI	The Awakening of Ecuador's Indians (in Quechua)
FCS	Federación de Centros Shuar/Shuar Federation (Ecuador)
FEDERCAMARAS	Venezuelan Federation of Chambers of Commerce and Production
FEINE	Ecuadorian Federation of Evangelical Indigenous
FEVA	Federación Venezolana de Abogadas/Venezuelan Federation of Women Lawyers
FIDEG	Fundación Internacional para el Desafío Económico Global/International Foundation for the Global Economic Challenge (Nicaragua)
FMLN	Frente Farabundi Martí para la Liberación Nacional/Farabundo Martí Front for National Liberation (El Salvador)
FSLN	Frente Sandinista para la Liberación Nacional/Sandinista Front for National Liberation (Nicaragua)
GEM	gender empowerment measurement

GNP	Gross National Product
ICCPR	International Covenant on Civil and Political Rights
ICESCR	International Covenant on Economic, Social and Cultural Rights
IDB	Inter-American Development Bank
IELSUR	Uruguayan Institute of Legal and Social Studies
ILO	International Labour Organisation
IML	Instituto Médico-Legal/Legal Medical Institute (Brazil)
IMM	Intendencia Municipal de Montevideo/Muncipal Government of Montevideo
INFM	Instituto Nacional de la Familia y la Mujer/National Institute for the Family and Women (Uruguay)
IPRE	Institute for the Prevention of Domestic Violence and Rehabilitation of Victims (Uruguay)
MNR	Movimiento Nacional Revolucionario/National Revolutionary Movement (Bolivia)
MUDE	Mujeres por la Democracia/Women for Democracy (Peru)
NGOs	Nongovernmental Organisations
NTAEs	non-traditional agricultural exports
OAS	Organisation of American States
OLM	Oficina Legal de la Mujer/Women's Legal Office (Nicaragua)
OMN	Oficina Nacional de la Mujer/National Women's Office (Venezuela)
PAIT	Programa de Apoyo de Ingreso Temporal/Temporary Aid and Income Programme (Peru)
PROMUDEH	Ministerio por la Promoción de la Mujer y del Desarrollo Humano/Ministry for the Promotion of Women and Human Development (Peru)
RSMLAC	Red de la Salud de las Mujer Latinoamericanas y del Caribe/Latin American and Caribbean Women's Health Network
RUVDS	Network against Domestic and Sexual Violence (Uruguay)
SERNAM	Servicio Nacional de la Mujer/National Women's Agency (Chile)
SIM	Serviço de Informação à Mulher/Women's Information Service (Brazil)
SIN	National Intelligence Service (Peru)

SNA	System of National Accounts
STJ	Superior Tribunal de Justiça/Higher Justice Court (Brazil)
UN	United Nations
UNDP	United Nations Development Programme
UNHR	Universal Declaration of Human Rights
UNICEF	United Nations Children's Fund
WID	Women in Development

Acknowledgements

This edited volume emerged out of a conference organised by the editors with the help of Virginia Vargas, which was held at the Institute of Latin American Studies of University of London. Thanks are due to the Institute of Latin American Studies for supporting the conference and to Tony Bell at ILAS who helped with the practicalities. The editors would like to thank Georgina Ashworth, Georgina Waylen, Teresa Sacchet, Karen Newman, Marilyn Thompson and Sîan Lazar who gave papers at the conference and to all who participated in the debates. We would also like to thank Niki Johnson and Anne-Marie Smith for their assistance with Gina Vargas' translation, and all the many women activists in Latin America who gave their time in interviews on the question of rights.

Notes on the Contributors

Nikki Craske is Director of the Institute of Latin American Studies, University of Liverpool. She has written extensively on Mexican politics and is author of *Women and Politics in Latin America* (1999). She is currently writing a book with Sylvia Chant, *Gender in Latin America* and is preparing a manuscript entitled *The Feminisation of Politics in Mexico*.

Elisabeth Jay Friedman is Assistant Professor of Comparative Politics in the Political Science Department at Barnard College, Columbia University. Her work focuses on the intersection(s) of gender, women's organising, civil society and democratisation in Latin America, as well as on the development of global civil society. In addition to her book *Unfinished Transitions: Women and the Gendered Development of Democracy in Venezuela, 1936–1996* (2000), she has published in journals such as *World Politics*, *Latin American Research Review*, and *Women and Politics*.

Jasmine Gideon is based at the University of Manchester, where she has been researching socioeconomic and gender issues. Her main areas of research include economies as gendered structures, health sector reforms and NGOs, and she has published in all these fields. She has recently completed her PhD on primary health care delivery in Chile.

Mala N. Htun is Assistant Professor of Political Science at the Graduate Faculty of Political and Social Science of New School University. She is author of a book on gender rights in Latin America to be published by Cambridge University Press and several articles on women in politics and public policy. She acts as advisor to the Inter-American Dialogue's Women's Leadership Conference of the Americas.

Niki Johnson was awarded her PhD in Politics in April 2000 from Queen Mary and Westfield College, University of London. Her doctoral thesis looked at gender citizenship, the women's movement and the state in Uruguay. She is currently living in Montevideo, Uruguay, and taking part in a research project on women's political participation at the Instituto de Ciencia Política of the Universidad de la República.

Mark P. Jones is Associate Professor in the Department of Political Science at Michigan State University. His work focuses on the influence of electoral laws and other political institutions on party systems, elite and mass political behaviour, and representation. In addition to *Electoral Laws and the Survival of Presidential Democracies* (1995) he has published widely, including recent articles in *Comparative Political Studies*, *Journal of Development Economics* and the *Journal of Politics*.

Fiona Macaulay is Research Fellow at the Institute of Latin American Studies at the University of London, and also participates in the Centre for Brazilian Studies, University of Oxford. She was previously Brazil Researcher at Amnesty International. Her present area of research concerns human rights and the reform of the criminal justice system in Brazil. She has also published articles on violence against women in Latin America and state gender policy and political parties in Brazil and Chile.

Maxine Molyneux has written extensively in the fields of feminist theory, political sociology and development studies. Her recent books include *Women's Movements in International Perspective: Latin America and Beyond* (2000) and *Hidden Histories of Gender and the State in Latin America* (co-edited with E. Dore, 2000). She is Professor of Sociology at the Institute of Latin American Studies, University of London, where she teaches courses on Society and Development, and Gender and Politics in Latin America. She is also acting as consultant to UNRISD on a year-long project entitled Substantiating Rights in a Disabling Environment.

Sarah A. Radcliffe (Department of Geography, University of Cambridge) researches issues of gender, race/ethnicity and nationhood in the Andes. Her work has covered themes of migration, Andean indigenous women, social movement organisations, the formation of national identities, and geographical and feminist social theory. Her books include *Viva: Women and Popular Participation in Latin America* (1993, edited with S. Westwood) and *Re-making the Nation: Place, Politics and Identity in Latin America* (1996, co-author).

Virginia Vargas is currently completing a Ford Foundation study of women's movements in four Latin American countries and is a member of the Peruvian NGO Centro de Mujeres: Flora Tristán. She has held teaching and research posts in Europe and Peru and has attended seminars, meetings and workshops around the world. In 1995 she was

Coordinator of Latin American and Caribbean NGOs for the IV World Conference of Women. She has published widely on the Latin American women's movement in Spanish and English.

Ceri Willmott completed her PhD in Anthropology at the London School of Economics in 1998. Her thesis, 'Gender, Citizenship and Reproductive Rights in the *Poblaciónes* of Santiago', examines the influence of cultural factors on women's ability to exercise their rights. She is a qualified lawyer. Until recently she was Head of Projects at a social development consultancy and is currently working as a freelance consultant in the field of social development.

1

The Local, the Regional and the Global: Transforming the Politics of Rights[1]

Maxine Molyneux and Nikki Craske

This book addresses the recent evolution of women's movements in Latin America, and, in so doing, seeks to demonstrate the wider relevance of this history for the comparative study of women's rights. To those who live in conditions of stable democracy, issues of rights and legal reform tend not to appear urgent or pressing unless as occurred in regard to reproductive rights, social movements make them so. In Latin America where liberal guarantees had been violated by decades of authoritarian rule, women's movements from the 1980s placed a special value on the 'right to have rights' and worked for the restoration of the rule of law, democracy and basic civil liberties. But at the same time, the language of rights and citizenship was deployed not only to restore or to improve upon formal legal rights, but also to deepen the democratic process. The affirmation of a culture of rights grew out of popular social movements in Latin America. 'Rights talk' was used to raise awareness among the poor and the socially marginalised of their formal legal rights, but also to call into question their lack of *substantive* rights. The language of rights thus became a way of making claims for social justice as well as for recognition in an idiom that framed such demands 'as a basic right of citizenship' (Baierle 1998: 124).

The focus of this book is on a central political issue facing Latin American women's movements, that of the potential and limits of post-authoritarian democracies as vehicles for the promotion of greater gender justice. The 1980s in Latin America were marked by the human and social costs of stabilisation and adjustment policies on the one hand, and the transition from authoritarian rule on the other.

By the 1990s, however, the end of the Cold War signalled a new international conjuncture which saw a more confident assertion of economic and political liberalism, but also a greater emphasis on human rights. The collapse of Soviet communism in 1989, coming after the painful reality of Latin America's 'lost decade' of economic crisis, was followed by a major reassessment of the goals of developmentagencies. In the 1990s a wave of UN Summits and Conferences sought to place issues of democracy, justice and rights on the development agenda. In the context of the continent-wide process of democratic consolidation that characterised the decade, women's movements were able to focus their attention on issues of rights and democracy in ways that were unthinkable in the 1970s and 1980s when the region's second wave feminism developed under the heel of military rule.

If issues of democracy, rights and justice were both revitalised and radicalised in the post-authoritarian democracies, this was a development that was also impelled by the international endorsement it received through the global summits that took place in the 1990s. This was an extraordinary period for international policy-making and standard setting in which UN conventions and regional agreements multiplied. Latin American governments readily signed up to many of these agreements to mark their re-entry into the international community. In so doing, they provided women's movements with the opportunity to advance reforms in women's position in a comparatively benign set of political circumstances.

The chapters in this volume analyse how, within specific national contexts, Latin American women's movements engaged the language of rights and the practice of democracy. They consider campaigns to change the law, including those which centred on improving female political representation through quotas, and those which made the issue of violence against women a major issue of public policy. Several authors examine critically the international instruments that served as a lever to press for reforms in the practice and letter of the laws pertaining to women. Others consider the ways that women's movements worked with notions of rights within poor communities. Taken together, these studies present a complex and contrasting picture of women's legal gains in post-authoritarian Latin America. While they show how the struggle for rights has potential for achieving greater gender equality, they also highlight the significant limits and difficulties of rights-based work.

Gender, rights and citizenship: twentieth-century developments

Women's activism around rights issues, including that engaged in by self-designated feminist organisations, has a long history in Latin America. In the late nineteenth century, feminist organisations, along with socialist and anarchist movements, demanded that women should be treated 'as equals not slaves' in the workplace and in the home. Suffrage movements were also active throughout Latin America, as were reform groups emerging from conservative Catholic and socialist currents campaigning for social rights and protection for mothers. Women therefore played an active part in the emergent civil societies of their nation-states, and through the course of the twentieth century came to occupy an increasingly visible role in political life as voters, movement and party activists and occasionally, as in the case of Eva Perón, as actors at the apex of political power.[2] Yet while some reforms were introduced over the course of the century, and women gained greater equality in the family and workplace as well as social rights as mothers, their presence in the public sphere as workers, professionals and traders co-existed with marked inequalities between the sexes in all areas of social life. This second class citizenship, both social and legal, was a source of growing female discontent. As the student movements of the late 1960s gathered momentum in Mexico, Argentina, Brazil and elsewhere, demands for equality, and for an end to illegitimate authority in the political and personal realms, became part of the language of revolt. In the 1970s following international trends, the region spawned a vibrant second wave feminism and an active and increasingly feminist popular[3] women's movement: these combined to provide the dynamic and support for women's demands in the region as a whole.

These movements were, however, overshadowed by the rise of military dictatorships in more than a dozen countries in the region. Some of these regimes resorted to forms of state terrorism, seeking not only to extinguish political life but engaging in extreme forms of human rights violations. In Central America and the Southern Cone where the repression was fiercest, many thousands were sent to their deaths, were 'disappeared' or were forced into exile. It was only slowly and where political conditions permitted, that the forces of civil society were able to regroup, and to demand the restitution of civilian rule. The literature on Latin America's transition from authoritarian rule has debated the relative importance, among other factors, of social movements and elite pacts in precipitating the demise of military rule.[4] Varied though the influence of these political forces was in the final outcome, few scholars doubted the importance of social movement activism in helping to accelerate regime change. Yet while the contribution of civil society as a whole was given early recognition in the transition literature, it took far longer for that of women's movements to be acknowledged. Feminist scholarship brought to light the *gendered* character of social movement activism and identified the multiple forms of women's movement that contributed to it.[5] Among the most celebrated were the protest movements of mothers of the disappeared such as the Madres de la Plaza de Mayo who succeeded in drawing international attention to human rights abuses in Argentina. However, also important were the feminist groups that worked in a wide range of activities such as publishing, advocacy and voluntary projects, and the sometimes extensive movements of low-income women who mobilised against the conditions of scarcity occasioned by the debt crisis and the stabilisation policies imposed to contain it.[6]

This gender-aware research demonstrated that women's activism in a variety of arenas made its own distinctive contribution to bringing the era of authoritarian states to a close. Women's movements contributed to the development of an autonomous civil society and helped to foster the spread of democratic and humanitarian values. They gained support from an international climate which was itself becoming more responsive to pressure from human rights movements both national and international. But, if women's movements were a vital force in the transition, and helped to create some of the conditions for revitalising democratic life, it was unclear if they would be able to sustain their momentum in the different conditions signalled by the return of civilian rule, and of 'politics as usual'. Some observers doubted that they could make the shift from being in opposition to securing a stake in the new 'masculinised' democracies that were emerging in the region (Safa 1990). Moreover, even if they did adapt their politics to take account of the new context, what role would these movements play, what campaigns would they advance, and what success would they have in meeting their demands?

The Latin American context

Here we come to the question of how far we can speak of a shared Latin American experience. While the case studies show that it is possible to identify many common trends in the strategies and perspectives of women's movements in Latin America, they also reveal considerable variations among countries with regard to outcomes. This reflects the region's historical, social and economic diversity. The specific evolution of state–society relations, the political complexion of post-authoritarian or post-conflict governments and the character and strength of civil society in particular countries have shaped the priorities, strategies and objectives of their women's movements. Latin America underwent major political change in the course of the last century, some provoked by external intervention, some reflecting the acute social tensions that accompanied the region's development. If its most recent convulsions were occasioned by brutal military regimes, its history from the 1930s was marked by the emergence of nationalist and populist leaders and by the impact of revolutionary upheavals in Bolivia, Cuba and Nicaragua. These more colourful moments, however, should not be seen as ideal-typical of Latin American formations: there were also states that managed to preserve stable democratic rule throughout these periods of change and to deliver a measure of well-being to their populations, Venezuela and Costa Rica among them.

Despite these contrasting histories, by the turn of the twenty-first century Latin America appeared to have achieved a consensus on core political values, with regional summits of the Organisation of American States (OAS) repeatedly affirming their commitment to institutional democracy and economic liberalism. Even so, political systems in Latin America and the Caribbean remained diverse, with liberal democracies co-existing with authoritarian quasi-democracies and, in Cuba, one case of state-centred socialism. In some countries too, the armed forces retained considerable influence over the political process.

Such political diversity is matched by a strikingly uneven range in the size of population and economic performance of Latin American States. At one extreme are the countries of five million or less inhabitants (Central America and Uruguay) and, at the other are the giants of the region, Brazil and Mexico with populations of over 170 million and 100 million respectively. Income per capita too, spans a wide spectrum from $1997 in Nicaragua to $12 730 in Chile, which are ranked 121 and 34 respectively in the global human development index.[7] This reflects the truism that there is no one 'Latin America', but a diverse range of dissimilar formations. While apparently united by a common history of Iberian colonialism, this too left markedly different traces across the continent. Those most adversely affected by the system of ethnic exclusion perpetuated by colonial rule, the indigenous and black populations, confronted distinctive legacies of rights and entitlements. It is only in recent decades that the significant numbers of Amerindian and Afroamericans have begun to realise their aspiration to be included as moral equals within their states and that governments, for their part, have began to recognise the multicultural character of their formations.[8]

The commonalities of Latin America reflect, in part, *global* trends. Latin American states are part of the global community and their policies respond both politically and economically to transnational forces and influences. If some of these influences may be judged benign, even positive in the region, others are contested, none more so than the policies associated with 'neoliberalism'. While it would be facile to attribute the spread of these policies in the region to external forces alone, the latter do wield considerable power, especially over the weaker states, through the practice of making aid conditional on compliance with donors' policy specifications. Governments frequently claim, often justifiably given these circumstances, that they have little room for manoeuvre over macroeconomic policy. Harsh and unpopular policies are said to be necessary if countries are to compete in an increasingly global and interdependent world, but in Latin America they have had a mixed economic record (ECLAC 2000). The human costs of such policies have been high and have fallen disproportionately on women.[9] The recessive conditions of the 'lost decade' and the accompanying stabilisation and adjustment policies sent millions into poverty. International agencies were slow to acknowledge the depth of the harm caused by the adjustment process. The policy instruments needed to protect the poor were not put in place until much damage had been done (Bulmer Thomas 1996; Green 1995; Cornia *et al.* 1987).

By the early to mid-1990s, however, Latin America had began its recovery; most countries registered positive growth rates. But international economic instability, including the South East Asian crisis of 1997, took its toll, and Latin America's average growth rate for the decade remained below 4 per cent. Poverty is a persistent feature in a region marked by deep and often growing income inequalities. Latin American countries register high levels of inequality when measured by the Gini coefficient (between 0.42 and 0.63 where 1 is absolute concentration of wealth). At 0.61 Brazil ranks as one of the most unequal societies in the world (compared with the UK at 0.32 and the USA at 0.35) (UNRISD 2000a: 12) and between 1990 and 1997 ECLAC notes that at least seven Latin American countries, including some of the stronger economies, became more unequal.[10] Bolivia, Honduras, Mexico and Uruguay saw slight improvements, but as the Bolivian experience shows, this was from such a low base that improvement still meant that the poorest 40 per cent's share of income only increased from 12 per cent to a paltry 13.5 per cent (ECLAC 1999: 61, fig. 11.1a). These inequalities, in turn, make attempts at achieving greater equality between women and men all the more difficult (ECLAC 2000: 6).[11] Poverty also remains a significant challenge and, while it has decreased relatively, it has increased absolutely, in that the number of those in poverty has gone up and is expected to continue to rise over the decade to come.[12] For the majority of Latin America's population, democracy has, in the 1990s, not delivered the results it promised; electorates have shown that they are capable of punishing governments which have failed them (Ecuador, Argentina) at times leading to considerable political volatility (Venezuela). The desire for radical change has sometimes resulted in maverick political choices, where unknown and untried independents have come to power (Peru). A distrust of political parties and government feeds voter disillusion, evident in low and declining electoral turnouts in a significant number of countries in the region.[13] Elsewhere, notably in Mexico, these trends have served to open up a sclerotic political system.

This social and political context helps in two ways to define the terrain upon which Latin American women's movements manoeuvre. First, their political agendas cannot ignore the painful reality of deepening socioeconomic inequalities and the limited scope offered for addressing them by neoliberal policies. Governments see themselves as caught between the twin imperatives of boosting economic growth and adhering to economic policies which limit both their capacity to redistribute and their commitment to social welfare. But at regional and international fora women's NGOs repeatedly demand greater attention to social inequality, not least because women are disproportionately represented among the region's poor and unemployed.[14] The return to civilian rule and democratic governance restored political and civil rights, but was accompanied by an erosion of some of the social and economic rights that were associated with earlier developmental and populist states. For many women's rights campaigners these rights are indivisible and cannot be separated.

Second, democracy is far from consolidated in the region. Following an initial period of optimism, there was growing concern about the character of the 'new' democracies that were being put in place. As these democracies were consolidated throughout the 1980s and 1990s many were judged to be deficient; if electoral processes were in the main respected, forms of corruption and clientelism continued to dog attempts to establish 'good governance'. In some countries (notably Mexico) accusations of rigged elections undermined government legitimacy. In others, rulers manipulated the limits of the constitutionally permitted period of office (both Fuijmori in Peru and Menem in Argentina rewrote constitutions to their advantage). Furthermore, charges of corruption brought some governments to electoral defeat,[15] while many repeatedly failed to deliver policies adequate to growing social needs and popular expectations. Issues of women's rights, indeed of rights in general, could not be detached from the broader question of the quality and character of democratic rule. This, as we shall see, faced women's movements with a series of political dilemmas.

International developments and the women's movements(s)

These shared, regional concerns were however addressed within a broader international context. While Latin American women's movements were active participants in the national struggles and debates that attended the turn to democratic rule, it was during the years of authoritarian rule that they also engaged with the international arena. The first international women's conference, held in Mexico in 1975, ushered in the UN Decade for Women (1976–85) and during this period Latin American women's movements became increasingly involved in 'transnational networking' (Keck and Sikkink 1998). At the same time, the changing geopolitical circumstances of the late twentieth century gave international conferences and conventions a new significance. No longer were they caught up in the bi-polar world of the Cold War, but they were able, potentially, to aid democratisation in many parts of the world that had been junior, but significant, players in the hostilities.

The international terrain was one where Latin American women were particularly active and influential. It is no exaggeration to say that the movement became even more internationalised in the 1980s and 1990s that at any time in its history.[16] This was so in three main ways. First, activists made full use of international networks and institutional arenas to give movements additional organisational capacity, to coordinate campaign strategies and to harness resources. Second, these instruments were used in popular education campaigns to inform both women and men of their rights and to debate how they should be interpreted. Third, such international agreements were used to hold governments accountable and to press for policy shifts consistent with them; if modern statecraft is forged with an eye to external approbation this could itself allow women's movements some additional leverage.

While this process placed specific national movements in an international context, it was also accompanied by a critique, and revision, of existing policy and of rights themselves. The international human rights movement had emerged in the immediate aftermath of World War II and its declarations resonate with that political moment, reflecting a horror of the abuses of war and in particular of genocide. The United Nations has been the focal point of these declarations, although some human rights instruments have been developed in regional fora such as the OAS. The 1948 Universal Declaration of Human Rights remains the reference point for subsequent rights-based conventions and has itself undergone numerous revisions. To reinforce basic human rights, the 1960s saw the focus shifting to particular bodies of rights and the development of new covenants: political and civil rights (ICCPR), and economic and social rights (ICESCR). The former embodied a liberal democratic perspective where procedural democracy was highlighted, whilst the latter, promoted by the Soviet bloc, placed greater emphasis on social and economic rights, rather than civil liberties. In the event, both covenants were adopted for signature in 1966,[17] although they only came into effect in 1976. They too reflect the limitations of their moment of conception.

The expansion in rights instruments was, however, accompanied by a questioning of women's place within them. Feminist and other critics argued that useful though these international human rights instruments were, they were insensitive to specific needs related to gender and ethnicity. Some, following feminist democratic theorists such as Pateman (1988) and Elshtain (1981), argued that their gender blindness derived from premises based on masculine norms.[18] Where gender was incorporated it generally focused on discrimination against women but without questioning women's structural marginalisation; as such, the focus was on negative rather than positive rights. Moreover, in their original conception human rights did not apply to the 'private' sphere of relations within the family, thereby ignoring many of the ways in which women were at risk from violence, and denied justice (Cook 1994).

Throughout the 1960s and 1970s, the international policy debate had been less concerned with women's *rights* than with how to incorporate women into the development process. At first such efforts at incorporation were restricted to welfare issues but later attention was paid to 'integrating' women into the modern economy (Moser 1989). Ester Boserup's (1970) path-breaking book on women in development challenged many of the assumptions of these policies, stressing that women were already 'integrated' even though the work that they did was more often than not unpaid and undervalued. Boserup drew attention to the importance of making women's reproductive, non-monetised and subsistence work visible while she highlighted their exclusion from decision-making processes.

These, and other theoretical advances within the gender and development field, challenged the ways in which women were seen (and saw themselves) and coincided with the spread of feminist movements and ideas across the world. A new gender awareness gave rise to, and was reinforced by, the UN's Commission on the Status of Women (CSW). Set up in the early 1970s this was 'the only international institution specifically assigned to attend to issues of justice for women' (Freeman 1999: 519). The CSW was responsible for the Decade for Women and the four international women's conferences that followed, and it drafted the UN Convention on the Elimination of all forms of Discrimination Against Women (CEDAW) adopted in 1979. Although these were important steps forward, the CSW 'concentrated on analyzing development-based economic and social issues concerning women rather than defining and pursuing rights issues' (ibid. 519–20). Further theoretical and methodological developments at this time also side-stepped rights. Molyneux's analytic distinction (1985), focused attention on strategic and practical gender interests, and Caroline Moser (1989), drawing on this work differentiated between types of *needs*,[19] rather than rights. While international conferences in their different ways offered some scope for focusing attention on women and their position in society, it was not until the 1990s that the focus shifted to questions of how rights could be incorporated into a general questioning of women's place in their own societies.

It was during this decade, with UN summits on the environment, social welfare, human rights and population, that rights came to the fore.[20] Of particular interest for women activists in Latin America and elsewhere were the Vienna Conference in 1993 on human rights, the Cairo Conference in 1994 on population, and the Fourth World Conference on Women held in Beijing in 1995. At Vienna the major step was taken of recognising that women's rights are human rights; this revitalised rights-based discourses as a strategic tool as well as placing violence against women on the human rights agenda.[21] In Cairo the thorny issue of sexual and reproductive rights was debated and was partially incorporated into health policy issues. Whilst this latter conference may not have gone as far as some would have liked on the question of decriminalising abortion, it did clarify many issues and it made reproductive choice part of the human rights agenda, by reinforcing woman's right to choose the number and spacing of her children (Lyklama à Nijeholt *et al.* 1998). At the regional level, significant developments occurred in 1994 at summits held in Mar del Plata in Argentina and in the Brazilian town of Belem do Pará both of which tackled the issue of violence against women. The global campaign against such violence has been one of the great successes of the 1990s and was both important and effective in Latin America.

The Beijing conference of 1995, attended by some 30 000 women (20 000 of whom participated in the NGO Forum), was of particular significance in advancing the commitment to pursue women's rights issues. It saw the ratification of the Cairo agreements and went further in tacitly recognising sexual rights. Its final document, the Platform for Action, contained a set of policy recommendations, which were adopted by 189 countries and served as a basis for NGO advocacy.[22] The UN committed itself to a five-year review of the progress achieved on the recommendations, and this was conducted at the Special Session of the UN General Assembly in New York in 2000. These regional and international events were important for women activists in several ways. First, governments were required to report to the relevant committees on their actions in relation to specific agreements.[23] These reports are normally biannual and they force states to account for their policy commitments. Whilst governments endeavour to put their accomplishments in the best possible light, their reports are submitted along with 'alternative' accounts produced by NGOs and other actors within civil society. Women's NGOs held their own follow-up conferences to monitor government compliance with conventions and produced documents that were often highly critical.[24] Second, they provide organised women with an opportunity for lobbying governments and highlighting particular areas of concern. The more effective the women's organisations within civil society, the better they are able to use such opportunities to advance their demands and to put pressure on governments to fulfil their commitments.

The growth in the number of international conventions coincided, as we have seen, with the consolidation of democracy in Latin America. States participated in debates at regional and international levels over how to respond to the new conventions, and the preparatory and follow-up meetings of these events brought new opportunities for debate and exchange between governments and women activists. At the regional level Latin America participated in a number of agenda-setting institutions all of which began to take up gender issues as part of their broader remit. The OAS, of which all Latin American states are members, has its own commission on women (CIM).[25] There is also an Inter-American Commission for Human Rights which had new life breathed into it in this period. Latin America is also peculiarly advantaged by the presence of ECLAC which pursued an active research and policy agenda on women. These institutions have reinforced the participation of Latin American states in UN deliberations and have helped to encourage a regional perspective on these global developments.

It is against this background that we can assess the changes of the 1990s. International developments interacted in important ways with Latin American politics and were particularly significant for women's rights campaigns. Women's organisations played a leading role in promoting a more inclusive and socially aware view of development and of citizenship, while human rights, and specifically women's rights became a focus of organisational strategy. As governments signed international agreements to respect democratic principles and human rights, women's movements were able to use these instruments to press for reforms, as issues of equal opportunities, positive discrimination and female representation in parliament became the focus of campaigns across the region. Through public discussion and debate, the issue of women's right to be treated as moral equals became in the words of one scholar, 'part of the common sense of the region'.[26] Where democratic institutions acquired a more secure foundation, Latin American women's movements showed themselves to be adept at adjusting to the new political context. They made the move from being an oppositional force whose efforts were pitched against the state, to being an effective force for reform.

National developments and international processes

These advances raised, however, difficult questions about the limits of participation, ones familiar to women's movements elsewhere. As noted earlier, the highly uneven and in many cases partial process of democratisation helped to determine what was achieved in the political and policy domains. Faced with the dilemmas posed by such 'democratic deficits', the region's social movements feared that collaboration with flawed democracies might serve to arrest rather than to advance more general democratic reform. Even in states with a credible record of good governance in the post-transition period, women's movements divided over whether to remain outside government or to enter into the power struggle being waged within. Those who chose to work with governments found the new terrain of institutional politics unfamiliar and difficult to navigate. This challenge was expressed as one of moving from 'la protesta a la propuesta' (from protest to proposal) and as requiring new strategies to deal with the changed political reality. The state, formerly a hostile force, was now offered as a site of engagement; many former opposition activists were faced with the possibility of working with, or even within, government as women's units, sometimes women's ministries, were established or reactivated with new 'women-friendly' briefs. Tensions between those who chose to work with or within the state and those who worked within civil society remained, however, and were particularly marked in Chile, Mexico and Peru.

Despite these differences, over the course of the 1990s women's movements increasingly directed their attention to securing improvements in women's legal and political status through a combination of pressure from below and working with the state. The period of democratic consolidation coincided with a growth in the importance of nongovernmental organisations (NGOs) matched by a corresponding rise in responsibility and international funding. Many women's movements took advantage of this development to institutionalise themselves, and in the process submitted to the pressures on them to professionalise their work, and to develop goals commensurate with donors' agendas. In Latin America, as a consequence, the distinction between women's movements and NGOs in the post-transition period was not always clearly drawn, as some NGOs owed their existence to women's movements, were managed by activists from the movement, and maintained close ties with the movement.

At the same time, a new regional collaboration developed. From the outset, Latin American women's movements worked on a transregional level, creating strong networks, some of which were formed during the experience of exile from military rule (Vargas 1992), and were subsequently fortified by the international initiatives discussed above. Latin American NGOs participated actively in the UN women's events and advisory committees. As these networks developed, they enabled those involved to prepare their suits, achieve some unity on core issues and to speak with conviction within international and national policy arenas.

Transregional networking was not only evident in regard to public institutional fora but was also a crucial resource in the practice of civil society organisations. Important among these were the series of regional feminist meetings (*Encuentros*) which, from 1981, occurred every 2–3 years (Sternbach *et al.* 1992). These regional initiatives fostered an exchange of ideas and experiences and helped to keep governments alive to gender issues. Networks could at times generate tensions and sharp disagreements, but they did enable both coordination on specific campaigns and a sharing of collective learning experiences that deepened the impact of in-country initiatives.

Such regional networks have worked both nationally and internationally to considerable effect. They were crucial in advancing specific campaigns such as the struggle for quota laws and the campaigns around domestic violence, and for legal literacy. Among the most notable networks have been those concerned with health, the Latin American and Caribbean Women's Health Network (RSMLAC), domestic violence (the Network against Violence towards Women), and the women's human rights organisation, the Latin American and Caribbean Committee for the Defence of Women's Rights (CLADEM). CLADEM has taken the lead in promoting women's access to rights in terms of engendering rights and in making political institutions take women's human rights seriously. The organisation emerged in the aftermath of the third UN conference on women in Nairobi 1985 which brought together a group of legal activists from across the region. They took a critical view of the law arguing, 'Power is legitimised through law and law legitimises women's subordination.'[27] Within two years, in July 1987, CLADEM was founded in Costa Rica and has subsequently grown into a campaigning organisation that has offices or links in sixteen of the region's countries, as well as links with other organisations and networks. CLADEM sees these regional links as a 'spider's web without hierarchies'.[28] Its activities focus principally on promoting women's human rights in international fora and in monitoring government compliance, but their engagement with the juridico-institutional terrain is complemented by work within communities and with social movement organisations. They have developed a regional perspective on legal reform which helps in the formulation of new legal projects at national level as well as comparing government efforts to comply with international agreements. Whilst Latin America may not be unique in its regional organisations, these contribute to the continued struggle for engendered citizenship and women's rights in key ways, as well as helping to support local civil society activity through an exchange of expertise and experiences. The regional dimension of these campaigns has been one of the strengths of the women's movement as well as a distinguishing feature of it.

Issues and cases

The case studies that make up this book illustrate the dynamic interaction between international factors and regional particularities within women's rights campaigns. The following eight chapters examine what have been, over the last decades, the central campaigns for women's rights and demands for full citizenship in the region: these are reproductive rights, protection from domestic violence, socioeconomic rights, democratic participation and representation, and issues of identity and difference.

Chapter 2 by Mala Htun and Mark Jones, and Chapter 3 by Elizabeth Friedman, focus on campaigns for greater gender equality in democratic representation. Htun and Jones examine one of the most radical measures taken to redress the under-representation of women in national parliaments; that of quota laws. Although in the United States support for such affirmative action measures has been diminishing in recent years, Latin America has followed the Northern European example in adopting quota laws to improve female representation in parliaments. However, while the European measures are voluntarily applied by political parties, the trend in Latin American is to go a step further and to write the requirement for gender quotas into national law.[29] Argentina initiated this trend when in 1991 it became the first democratic country to include a quota law in its electoral code.

The passage of these laws in Latin America resulted in the first place from the combined efforts of local and regional women's movements, but the success of the quota law campaigns also depended in large measure on cross-party and multisectoral collaboration by women parliamentarians and their male allies within the legislature itself.[30] The example of Argentina along with the impact of the Beijing Declaration in 1995 which called for quotas, and the regional meetings to discuss its import also helped to inspire women in other Latin American countries to press for quotas. As Htun and Jones attest, throughout the 1990s more than a dozen Latin American countries adopted legislation requiring parties to place between 20 per cent and 40 per cent of women on their lists.[31] Once in force, these laws resulted in almost doubling the average female representation in Latin American parliaments during the decade, from a low base of 6 per cent to 15 per cent for the lower house, and 14.4 per cent for senates in 2000.[32] This is higher than the UK, the United States and some European countries. Latin America comes third regionally to Nordic countries (at 38.8 per cent) and non-Nordic Europe (at 16.4 per cent). However, Htun and Jones point out that crucial to the effectiveness of quota laws in bringing about greater female representation is the electoral system itself: closed list systems such as in Argentina, are more likely to favour the election of women through quotas than open voting for candidates.[33] Such variations in electoral systems as well as in the letter of the quota laws themselves influence the results obtained. While all countries with quota laws have seen some increase in the number of female representatives, in some cases such as Brazil, the increase in women candidates was small. In the 1998 elections the results were only 5.7 per cent of women in the lower house and 7.4 in the senate, leaving Brazil in 85th place internationally. It is moreover arguable whether the small increase was due to the quota law. As Htun and Jones demonstrate, if quota laws are to have a greater impact on reducing inequality in political representation, and if they are indeed to serve as effective democratic mechanisms, they will need more teeth.

It has been widely acknowledged, however, that the mere presence of women in parliaments is no guarantee of greater gender sensitivity in policy-making. Latin American advocates of quotas argue that not only do they serve as a democratic mechanism for redressing persistent in-equalities in access to decision-making power, but that there are advantages in women constituting a critical mass in the decision-making process. Although not all women delegates necessarily serve the interests of their female constituencies, research has shown that in practice female representatives tend to collaborate on legislative matters concerning women and that gender legislation is more often put forward by women. Once in power, female representatives can be an important resource for civil society campaigners who call upon them to be responsive to women's demands (UNRISD 2000b). However, they also stress that to recognise these positive aspects of quotas does not imply that they remedy the structural gender inequalities which limit women's access to political and decision-making power in society.

In Chapter 3 Elisabeth Friedman examines the alliance-building process in a campaign to reform the labour code in Venezuela in the late 1980s. In the case of Venezuela, female parliamentarians from different parties combined with women active in trade unions and in independent women's groups to promote the reforms. Their success was due in part to the enhanced political clout that this gave to their campaign, but important too, was careful strategising in regard to securing consensus for the demands. Feminist activists sought to change provisions in the law that discriminated against women workers by promoting the principle of equal treatment, but they did so in a way that recognised rights related to maternity. Here, they aimed to reconcile principles of equality and difference in a context where motherhood retains significant cultural value and where equality feminism is far from being widely accepted. Catholicism has exerted an enduring influence on the region's gendered ideologies, and femininity is strongly associated with motherhood and domesticity in Latin America even as it is refigured though divisions of class, race and ethnicity. Laws concerning women and the family continue to reflect a traditional division of responsibility between the sexes in the family, as well as to restrict women's reproductive rights. Advocates of women's equality have had to formulate their demands in ways that take account of these sometimes tenaciously held motherist identifications. In the case of the revised Venezuelan labour code, women were recognised as having special responsibilities in the family, but whereas this had been a basis for discrimination under the previous code, employers were now required to hire women on the same terms as men. This represented a significant legal advance, with two qualifications. First it would take more than a reformed law to ensure that employers complied with it, and second, the law did not cover domestic workers, still a sizeable part of Latin America's female labour force. The women delegates, Friedman suggests, were not all ready to surrender their class privileges and embrace the cause of their own employees.[34]

In the following two chapters, other key issues of legal reform are examined in the context first of Brazil and then of Uruguay. In Chapter 4, Fiona Macaulay analyses the importance of advocacy as activism for the promotion of women's rights. In this context, advocacy work includes lobbying for changes in the law as well as in the *practice* of the law. Legal reform has been considered a fundamental part of the consolidation of democracy in Latin America, and many countries have embarked on reform programmes of different kinds. International development institutions, such as the World Bank, have been paying particular attention to this issue and have supported efforts to reform judiciaries and legal practice as part of their general support for good governance. Social movements across the continent have also campaigned in citizens' groups and networks for such reforms. The complex and often inefficient legal systems in much of Latin America have made claims on rights all the more difficult since access to the legal system is limited by its opaqueness and expense. Making the legal system open and accessible is seen by legal advocacy campaigners as central to deepening the democratic process. It is a strategy which operates at different levels in society, aimed as much at legal practitioners at the highest levels of the justice system as forming part of the practice of grassroots organisations. The efforts of Latin American women's movements to promote legal advocacy need to be seen as one of several strategies in the pursuit of greater gender justice and women's citizenship. Macaulay's examination of the innovative work of a feminist organisation shows how it has worked to promote legal literacy and trained 'paralegals' among women from the popular classes in Porto Alegre, Brazil. If women are aware of their rights they will also be able to be more effective in claiming them, and their capacity to exercise political agency can be enhanced.

The contrasting example of the development of the law on domestic violence in Uruguay is analysed in Chapter 5. Niki Johnson traces the evolution of the campaign to improve women's legal rights in this area by making bodily integrity central to gendered understandings of citizenship. As noted earlier, the campaign against domestic violence has been, perhaps the most successful across Latin America as well as having a powerful international resonance.[35] The entire region signed up to CEDAW between 1980 (Cuba) and 1989 (Chile) and this provided some basis for legal change. Over the course of the 1990s several countries made significant changes in their laws and state provision in protecting women and children. As an issue, violence against women received support from international human rights declarations as well as from the church. Here again, within specific countries, the importance of cross-party collaboration and links with civil society organisations made a decisive difference to the outcomes. Johnson, like Friedman, demonstrates the complexities involved in developing laws which are acceptable both to the campaigners and to the more conservative lawmakers. She also raises the important issue of how women's rights campaigns can succeed in changing laws, but in ways that were not envisaged or desired by women's movements. In Uruguay campaigners demanded educational measures to support changes in attitudes towards women. Instead, what eventuated were tougher laws for the perpetrators of violence against women. In other words governments can react selectively to social movement campaigns, and can use their demands to push through changes that otherwise might have been resisted.

Another issue that emerged in the Latin American region during the campaign on domestic violence was that of whether and to what extent it was desirable to make its gender dimensions explicit. In Uruguay, as Johnson shows, women activists campaigned to highlight the gender dimension of the violence and to link it specifically to the extension of *women's* rights rather than calling for measures which were focused on the family. In contrast, in Mexico the government decided to focus on 'intra-family' violence. This downplayed the fact that women make up the bulk of the victims and derailed the legislative and policy provision for women, causing concern not only among women activists in Mexico but also in other parts of Latin America.

The broadening of the definition of rights by women's movements to include issues of bodily integrity is also the subject of Ceri Willmott's Chapter 6 on Chile. The idea that women have the right to choose in relation to such contested areas as sexuality and reproductive rights is at odds both with Catholic teaching and with Chilean law. Reproductive rights are a sensitive and bitterly disputed issue in Latin America. Abortion rates remain high with the least advantaged women at greatest risk from death and illness from illegal terminations. Conservative, religious opposition to women's reproductive rights strengthened in recent decades; the Vatican under John Paul II has promoted a strict policy on contraception while reinforcing its refusal to permit abortion under any circumstances. If attitudes towards contraception have been changing under the impact of the AIDS epidemic, abortion remains a deeply contentious issue. It is completely illegal in Chile (which with Peru has the highest per capita number of abortions) and whilst legal in some form in the rest of the region, in reality access to safe abortion is extremely restricted and affordable only by an advantaged minority.[36] That the abortion debate in Latin America can be highly politicised, and risks being captured by conservative forces was brought into sharp relief in Mexico in the summer of 2000. The state of Guanajuato attempted to increase the penalties even in the case of rape. The subsequent protest meant that abortion was discussed in all the media, opening up public debate for the first time. The law in Guanajuato was eventually vetoed by the governor but, at the same time, attempts to liberalise the law in Mexico City were also shelved. Although official views on abortion remain conservative, surveys in Chile and Mexico indicate that there is public support for its legalisation in many circumstances and that a majority favours legalisation. Much rests on *how* the question is asked with many questionnaires prone to bias.[37] Furthermore, whatever the law and opinion surveys say, women do resort to terminations, often in very difficult and dangerous circumstances. It is estimated that abortion is the main cause of maternal death in Argentina (30 per cent) and Chile (26 per cent) and there is no reason to suppose that these two countries are worse than others in the region (ECLAC 2000: 39–40).

Within Latin America, Chile stands out as one of the most socially conservative nations, with predominantly negative attitudes towards women's rights and equality.[38] Whilst it scores highly in the human development index, where it is ranked 34th, in terms of gender empowerment it ranks 54th. This compares poorly with high-ranked Costa Rica (45th and 23rd respectively), and low-ranked Ecuador (72nd and 29th) and Guatemala (117th and 44th) (see Table A.1 on p. 222). The combination of these factors has affected women's own perception of their sexuality and reproductive needs. Drawing on research in low-income settlements in Santiago, Willmott shows how reproductive rights and sexuality are being refigured as sites over which women *can* exercise more individual choice. While women often found these issues painful and difficult, Willmott argues that women's groups have opened up these issues for discussion, allowing their experiences to be shared, needs to be expressed, and rights reconsidered.

Chapter 7 by Sarah Radcliffe examines questions of identity through a discussion of indigenous women in the Andean region. With reference to Peru and Ecuador she shows that with few exceptions, indigenous women were historically excluded from citizenship in Latin America and how they have, in recent times, sought to assert their claims in ways that recognise both their ethnic identities and their rights as women. The indigenous or Amerindian population of Latin America is estimated at 40 million, or around 8 per cent of the region's total population. The majority lives in conditions of poverty and fares badly on all human development indicators. If issues of Amerindian rights gradually achieved some limited recognition from the 1960s onwards, it was only in the 1990s that an effective regional movement emerged. The catalyst was the quincentenary celebration in 1992 of Columbus's arrival in the Americas. This sparked a global campaign challenging the premises of the celebration from the perspective of those who had been at the sharp end of the colonisation process. Campaigners were able to highlight questions of rights and identity, promote common interests, and work towards developing an agreed platform. From the late 1980s there had been a shift away from the assimilationist policies favoured by governments and development agencies towards a greater emphasis on cultural rights and indigenous identities. This move was accelerated with constitutional and legal reforms recognising Amerindian rights introduced *inter alia* in Argentina, Bolivia, Brazil, Chile, Ecuador, Para-guay and Colombia (Brysk 2000). However, as Radcliffe shows, while these developments have been welcomed by indigenous women, they have also generated tensions between their individual rights and their group rights. Indigenous women, so often made responsible for preserv-ing 'ethnic authenticity' in a way that can undermine their individual rights as women, have found it difficult to reconcile the prevailing version of authenticity with their own claims for rights and recognition.

The final two Chapters, 8 and 9, focus on some important challenges faced by women's movements. Whilst significant gains have been made in securing women's rights and political representation in recent times, and while the emphasis on rights has served as a useful strategic resource, these gains have occurred in a region still gripped by major social and economic problems. For women's movements two major questions remain unresolved: how to make macroeconomic policy more gender-sensitive, and how to negotiate with states that may well fall short of fulfilling their commitment to democracy while using their support for women's rights in an instrumental fashion.

Chapter 8 by Jasmine Gideon is concerned with international instruments such as the 1966 International Convention on Economic and Social Rights (ICESCR). She considers to what extent they can be said to be effective and to be appropriately sensitive to gender difference. At the Beijing conference the indivisibility of economic and political rights was reaffirmed, and this together with the impact of the feminist critique of structural adjustment policies drew attention to the need for gender-sensitive macroeconomic policies.[39] The extreme poverty of Central America makes these issues all the more urgent, but as Gideon argues, while states have signed up to these agreements, the results have been limited. This is in part because of deficiencies in the formulation of the agreements; women's unpaid work, in agriculture for example, is not recognised as work. But they are also ineffective because adherence to them would commit states to making active policy commitments and to providing financial and other resources. Governments, however, are reluctant to expand their responsibilities in the economic domain, and are under pressure to shrink public sector expenditure in conformity with the neoliberal agenda. If international agreements themselves are insufficiently gender aware, their usefulness as campaigning tools for women activists is limited. Gideon suggests where improvements could be made in the ICESCR to promote greater gender sensitivity.

The failure to make socioeconomic rights more meaningful is disappointing given that the original focus of the UN's Commission on the Status of Women (CSW) was on socioeconomic issues, in keeping with the then prevalent welfarist approach. At that time in the 1960s and 1970s it was women's civil and political rights that were ignored in favour of encouraging development (Freeman 1999: fn. 14). It was only in later years that the focus shifted to the political arena. As Gideon argues however, the key issue is the *indivisibility* of different types or generations of rights, with each reinforcing the others; only policies which recognise this interdependency will succeed in tackling the multiple forms of female deprivation that are such a persistent feature of the Central American region.

Virginia Vargas (Chapter 9) echoes this sober reflection on the limits of the process of generalising rights agendas. Vargas is one of Latin America's most prominent feminist activists, founder of the Flora Tristán Women's Centre in Peru, and coordinator of the Latin American and Caribbean NGO delegation to the Beijing Conference. Drawing on her considerable experience at both national and international levels, she addresses a major and continuing problem for feminists and women's movements; that of how to interact with states. Whilst acknowledging the importance of the state as a terrain of engagement, she emphasises that there are dangers of cooption and over-reliance on the state to fulfil feminist agendas. For over a century, feminists have struggled for greater state recognition of their demands, but Vargas argues that women's movements should maintain a distance from the state and that their own organisational autonomy should not be placed at risk of being colonised by the state or instrumentalised into fulfilling its agenda. This was a particular concern during the Fujimori administration (1990–2000) which increasingly suspended democratic guarantees. Women's issues achieved considerable prominence and their representation within the state increased, but not without costs. There is always a risk that women's organisations might serve as a vehicle for the realisation of government goals as the latter coopt movements for their own ends. In countries where this has occurred, it is unsurprising to find women's organisations wary of close interaction with the state. Yet, at the same time, states can offer valuable opportunities and resources to campaigning organisations. Vargas shows how the old tension between autonomy and integration remains a particular challenge in Latin America. It is, perhaps, in Mexico under the PRI, and in Peru under Fujimori, where this has been a major problem, and with the demise of both administrations in 2000, these countries are undergoing significant political change. But this tension has been more widely debated in Latin America, and even in the democratic administrations which succeeded Pinochet in Chile from 1990, there has been criticism of the close relationship between feminist NGOs and the state women's committee, SERNAM.[40]

Conclusions

While the Latin American experience shares some common elements with other parts of the world, the region's recent history of authoritarian rule has given to struggles for democracy, citizenship and rights a special significance. Yet the case studies in this volume highlight the variability and contingency of rights-based struggles in the region. Issues of rights and citizenship, while apparently universal and occupying such a central a place in women's demands for full citizenship, are nonetheless associated with different political objectives, and are contested, reframed and reinterpreted by different political forces. In the 1980s and 1990s women's movements in Latin America worked to promote and to spread awareness of women's rights in their 'actually existing democracies', but they also helped to shape, through their active participation in a variety of arenas, the international and regional legal instruments that were developed in this period.

However successful women's movements have been in this domain, and however committed many remain to extending and deepening the meaning and effectiveness of rights, there is a keen awareness among activists of the pitfalls and limitations of such rights-based strategies. International and national legal instruments can be unwieldy; working with them requires long-term commitments of time and energy on the part of campaigners, as well as a favourable policy environment in which to work. Such instruments are themselves still far from meeting standards consistent with the principles of equality and fairness promoted by the international women's movement (Charlesworth *et al.* 1991).[41] Gideon's critique of the assumptions of the 1966 International Convention for its focus on the paid economy and for overlooking women's unpaid work, is an illustration of these limits. Moreover, since these instruments must be accepted by often widely differing states, they can often lack teeth in having the character of 'lowest common denominator'. They are also vulnerable to attacks from opponents: at the CEPAL Beijing + 5 meeting in Peru in February 2000, and at the June 2000 meeting in New York, opponents of the Platform for Action recommendations tried to subvert agreement to continue pressing for implementation and questioned the document's terminology and formulations.[42] As many participants in these fora have argued, the recommendations which eventuate from international conferences need clearer benchmarks, measurable goals and time-bound targets if they are to move off the paper and into policy.[43] In practice, too, these instruments are only useful if the rights enshrined in them can be put into effect at the nation-state level, and if they serve to promote policy changes that impact positively on the lives of women. Governments more often than not lack the political will to implement the measures and to put the necessary resources into making compliance meaningful; without continued pressure by activists most states are content to treat these agreements as mere window-dressing.[44] It was not for nothing that NGO forum activists demonstrated at the Latin American UN governmental fora with tee shirts and placards reading 'Deeds not Words!' Moreover, as Macaulay shows, while valuable and innovative work in legal education is being undertaken at the grassroots level in Brazil, the effectiveness of such work is hampered by the absence of a broader process of legal reform.

A second set of reservations concerns the political risks associated with working with rights-based agendas. Legal reform in matters of women's rights is often a highly politicised process and campaigns can eventuate in unintended outcomes. If these can sometimes be judged broadly positive, at other times they can be thwarted, diluted or captured by states to serve their own ends. As Vargas illustrates in the case of the Fujimori administration in Peru, women's movements in Latin America have had to be especially cautious in regard to engaging with states given the dangers of co-optation and resulting loss of autonomy. More women in government as a result of the quota laws is a step in the direction of equality as Htun and Jones argue, but where those governments serve authoritarian and or corrupt states, the gains are minimal or nullified. Women, many of whom are former movement activists, have entered the institutional domain in large numbers. While they could make an impact on legislation, service delivery and policy, there was a danger that this 'institutionalisation' might be at the expense of reduced links with the movement and a corresponding bureaucratisation of women's issues. Campaigns around women's rights can also serve to mobilise conservative opposition or to create acrimonious divisions among women themselves over the interests advanced and the tactics and strategies deployed. While women's coalitions and networks have shown themselves able to overcome many social and political differences in the pursuit of legal reform, vested interests often remain important, as evidenced by Friedman in the case of the failure to address the rights of domestic workers, and by Radcliffe's discussion of the marginalisation of indigenous women's voices in political policy debates. Many questions remain concerning the ability of universal discourses of rights to recognise and respect difference. Indigenous and Amerindian rights involve acknowledging a history of colonial oppression and racialised systems of inclusion and exclusion, a process which has only just begun in Latin America.

This volume therefore provides evidence not only of the considerable advances secured by women's movements in the domain of rights and policy, but also serves to highlight the significant difficulties that attend such strategies. The accelerated pace of globalisation over the past two decades has had contrasting effects. On the positive side the proliferation of international fora, conventions and agreements have helped to reinforce rights and have served as a lever for women's rights campaigners. The focus on rights has introduced new tactics and strategies into women's movements and has delivered some notable gains. Of these three stand out as of particular significance: the passage of quota laws in more than a dozen countries (with more awaiting confirmation); greater protection for women from violence through better legal framing, police training and provision of support for the victims of abuse; and legal and policy reforms to provide for greater equality in the family and at work, through promoting greater gender-sensitivity in policy making.[45]

At the same time however, these gains made only a small contribution to alleviating the human cost of the adjustment policies,[46] and without a corresponding rise in economic returns poverty and inequality stalk the region. The focus on rights has made states responsible and accountable in new ways, but even where new rights have been achieved or where existing rights have been put in the spotlight, constant campaigning is required both to ensure that women's rights are understood as central, not marginal, to human rights, and that women are aware of their rights and can defend them if need be. As noted earlier, activists are duly sceptical of the narrow individualism that can be associated with normative definitions of rights. In Latin America, where social policy issues remain urgent, the struggle for rights has to be accompanied not only by considerations of need, but also of the diversely situated demands of indigenous populations. If rights are not promoted in a way which makes them accessible and acceptable to the disadvantaged, they remain the preserve of the privileged few. Women's movements have emphasised the need to radicalise and popularise rights demands, while they have stressed the indivisibility of rights and the need for political guarantees to protect and advance those rights. The pursuit of rights in themselves, divorced from broader questions of democracy and social justice, has little meaning if they are not accompanied by the conditions which make it possible to claim them. As Virginia Vargas argued in her address to the NGO forum at the Beijing + 5 conference in New York 2000, speaking for many in the region:

> The twenty-first century will be a 'women's century' only if it also democracy's century, [democracy understood in its] political, social, economic and cultural aspects. Only with democratic governments that fulfil their political and juridical commitments and with strong civil societies with the capacity to monitor the management of public resources and formulate proposals will we be able to face the challenges that the new millennium poses. (REPEM 2000)

Notes

1   This chapter draws on the authors' interviews with women's rights activists in Latin America and on other thematic discussions in related areas. See in particular: Craske (1999, 2000), Molyneux (2000a, 2000b, 2000c), and Molyneux and Lazar (2002). We would like to thank Fiona Macaulay for her helpful comments on an earlier draft.

2   For the history of women's movements and rights struggles in Latin America see Dore and Molyneux (2000), Lavrin (1995), Miller (1991) and Stoner (1988).

3   'Popular' in Latin American usage means of the working or subaltern, classes.

4   For those emphasising elite settlements, see, among others, Diamond, Hamlyn, Linz and Lipset (1999), Mainwaring and Shugart (1997), O'Donnell, Schmitter and Whitehead (1986). For greater emphasis on social movements and the (re)-building of civil society see Escobar and Alvarez, (1992), Drake and Jaksić (1991), Foweraker and Craig (1990) and Eckstein (1989).

5   See, among others, Alvarez (1998, 1990), Jaquette and Wolchik (1998), Waylen (1996a, 1996b, 1994), Jaquette (1994), Fisher (1993), Jelin (1990), Molyneux (1985).

6   The 'Glass of Milk' programme involved tens of thousands of women in Peru in running this service for low-income households. See Barrig (1994), Blondet (1995).

7   These figures refer to real GDP per capita. According to UNDP data four Latin American countries, Chile, Argentina, Costa Rica and Uruguay, rank in the 'high human development' category whilst the remaining fifteen are ranked as medium. There are significant differences, however, in the standards of living of these medium ranked countries with GDP per capita ranging from over $8000 for Mexico and Venezuela to less than $3000 for El Salvador, Bolivia, Honduras and Nicaragua (UNDP, 1999 tab. 1).

8   For a discussion of the indigenous rights movements of Latin America see Brysk (2000). On the relationship between indigenous people and state reform see Assies, van der Haar and Hoekama (2000) and for conceptual issues concerning indigenous rights see Stavenhagen (1996).

9   Women outnumber men among the poor and unemployed in Latin America, see ECLAC (2000).

10   These are Argentina, Brazil, Chile, Costa Rica, Ecuador, Panama, Paraguay and Venezuela (ECLAC, 1999: 61, fig. 11.1a).

11   The UNDP's gender analysis indicates that in many parts of the region gender disparities make conditions worse for women and that relatively wealthy countries such as Brazil, Chile and Uruguay often display greater gender disparities than their poorer neighbours. Table A.1 on page 222 offers selected data on gendered development in the region.

12   Furthermore, although the percentage of people living in poverty in Latin America has declined from 41 per cent to 36 per cent between 1990 and 1997, it is still above the percentage for 1980 (35 per cent) and, in absolute numbers, the number of poor has increased. Although the number of indigents has declined from 93 400 to 89 800, it is much higher than the 62 400 recorded in 1980 (ECLAC, 1999:18 tab. 1).

13   *Comisión Andina de Juristas* 2000a. A poll of 17 Latin American countries showed that only 37 per cent of those interviewed were content with the

way their democracy worked in practice. Roughly two out of three had little or no trust in their politicians, parties, congresses, police or judiciaries (*The Economist* 13 May 2000, 66).

14 It is illustrative that in Chile, Latin America's highest ranking country in human development terms, men's real per capita GDP is $19 749 whilst women's is $5853 (UNDP, 1999 tab. 2 gender-related development index).

15 Venezuelan president, Carlos Andrés Perez, and Brazilian president, Fernando Collor, were both impeached on charges of corruption.

16 As Francesca Miller (1991) has shown the Latin American feminist movement from the early twentieth century was active in international fora and spawned its own international organisations.

17 The Soviet Union became a party to both on 16 October 1973, whilst the USA became a party to the ICCPR in June 1992 and a signatory to the ICESCR on 5 October 1977.

18 For a critique of international legal instruments from a gender perspective see Cook (1994), and Charlesworth *et al.* (1991).

19 See Molyneux (2000a) for a discussion of the needs/interests debate.

20 The 1980s had already seen further developments in the international arena with attention to children's rights (CRC: 1989), Convention Against Torture (1984), and the 1989 ILO Convention 169 on ethnic and minority rights (the only statutory international instrument on indigenous rights).

21 See Keck and Sikkink (1998) for a discussion of the global and specifically Latin American campaigns on this issue.

22 Despite some hard fought gains in the areas of sexual preference, as concerns economic rights and abortion less was achieved than was hoped for, largely on account of conservative religious opposition.

23 On CEDAW commitments they report to the Commission on the Elimination of all forms of Discrimination Against Women, for ICCPR they report to the Commission for Human Rights (CHR); for the ICESCR to the Commission for Economic and Social Rights (ECOSOC).

24 An index of the participation in these issues can be gained from one example: 500 Chilean women attended a conference on 'Beijing one year afterwards' in 1996 (Valdés and Weinstein n.d).

25 The Comisión Interamericana de Mujeres is a permanent committee of the OAS on which each member country has a representative. The committee is obliged to report back regularly to the OAS on progress achieved in meeting regional agreements.

26 Molyneux interview with Cecilia Blondet, Lima 2000.

27 See CLADEM website: http://www.derechos.org/cladem/index.html.

28 As in note 27.

29 Some laws are specifically to increase women's representation whilst others aim for gender balance and thus are to ensure that no more than 70 per cent of the chamber is made up of one sex.

30 Presidential support was arguably a decisive factor as in the cases of Menem in Argentina and Fujimori in Peru.

31 The most radical, as well as highly controversial, to date, has been the recent decision by the government of the province of Córdoba, Argentina, to instigate 50 per cent quota laws for elected and 'intermediate organisations' positions (*Clarín* 4 Dec. 2000).

32   See data from the Inter-Parliamentary Union http://www.ipu.org/.
33   In closed list systems the voter is presented with lists controlled by parties rather than voting for individual candidates, consequently voters have to vote for women if they are listed and can't 'cherry pick' from a list of candidates put forward by the party.
34   Domestic work continues to be the major employment available to women in Latin America.
35   Keck and Sikkink (1998) suggest that the degree of international consensus on this issue was unusual and due to careful discursive strategising to make issues of bodily integrity capable of having meaning in a variety of cultures.
36   It is debatable whether abortion is legal under any circumstances in El Salvador but in Chile protecting life from the moment of conception was one of the last acts of the Pinochet dictatorship. For full details on the region's abortion laws see www.undp.org.popin/wdtrends/abt/batplac.htm.
37   For Chile see *Encuesta Nacional* (1999) carried out by the Grupo Iniciativa Mujeres, for Mexico see *GIRE Boletín* No. 17, June 1998.
38   Public Opinion Surveys, cited in *Comisión Andina de Juristas* 2000b.
39   This work built on the theoretical insights of feminist economists such as Diane Elson. See Elson 1991.
40   For critical discussion see Craske (2000), Schild (1998), Barrig (1997), Waylen (1996b), Valdés, T. (1998).
41   An example is the Belém do Pará Convention on violence against women where there is the requirement that states exercise 'due diligence' in preventing violence against women. Nowhere, however, is there a normative definition of what might constitute 'due' – or sufficient – diligence on the part of a state. A UN Special Rapporteur was appointed to carry out a country study of Brazil where implicit benchmarks are employed (Macaulay, personal communication).
42   The role of the Vatican in coordinating conservative Catholic opposition during the Beijing process is discussed by Keck and Sikkink (1998), and by Lyklama á Nijehold *et al.* (1998).
43   Molyneux's interviews with participants at the CEPAL meeting in Lima, Peru 2000 and the UN Special Session on Women in New York 2000.
44   See the Comisión Andina Reports 2000a and 2000b, for a critical review of government action.
45   By the end of the decade (1995–2000) there had been a 50 per cent rise in female participation in the legislature and a sharp rise in the number of women in ministerial posts; 11 Latin American countries promulgated quota laws and 12 passed laws on violence against women.
46   ECLAC (2000) estimates that without the gains made by the women's movements inequality and poverty would be far worse in the region.

Bibliography

Alvarez, Sonia (1990) *Engendering Democracy in Brazil*, Princeton, NJ: Princeton University Press
Alvarez, Sonia (1998) 'Latin American feminisms "go global": trends of the 1990s and challenges for the new millenium' in S. Alvarez, E. Dagnino and A. Escobar

(eds) *Cultures of Politics/Politics of Cultures: Revisioning Latin American Social Movements*, Boulder, Colo.: Westview Press

Assies, Willem, Gemma van der Haar and André Hoekama (eds) (2000) *The Challenge of Diversity: Indigenous People and Reform of the State in Latin America*, Amsterdam: Thela Thesis

Baierle, Sérgio Greg (1998) 'The explosion of experience: the emergence of a new ethical-political principle in popular movements in Porto Alegre, Brazil' in S. Alvarez, E. Dagnino and A. Escobar (eds) *Cultures of Politics/Politics of Cultures: Revisioning Latin American Social Movements*, Boulder, Colo.: Westview Press

Barrig, Maruja (1994) 'The difficult equilibrium between bread and roses: women's organizations and democracy in Peru' in J. Jaquette (ed.) *The Women's Movement in Latin America: Participation and Democracy*, Boulder, Colo.: Westview Press, 151–76

Barrig, Maruja (1997) 'De Cal y Arena: ONGs y movimientos de mujeres en Chile', mimeo

Blondet, Cecilia (1995) 'Out of the kitchens and onto the streets: women's activism in Peru' in Amrita Basu (ed.) *The Challenge of Local Feminisms: Women's Movements in Global Perspective*, Boulder, Colo.: Westview Press

Boserup, Ester (1970) *Woman's Role in Economic Development*, London: Allen & Unwin

Bouvard, Marguerite Guzman (1994) *Revolutionizing Motherhood: the Mothers of the Plaza de Mayo*, Wilmington Del.: Scholarly Resources

Brysk, Alison (2000) *From Tribal Village to Global Village: Indian Rights and International Relations in Latin America*, California: Stanford University Press

Bulmer, Thomas, Victor (ed.) (1996) *The New Economic Model in Latin America and its Impact on Income Distribution and Poverty*, London: ILAS/Macmillan Press – now Palgrave

Charlesworth, Hilary, Christine Chinkin and Shelley Wright (1991) 'Feminist approaches to international law' *American Journal of International Law*, 85 (4) 613–45

Comisión Andina de Juristas (2000a) *Democracia en la Encrucijada*, Lima, Peru

Comisión Andina de Juristas (2000b) *Protección de los Derechos Humanos de la Mujer: Estándares Internacionales*, Lima, Peru

Cook, Rebecca (ed.) (1994) *Human Rights of Women: National and International Perspectives*, Philadelphia: University of Pennsylvania Press

Cornia, Giovanni A., R. Jolly and F. Stewart, (1987) *Adjustment with a Human Face*, Oxford: Clarendon Press

Craske, Nikki (1999) *Women and Politics in Latin America*, Cambridge: Polity Press

Craske, Nikki (2000) *Continuing the Challenge: the Contemporary Latin American Women's Movement(s)*, ILAS research paper #23, Liverpool: ILAS

Diamond, Larry, Jonathan Hamlyn, Juan Linz and Martin Seymour Lipset (eds) (1999) *Democracy in Developing Countries: Latin America*, Boulder, Colo.: Lynne Reinner

Dore, Elizabeth and Maxine Molyneux, (eds) (2000) *Hidden Histories of Gender and the State in Latin America*, Durham: Duke University Press

Drake, Paul W. and Iván, Jaksić (eds) (1991) *The Struggle for Democracy in Chile 1982–1990*, London: Nebraska University Press

Eckstein, Susan (ed.) (1989) *Power and Popular Protest in Latin America*, Berkeley, Calif.: University of California Press

ECLAC (1999) *Social Panorama of Latin America 1998*, Santiago de Chile: ECLAC

ECLAC (2000) *The Challenge of Gender Equity and Human Rights on the Threshold of the Twenty-First Century* Chile: ECLAC

Elshtain, Jean B. (1981) *Public Man, Private Woman*, Princeton, NJ: Princeton University Press

Elson, Diane (ed.) (1991) *Male Bias in the Development Process*, Manchester: Manchester University Press

Escobar, Arturo and Sonia Alvarez (eds) (1992) *The Making of Social Movements in Latin America*, Boulder, Colo.: Westview Press

Fisher, Jo (1993) *Out of the Shadows: Women, Resistance and Politics in South America*, London: Latin American Bureau

Foweraker, Joe and Ann Craig (eds) (1990) *Popular Movements and Political Change in Mexico*, Boulder, Colo.: Lynne Reinner

Freeman, Marsha (1999) 'International institutions and gendered justice' *Journal of International Affairs*, 52 (2) 513–32

Green, Duncan (1995) *Silent Revolution: the Rise of Market Economics in Latin America*, London: Cassell

Jaquette, Jane (ed.) (1994) *The Women's Movement in Latin America*, 2nd edn. Boulder, Colo.: Westview Press

Jaquette, Jane and Sharon L. Wolchik (eds) (1998) *Women and Democracy: Latin America and Central and Eastern Europe*, Baltimore; Md.: Johns Hopkins Press

Jelin, Elizabeth (ed.) (1990) *Women and Social Change in Latin America*, London: Zed Books

Jelin, Elizabeth and Eric Hershberg (eds) (1996) *Constructing Democracy: Human Rights, Citizenship, and Society in Latin America*, Boulder, Colo.: Westview Press

Keck, Margaret and K. Sikkink (eds) (1998) *Activists Beyond Borders: Advocacy Networks in International Politics*, Ithaca, NY: Cornell University Press

Lavrin, Asunción (1995) *Women, Feminism and Social Change in Argentina, Chile and Uruguay 1890–1940*, Lincoln, Nebr.: University of Nebraska Press

Lycklama à Nijeholt, Geertjee, V. Vargas, and S. Wieringa (eds) (1998) *Women's Movements and Public Policy in Europe, Latin America, and the Caribbean*, New York: Garland

Mainwaring, Scott and Matthew Shugart (eds) (1997) *Presidentialism and Democracy in Latin America*, Cambridge: Cambridge University Press

Miller, Francesca (1991) *Latin American Women and the Search for Social Justice*, Hanover, NH.: University Press of New England

Molyneux, Maxine (1985) 'Mobilisation without emancipation? Women's interests, state and revolution in Nicaragua' *Feminist Studies*, 2 (2) 227–54

Molyneux, Maxine (2000a) *Women's Movements in International Perspective*, London: ILAS/Macmillan Press – now Palgrave

Molyneux, Maxine (2000b) 'State formations in Latin America' in Elizabeth Dore and M. Molyneux (eds) *Hidden Histories of Gender and the State in Latin America*, London: Duke University Press

Molyneux, Maxine (2000c) 'Gender and citizenship in comparative perspective' in J. Cook, J. Roberts and G. Waylen *Towards a Gendered Political Economy*, Basingstoke: Macmillan Press – now Palgrave

Molyneux, Maxine and S. Lazar (forthcoming 2002) *Rights Citizenship and Participatory Development in Latin America*, London: ILAS discussion paper

Moser, Caroline (1989) 'Gender planning in the Third World: meeting practical and strategic needs' *World Development*, 1 (11) 1799–825

O'Donnell, Guillermo, Phillippe Schmitter and Laurence Whitehead (eds) (1986) *Transition from Authoritarian Rule*, (4 vols) Baltimore Md.: Johns Hopkins University Press

Ortiz, Adriana, A. Amuchástegui and M. Rivas 'Because they were born from me: negotiating women's rights in Mexico' in R. Petechesky and K. Judd (eds) *Negotiating Reproductive Rights*, London: Zed Books

Pateman, Carol (1988) *The Sexual Contract*, Cambridge: Polity Press

Rai, Shirin (ed.) (2000) *International Perspectives on Gender and Democratization*, Basingstoke: Macmillan Press – now Palgrave

REPEM (2000) Second Report Beijing + 5: Women (http.www.repem2@chasque.apc.org)

Safa, Helen (1990) 'Women's social movements in Latin America' *Gender and Society*, 4 (3) 354–69

Schild, Veronica (1998) 'New subjects of rights? Women's movements and the construction of citizenship in the "New Democracies"' in S. Alvarez, E. Dagnino and A. Escobar (eds) *Cultures of Politics/Politics of Cultures: Revisioning Latin American Social Movements* Boulder, Colo.: Westview, Press, 93–115

Stavenhagen, Rodolfo (1996) 'Indigenous rights: some conceptual problems' in E. Jelin and E. Hershberg (eds) *Constructing Democracy: Human Rights, Citizenship and Society in Latin America*, Boulder, Colo.: Westview Press

Sternbach, Nancy Saporta, Marysa Navarro Aranguren, Patricia Chuchryk and Sonia Alvarez (1992) 'Feminisms in Latin America: from Bogotá to San Bernardo' in Arturo Escobar and Sonia Alvarez (eds) (1992) *The Making of Social Movements in Latin America*, Boulder, Colo.: Westview Press

Stoner, C. Lynne (1988) *From the House to the Streets: the Cuban Women's Movement for Legal Reform*, Durham, NC: Duke University Press

UNDP (1999) 'Globalization with a human face: human development report', www.undp.org/hdro/99.htm.

UNRISD (2000a) *Visible Hands: Taking Responsibility for Social Development*, Geneva: UNRISD

UNRISD (2000b) 'Gender justice, development and rights: substantiating rights in a disabling environment' report of the UNRISD Workshop, New York, 3 June

Valdés, Teresa (1998) 'El Control Ciudadano de la Plataforma de Beijing: Un proceso social en Construcción' in *Entre la II Cumbre y la detención de Pinochet'*, Flasco, Chile

Valdés, Teresa and Marisa Weinstein (n.d.) 'Corriendo y descorriendo tupidos velos' FLACSO mimeo

Vargas, Virginia (1992) 'The feminist movement in Latin America: between hope and disenchantment' in *Development and Change*, 23 (3) 195–214

Vargas, Virginia (1998) *Caminos a Beijing*, Lima: Flora Tristán

Waylen, Georgina 1994 'Women and democratization: conceptualizing gender relations in transition politics' *World Politics*, 46, 327–54

Waylen, Georgina (1996a) *Gender in Third World Politics*, Milton Keynes: Open University Press

Waylen, Georgina (1996b) 'Democratization, feminism and the state in Chile: the establishment of SERNAM' in Shirin Rai and G. Lievesley, (eds) *Women and the State: International Perspectives*, London: Taylor & Francis

2
Engendering the Right to Participate in Decision-making: Electoral Quotas and Women's Leadership in Latin America

Mala N. Htun and Mark P. Jones

Since elite women mobilised around suffrage rights in the nineteenth century, gaining access to decision-making power has been a central objective of women's movements in Latin America. Today these demands appear to have been realised. Between 1991, when Argentina became the first democratic state in Latin America to establish a strict women's quota, and 2000, when Colombia became the most recent country in the region to do so, 12 Latin American countries enacted national laws establishing a minimum level of 20 to 40 per cent for women's participation as candidates in national elections. The regional trend toward the enactment of quota laws is unprecedented in world history. Only Belgium and Taiwan have similar quota legislation. Today (December 2000), women occupy 13 per cent of the seats in the lower houses of parliament in Latin America. The region ranks behind Northern Europe (at 39 per cent), and compares with the world average, the rest of Europe, as well as the United States (all at 13 per cent).[1]

This chapter analyses whether quotas have achieved the goals invested in them by women's movement activists. We develop two arguments about the effects of quotas on the election of women and on gender-related policy outcomes. First, we show that quota laws have been only mildly effective in increasing women's presence in legislatures. Many of Latin America's electoral systems make it hard to apply a women's quota, and political parties tend to comply with quotas in a minimalist manner. Data from the most recent round of elections show that, on average, quotas helped to boost women's presence in national congresses by five percentage points. Next, we present preliminary evidence suggesting that when quotas work, women's greater presence in politics serves to shift the terms of legislative debates. Yet quotas alone do not generate the political alliances necessary to change policy.

Quotas, like other policy measures addressed to women in the 1990s, represent an unprecedented breakthrough in the state's recognition of certain rights, such as the right to participate in decision-making, the right to be free from domestic violence and the right to decide on the number and spacing of children. International agreements such as the 1995 Platform for Action endorsed by governments at the Fourth World Conference on Women were instrumental in diffusing these broader understandings of rights. Yet, the dilemmas engendered by quotas are representative of difficulties in making concrete women's new formal rights in general. Quotas have produced small and uneven gains in women's leadership because of a failure to reform the institutions necessary to make quotas work. Institutional pathologies – corruption, inefficiency, low accountability – help to explain the low enforcement not only of quotas but also a wide array of women's other 'new rights'.

Background

The quota laws passed in twelve countries – Argentina, Bolivia, Brazil, Colombia, Costa Rica, the Dominican Republic, Ecuador, Mexico, Panama, Paraguay, Peru and Venezuela – are the product of women's movement demands at the national and international level for governments to take action to increase women's participation in politics.[2] The growth of women's movements in the 1970s, and the roles played by women in the struggle against authoritarianism, placed the question of women's representation on the policy agenda of new democratic governments in the 1990s. Meanwhile, international agreements such as the United Nations Convention on the Elimination of all Forms of Discrimination Against Women (CEDAW), and the Beijing Platform for Action, contributed to the spread of global norms and understandings of gender equality in decision-making. Latin American leaders responded by adopting new laws and public policies aimed at furthering women's equal opportunities in the polity, economy and society. Governments created women's agencies to propose, advise, and coordinate public policies on women; modified discriminatory parts of civil and criminal codes to grant women equal rights and obligations; incorporated principles of equality in new or reformed constitutions; and adopted policy initiatives targeted at women such as microcredit programmes, literacy drives and daycare for children (Htun 1998, 1999, n.d.).

Why and how did Latin Americans opt for quotas over another policy mix? Women activists in Latin America argue that democracy, equality and fairness demand that women participate in political decision-making on equal terms with men. The gender biases of political institutions, reinforced by decades of women's exclusion, mean that more gradualist forms of affirmative action will only produce results in the very long term. By guaranteeing a certain level of women's representation in congress, quotas aim to close the gap between women's presence at the bottom and their representation at the top. Women make up over half of the eligible voters in most Latin American countries, and amount to approximately one-third of political party members. Women's presence in congresses (at an average of 13 per cent) is high by world standards, but lags behind women's participation in the public sphere at large. As Brazilian congresswoman Marta Suplicy put it: 'In Brazil today, [the quota] is more than a new instrument in women's struggle for equality and the construction of true democracy, it is an imperative of justice' (Suplicy n.d.: 1).

Other arguments for quotas focus on anticipated outcomes. Women leaders are seen to better represent the interests of women citizens and to introduce women's perspectives into policy-making. Having a 'critical mass' of women in power facilitates debate and legislation on women's issues (Staudt 1998). Mexican Senator María de los Angeles Moreno reports that only when at least one quarter of the people in the room are women is it possible to conduct a civilised debate on issues of concern to women, such as rape and domestic violence.[3] A final argument centres on the symbolism of quotas. Quotas help to educate the public about gender equality and demonstrate that society is inclusive and egalitarian. As Peruvian congresswoman Beatriz Merino explains: 'When women opine on important public issues – like the management of the economy – civil society sees that women are able to face the challenge of leading the country' (PROMUJER 1998: 44).

The quota movement gained momentum at regional and international meetings, particularly the September of 1995 United Nations fourth World Conference on Women in Beijing. Earlier in the year, Latin American congresswomen gathered at the Latin American Parliament in São Paulo to discuss Argentina's quota experiment and quota politics around the world. The regional meeting 'was the spark that ignited a call to action' for many of the women politicians present (Suplicy 1996: 9). Then, the Platform for Action endorsed the notion that women had a right to participate in decision-making. It called on governments to ensure 'women's equal access to and full participation in power structures and decision-making', and to consider adopting affirmative action policies to achieve equal representation of women and men.

The Beijing Platform legitimised the idea of quotas at the international level and served as a focal point for domestic mobilisation. To generate support for the quota, Mexican deputy María Elena Chapa recalled, 'we travelled around the entire country organising meetings about women's participation in diverse areas and women's common concerns: health, education, employment, politics, poverty, self-image, environment, violence, children, among others, in line with the issues granted global attention by the Beijing Platform for Action.'[4] The fact that many Latin American female politicians went to Beijing served to unite women around the idea of the quota.[5] The Beijing conference also provided normative leverage: since governments had already endorsed the Beijing Platform, activists could argue that quota laws furthered governmental compliance with commitments made in international forums.

Although pressure from women politicians and international norms were the central causes of quotas, presidential interest has also been important. Presidents and other senior male officials supported quotas for a variety of reasons: out of embarrassment over the low levels of women's representation in their countries; the desire to court women's votes and the support of women politicians; the need to meet commitments enshrined in international agreements.[6] These politicians responded rationally to the way that principles of gender equality have been gradually incorporated into prevailing understandings of democracy and modernity.

There is no consensus on the desirability of quotas, however. Opponents of quotas, many of whom are women, argue that they discriminate against men, will elevate underqualified women to power, and above all, are unnecessary, since qualified women will rise to power on their own merits. They are also concerned that women beneficiaries of a quota will be stigmatised as owing their position to the quota and not to their own efforts.

To sum up, advocates of quotas make three claims. The first is *normative*: fairness and equality require that women be present in decision-making affecting society at large. Quotas, which guarantee women's presence in the short term, are the most effective means of achieving this objective. The second is *consequentialist*: quotas, which mean that more women are in power, will place fresh items on the political agenda and change policy outcomes to better reflect women's concerns. The last is *symbolic*: quotas educate the public about gender equality and demonstrate society's commitment to a democracy based on inclusiveness. The rest of the chapter evaluates the effectiveness of quotas in meeting these expectations.

Preliminary evaluation of quotas

The enactment of laws establishing a minimum level of women's participation as candidates in national elections in 12 Latin American countries is a truly novel phenomenon. Rarely have so many countries adopted strikingly similar legislation on women's rights within such a short period of time. The quota trend reveals an unprecedented commitment to women's participation in decision-making on the part of the region's leaders. Do quotas work? In this section, we analyse Latin American quota laws along three dimensions. First, we show that features of a country's electoral system and institutions determine whether quotas help more women get elected. A closed-list system, a placement requirement, large district magnitude and good-faith compliance by political parties are the factors that make quotas work. Second, we explore the consequences of quotas. Preliminary evidence from Argentina suggests that quotas have spillover effects and that women elected with a quota have different policy priorities than their male counterparts. Nonetheless, quotas do not seem to make women's political alliances, the key factor in enacting gender-related legislation, any stronger. The final section offers a few remarks on the symbolic dimensions of quotas.

Quotas and the election of women

In general, quotas have been only mildly effective in increasing the number of women elected to Latin American legislatures. In the 11 countries with quotas, women made up an average of 9 per cent of the legislature prior to the quota. Following the implementation of the quota, this increased to 14 per cent. In other words, the quota served to boost women's presence by five percentage points. In historical perspective, a five-point gain is an impressive jump from one election to another. Still, in very few instances did women's presence actually reach the level of the quota. To make sense of these results, we must examine the interaction of quotas and national electoral systems. Women's presence approximated the level of the quota only in the Argentine Chamber of Deputies and the Paraguayan Senate. The success of quotas in these two countries owes to the closed-list system, placement mandate, moderate to large-sized electoral districts and good-faith compliance by political parties.[7]

All 11 countries with quota laws elect their legislators from party lists in multimember districts using proportional representation (PR), although in some countries a fixed percentage of the legislature is elected from single member districts.[8] Beyond these basic features, the laws vary significantly (see Table 2.1). The table shows that the minimum level of women's presence (or quota percentage) varies from 20 to 40 per cent. Whether this quota is actually reached by the election of women legislators depends in large part on three institutional factors: the type of party list (closed or open), the existence of a placement mandate, and the size of the districts from which the legislators are elected (the district magnitude).

Type of party list

The type of party list (closed or open) is highly consequential for the effectiveness of a quota law. When party lists are closed, political parties present a rank-ordered list of candidates in each of the multimember districts where they are contesting seats. Voters cast a ballot for the entire list; they cannot alter the ordering of the candidates. Once a party's seat allocation has been determined (using a proportional representation allocation formula), its seats are distributed based on the list's rank ordering. For example, if a party wins three seats, the first three people on its list are elected: Argentina, Bolivia, Costa Rica, the Dominican Republic, Mexico, Paraguay and Venezuela use closed lists.

Although parties present a list of candidates in an open-list system, there is no rank ordering. Voters are required to select a candidate on the party list (also called exercising a preference vote).[9] The seats are allocated among the parties based on the percentage of the vote each party received (similar to the closed-list systems). However, the seats are distributed among the party's candidates based on the number of 'preference' votes received, not based on their ordering on the list. For example, if a party wins three seats, the three party candidates who obtained the most preference votes are elected: Brazil, Ecuador, Panama and Peru use open lists.

In a closed-list system, parties compete against one another for votes. Every candidate has an incentive to maximise the vote for his or her party since seats are allocated based on the party's total vote. In an open-list system, there is fierce intra-party competition in addition to the inter-party competition. Because a candidate's preference votes determine whether he or she is elected, candidates from the same party

Table 2.1 Quota laws in Latin America

Country	Year adopted	Legislative branch	Quota percentage	Open vs. closed list	Placement mandate	Average district magnitude
Argentina	1991	Chamber of Deputies	30	Closed	Yes	5
	1991 (2001)[a]	Senate	30/50[a]	Closed	Yes	3
Bolivia	1997	Chamber of Deputies	30[b]	Closed	Yes	7
		Senate	25	Closed	No	3
Brazil	1997	Chamber of Deputies	25/30[c]	Open	No	20
Costa Rica	1997	Chamber of Deputies	40	Closed	No[e]	7
Dominican Republic	1997	Chamber of Deputies	25	Closed	No	5
Ecuador	1997	Chamber of Deputies	20/33[c]	Open	No	6
Mexico	1996	Chamber of Deputies	30	Closed	No	40
		Senate	30	Closed	No	4
Panama	1997	Chamber of Deputies	30[b,d]	Open	No	4
Paraguay	1996	Chamber of Deputies	20[d]	Closed	Yes	4
		Senate	20[d]	Closed	Yes	45
Peru	1997	Chamber of Deputies	30[c]	Open	No	5
Venezuela	1998	Chamber of Deputies	30[b]	Closed	No	4
		Senate	30	Closed	No	2

[a] The first Senate election where quotas will be used takes place in 2001. Since each list can elect a maximum of two senators, the *de facto* quota is 50% (the *de jure* quota is 30%). Combined with the electoral rules governing the Senate election (two seats for the plurality party and one for the first runner-up), the quota law insures that at a minimum 33% of the senators will be women.

[b] Approximately one-half of the Chamber legislators in Bolivia and Venezuela, three-fifths in Mexico, and one-third in Panama, are elected from single-member districts (SMD). The quota law does not apply to these SMD elections. The district magnitude data are based on the multimember district seats governed by the quota law. All Venezuela data are for the pre-2000 period. In the 2000 Venezuelan election (for a unicameral legislature) no quota law was in force.

[c] The Brazilian quota percentage was 25% for the 1998 election (it will be 30% in future elections). The Ecuadoran quota was 20% for the 1998 election (it will be 33% in future elections). The initial Peruvian quota was 25% (the quota used in the free and fair 2001 elections was 30%).

[d] The Panamanian and Paraguayan quotas are for the party primary elections.

[e] A placement mandate will be in force for the next election, to be held in 2002.

compete against one another for preference votes in the general election. As relative newcomers, women generally have fewer resources than their male colleagues, a major handicap in intra-party competition.

Placement mandate

The second factor shaping the effectiveness of quota laws is the existence of a placement mandate in closed-list systems. The purpose of this mandate is to prevent parties from clustering women at the bottom of the party list where they have no realistic chance of getting elected. For example, the Argentine Ley de Cupos (1991) requires that women account for a minimum of 30 per cent of the candidates on the party list and that these women be placed in *electable* positions. The second requirement has been interpreted to mean that every third (and sixth, ninth, etc.) candidate on the party list must be a woman (except in districts where a party is renewing two seats, where the second candidate, at the minimum, must be a woman). The Bolivian law is similar to the Argentine Ley de Cupos since at least one of every three positions on the list must be occupied by a woman. The Paraguayan law establishes a 20 per cent quota (for the party primaries) and mandates that at least one of every five candidates on the lists presented in these primaries be a woman.

The quota laws in the Dominican Republic, Mexico and Venezuela respectively stipulate that women occupy at least 25 per cent, 30 per cent and 30 per cent of the positions on the party list. Yet, these laws say nothing about the location of women on the list. As a result, parties tend to place women at the bottom of the party list, where they have little chance of getting elected. Costa Rica's quota law (40 per cent) originally contained no placement mandate. In 2000, however, the country's Supreme Electoral Court ordered political parties to comply with the quota by placing women in *electable* positions, thereby establishing a placement mandate. To be effective in a closed-list system, quota laws must include a placement mandate.

District magnitude

Small district magnitudes, particularly when combined with a large number of parties winning seats in the legislature, severely limit the effectiveness of quotas, since parties normally win only one or two seats in a district. In closed-list systems, the top positions on the party list (which are the only electable positions) are generally occupied by men. The larger the district magnitude, the more effective quotas are likely to be.

The average district magnitude varies considerably across these 11 countries. At the low end are the Argentine, Bolivian, Mexican and Venezuelan Senates and the Panamanian Chamber of Deputies with average district magnitudes of less than five representatives. At the other end of the continuum are the Brazilian Chamber of Deputies, Mexican Chamber of Deputies and the Paraguayan Senate. The average Brazilian and Mexican constituency (district) elects 20 and 40 legislators respectively, while Paraguay uses a single national district (with 45 legislators). The remaining cases occupy an intermediate position between these two extremes.[10]

In most countries, the absence of a placement mandate, the use of open lists, and/or the employment of small legislative districts reduced the effectiveness of quotas. With one exception (the Paraguayan Senate), the percentage of women elected with quotas did not reach the minimum percentage established by the quota in any country (see Table 2.2). After the Paraguayan Senate, the Argentine Chamber of Deputies came closest to reaching the minimum threshold (two percentage points lower than the quota). The Bolivian Senate, Costa Rican Chamber of Deputies and Venezuelan Senate remained the furthest from this minimum goal (each 21 percentage points lower than the quota). The Bolivian and Venezuelan results are not surprising, since a party can elect a maximum of two senators from each district and there is no placement mandate requiring the parties to locate a woman in one of the first two positions on the party list. In Costa Rica, the law stated that women must comprise 40 per cent of each party's district level lists, but did not regulate the placement of these women on the lists. The lack of a placement mandate was also the reason (along with a low district magnitude) behind the limited success of the quota laws in the Dominican Republic and Venezuela (Chamber of Deputies).

Successful cases

The Argentine and Paraguayan Senate cases highlight three elements that are crucial to the success of the quota: the utilisation of a placement mandate in a closed-list system, a moderate to high average district magnitude, and party compliance. The Argentine Ley de Cupos of 1991 contains two important requirements: a minimum of 30 per cent of candidates on the closed party lists in all of the country's 24 electoral districts must be women, and these women must be placed in electable positions on the lists and not in 'ornamental' positions from which there is no chance of election. Party lists that fail to comply with the law are rejected.[11]

Table 2.2 Quota laws and the election of women

Country	Legislative branch	Percentage of women prior to law	Percentage of women after law	Change (in % points)	Minimum percentage established in the quota law
Argentina	Chamber	6	28	22	30
Bolivia	Chamber	11	12	1	30
Bolivia	Senate	4	4	0	25
Brazil	Chamber	7	6	–1	25
Costa Rica	Chamber	14	19	5	40
Dominican Republic	Chamber	12	16	4	25
Ecuador	Chamber	4	17	13	20
Mexico	Chamber	14	17	3	30
Mexico	Senate	13	15	2	30
Panama	Chamber	8	11	3	30
Paraguay	Chamber	3	3	0	20
Paraguay	Senate	11	20	9	20
Peru	Chamber	11	18	7	30
Venezuela	Chamber	6	13	7	30
Venezuela	Senate	8	9	1	30
AVERAGE		9	14	5	28

In Argentina, the political party has control over access to the party list and the location of candidates on the rank-ordered list. In Chamber of Deputies elections, the quota law means that if a party wins six seats in a district, a minimum of two of the winning candidates will be women. If the open-list method were used, the quota law would provide no such guarantee. In the four open-list countries with quotas (Brazil (25 per cent), Ecuador (20 per cent), Panama (30 per cent), Peru (30 per cent)), the laws say nothing about placement. While these laws guarantee that there will be a significant increase in the percentage of women candidates, they provide no guarantee that there will be a corresponding increase in the percentage of women elected. The same conclusion also holds for the closed-list countries that lack a placement mandate in their quota laws (i.e. Costa Rica, the Dominican Republic, Mexico and Venezuela).

Second, a large district magnitude (combined with a one-in-five placement mandate) explains the relative success of the quota law in the Paraguayan Senate election of 1998. In Paraguay, the combination of the large single national electoral district (from which 45 senators are elected) and the strong performance by the two largest parties, Asociación Republicana Nacional (ANR) (which won 24 seats) and the Alianza Democrática (which won 20 seats) allowed women placed low on the list to get elected. No woman occupied one of the first ten positions on the ANR list, but four held positions between 11 and 20. On the Alianza's list, only one woman was located in the first ten slots (eighth), but three women occupied positions between 11 and 20. In all, nine women were elected to the Paraguayan Senate, five from the ANR and four from the Alianza.

The third crucial element for the success of the quota in getting women elected is good faith compliance by political parties. Compliance with the quota law has become routine in Argentina, and problems of non-compliance are virtually non-existent for Chamber elections. This present norm of compliance was only achieved by the tremendous efforts of women activists from across the political spectrum during the 1993–95 period. These women took parties to court to force them to comply with the law. Although parties eventually complied, it is important to note that they have largely done so in a minimalist manner, placing women in the lowest positions permitted by law. In the four Chamber elections held since 1993, three-quarters of the major party lists complied with the quota law in this way. In contrast to the success in Argentina, Brazil has experienced significant difficulties with compliance. There, women represented a mere 10 per cent of the Chamber of

Deputies candidates in 1998, in spite of a quota law that requires parties to reserve 25 per cent of candidacies for women.[12]

In sum, the combination of the use of open lists, the lack of explicit legislation mandating placement, small district magnitudes, and lack of good faith compliance contributed to the meagre advances in the election of women in most of the 11 countries. Given the features of each country's electoral system, the disappointing results should have been relatively easy to predict. In other words, adoption of the quota law in most countries never posed a major threat to the aspirations of male politicians. This might help to explain the relatively smooth and trouble-free passage of many of the quota laws in the 1996–2000 period.

Quotas in political parties

Many Latin American political parties have voluntarily adopted quota rules that establish minimum percentages of women to be included on the party lists. The first use in Latin America (and as far as we are aware in the world) of party quota rules occurred in Argentina in the early 1950s. Due to lobbying by Eva Perón, the Peronist Party applied a women's quota to congressional elections (Molinelli 1994). Combined with the electoral success of the Peronist Party, the quotas gave Argentina an impressive level of women's representation in the Chamber of Deputies (15 per cent between 1952 and 1954 and 22 per cent in 1955) (Inter-Parliamentary Union 1995). In 1955, Argentina (where deputies were chosen in contested elections, albeit under somewhat strained circumstances) had the world's fourth highest percentage of women national deputies, trailing the communist countries of East Germany, the Soviet Union and Mongolia. In Finland, the democracy with the most women legislators in 1955, women amounted to a mere 15 per cent of the legislature. Today, party quota rules are the most common form of positive action employed to increase the representation of women outside of Latin America, and are in large part responsible for the high levels of women's representation in Northern European countries (Caul 1999, Dahlerup 1998, Inter-Parliamentary Union 1997).

Several major political parties in Latin America use quotas for internal elections and to construct lists for general elections.[13] The use of a party quota rule by the Frente Farabundo Martí para la Liberación Nacional (FMLN) for the 1997 Salvadoran Legislative Assembly election and by the Frente Sandinista de Liberación Nacional (FSLN) for the 1996 Nicaraguan

National Assembly election provide evidence of the potential of party quota rules. In El Salvador and Nicaragua, deputies are elected from a combination of multimember districts and a single national level district using closed party lists. The FMLN and FSLN quotas specify that a minimum of 35 per cent and 30 per cent of the candidates on the party's lists for public offices be women.

Women amounted to 29 per cent of the FMLN Assembly candidates in El Salvador, 10 per cent more than that of the country's other major party, the Alianza Republicana Nacionalista (ARENA) (Luciak 1997). Thirteen women deputies were elected in 1997: nine from the FMLN (33 per cent of its 27 deputies) and four from ARENA (14 per cent of its 28 deputies). Neither of the country's two other relevant parties, the Partido de Conciliación Nacional (11 deputies) and the Partido Demócrata Cristiano/Partido Demócrata alliance (ten deputies), nor any of the four minor parties that won seats (eight total) had any women elected. In Nicaragua, 36 per cent of the National Assembly candidates presented by the FSLN were women. This figure dwarfs that of Nicaragua's other major political force, the Alianza Liberal (AL), where women represented a mere 9 per cent of candidates. Ten women deputies were elected in 1996: eight from the FSLN (22 per cent of its 36 deputies), one from the AL (2 per cent of its 42 deputies) and one from one of the nine minor parties that garnered a combined total of 15 seats. The relatively high percentages of FMLN and FSLN women deputies show that party quotas can work for parties who employ them.[14] Unlike a national law, however, they are not mandatory for all parties.

Quotas and policy outcomes

If quotas work, more women will get elected to public office. Does having more women present produce changes in law and policy that are more favourable to women's interests? To answer this question, we first consider evidence from Argentina. There, the most prominent effect of the national quota law has been to encourage the adoption of quotas at other levels and branches of government. Argentine evidence shows that women legislators have different policy priorities than men, although many women politicians demonstrate little interest in gender-related legislation. Next, we analyse the role of women's political alliances in getting legislation passed. Law and policy advances in the 1990s have been brought about by political alliances uniting women from different political parties. Yet, quota laws are neither necessary nor sufficient for the formation of such alliances.

Policy consequences of quotas: the Argentine case

Most Latin American quota laws were adopted between 1996 and 1999, making it premature to evaluate their effects on public policy. The Argentine law, however, dates from 1991, and was first applied in 1993. Data from Argentina suggest some preliminary generalisations about the policy consequences of quotas.

The most visible effect of the Argentine quota law has been the adoption of quota laws for provincial and municipal elections since 1991. Twenty-one of Argentina's 23 provinces, as well as the federal capital City of Buenos Aires, currently use quotas in the election of provincial and, in most cases, municipal legislators. This legislation has in many instances resulted in a dramatic increase in the percentage of women provincial and municipal legislators. In the 12 provincial legislatures elected using closed lists, the average percentage of women legislators increased from 7 per cent to 21 per cent. Some jurisdictions have gone even further with quotas. The 1996 Constitution of the City of Buenos Aires stipulates that members of appointed bodies with three or more members (such as the Judiciary and the Public Services Commission) should include no more than 70 per cent of the same sex. The city's constitution was itself drafted by a constituent assembly elected using quota legislation (women made up 32 per cent of the assembly).

Evidence from Argentina also suggests that women's legislative behaviour differs from men's. Two indicators of legislative behaviour are committee membership and bill introduction (Crisp *et al.* n.d.). Following consequentialist arguments for quotas, we would expect women to be over-represented on committees that deal with issues related to women's rights or issues of traditional interest to women, such as children and families, education, the elderly, the environment, health care, and housing (Dodson and Carroll 1991). Table 2.3 contains information on committee membership in the Argentine Chamber of Deputies in 1997, at which time 72 of the 257 legislators were women. The table shows that women were significantly over-represented on most committees of traditional interest to women (e.g. Education, Elderly, Family, Women and Minorities, Public Health and Social Action). Committee posts in Argentina are assigned by the party leadership based on the requests of legislators (Jones 1998).[15]

A second measure of legislator behaviour is bill introduction. The distribution of bills across thematic areas provides a good indicator of the policy priorities of a legislator. Table 2.4 displays information on bill introduction by legislators during the 1993–94 period in the Argentine

Table 2.3 Composition of ordinary committees in the Argentine Chamber of Deputies, 1997

Committee	Women overrepresented	Men overrepresented	Equal representation
Agriculture and livestock			x
Budget		x	
Commerce			x
Communications			x
Compliance with tax and social security norms			x
Constitutional affairs			x
Cooperative and mutal aid affairs			
Culture	x		
Drug addiction	x		
Economy		x	
Education	x		
Elderly	x		
Energy and fuel			x
Family, women and minorities	x		
Finance		x	
Foreign affairs		x	
General legislation			x
Housing			x
Human rights	x		
Impeachment			x
Industry		x	
Justice			x
Labour legislation			x
Maritime, river and fishing interests			x
Mining			
Municipal affairs			x
National defence		x	
Natural resources			x
Penal legislation			x
Pensions and social security			x
Population and human resources			x
Public health and social action	x		x
Public works			
Regional economic development			x
Rules			x
Science and technology			x
Sports			x
Tourism			x
Transportation			x

Note: Overrepresentation signifies that the sex difference was significant at the .05 level for a Chi-Square test, and that the members of that sex were overrepresented.

Source: Elaborated by the authors using data provided by the Centro de Estudios para el Desarrollo Institucional de la Fundación Gobierno y Sociedad.

Chamber of Deputies, when 36 of the 257 deputies were women. The results indicate that while women differed from men in their bill introduction in two of the highlighted areas (Women's Rights and Children and Families), no significant priority differences between male and female legislators were observed for any of the other categories often identified as of traditional interest to women (i.e. Health Care/Public Health, Education, Welfare/Social Security, Environment).

Although significant gender differences were detected in the areas of Women's Rights and Children and Families, it is important to note that this does not signify that *all* women prioritise these issues. The data in Table 2.4 show that 33 per cent of the women legislators presented a third or more of their bills in the Women's Rights area and 11 per cent in the Children and Families area. On the other hand, 58 per cent of the women legislators presented no bills in Women's Rights and 61 per cent presented no bills in Children and Families.[16]

Argentine evidence suggests that quotas, by getting more women into Congress, have helped to place gender-related issues on the legislative agenda. Have these women succeeded in enacting gender-related legislation? The next section explores the role of women's political alliances

Table 2.4 Policy priorities in the first 'Post-quota' legislative period in Argentina, 1993–94

Policy area	Significant differences in priority between male and female legislators*	Percentage of women who presented more than 1/3 of their bills in this area	Percentage of women who presented no bills in this area
Women's rights	x	33	58
Children and families	x	11	61
Women's rights + children and familes	x	50	39
Health care/public health		8	81
Education		11	83
Welfare/social security		8	83
Environment		6	86
Other	x	42	44

* Difference significant at the .05 level for a two-tailed test. For every policy area where there was a significant difference but 'Other', women prioritised the policy area to a greater extent than men.

Source: (Jones 1997).

in policy change. We will see that alone, quotas do not strengthen the political alliances necessary to get legislation passed.

Women's political alliances

In Argentina, women's higher presence in Congress led to the introduction of more bills on women's issues. Women legislators expressed policy priorities that were different from men's in some areas. What about getting legislation passed? In the 1990s, women politicians in various countries have joined in political alliances to lobby for legal and policy changes to benefit women. If we compare the results achieved by women's political alliances in countries with and in countries without quotas, however, the differences are not dramatic. Argentine women, in spite of the fact that they make up 28 per cent of Congress, have not achieved many more policy changes than women legislators in other countries where the numbers are smaller. Women politicians in Argentina were responsible for advances in the 1994 constitutional reforms, domestic violence legislation, and the Chamber of Deputies' approval of a reproductive health bill.[17] In Chile and Colombia, where there was no quota and women's presence in Congress amounts to 11 and 12 per cent respectively, similar policy changes have been enacted. In Colombia, the 1991 constitutional reforms recognised the principle of gender equality, including the equal 'right to participate in the formation, exercise, and control of political power' (Morgan 1992: 381–2).[18] By the mid-1990s Colombia had established around 250 family police stations nation-wide, and a domestic violence law was enacted in 1996. The Chilean Congress approved a domestic violence law in 1994 and major (though much-delayed) changes to family law in 1998.

Women's alliances have secured policy changes on some issues, but they have failed to produce change on all issues. Several factors mitigate the strength and the unity of such alliances. The first is the fact that gender issues are not the first priority of most women elected to public office. The vast majority of women who enter politics in Latin America do not campaign on women's issues (such as domestic violence, child care, equal opportunities or reproductive health), nor do they make such issues the central focus of their legislative careers. In Argentina, 58 per cent of women legislators did not present a single bill in the area of Women's Rights between 1993 and 1994. Rodríguez notes in the case of Mexico that 'gender concerns come in second within the majority of women's policy agendas, trailing behind whatever their principal policy area may be' (Rodríguez 1998: 7). For some politicians, this stems from pragmatism. Political society and the electorate have not proven immediately responsive, and in fact have at times been resistant, to the promotion of a 'women's agenda' in politics. As one Argentine congresswoman remarked: 'men have convinced women that talking about women's issues is of little importance. Women, in order to be important politically, can't talk about gender issues.'[19]

The second factor is party loyalty. Party loyalty frequently trumps gender identity in politics. Based on interviews with 80 Mexican women in politics, Rodríguez concludes that

> women's political loyalties, first and foremost, rest with the political party or organisation to which they belong. Gender loyalty, for all practical purposes, comes in (a distant) second. Even among women of the same party, it is noticeable that their solidarity and loyalty rest with policies and programs, political patrons and mentors, career plans and ambitions – not with the other women in the party. (Rodríguez 1998: 8).

Another recent study of Mexico concluded that gender-related policy changes came about only when they coincided with party interests, as in the case of domestic violence. When party interests contradicted women's strategic gender interests – in the case of quota laws, protection of women in the workplace, and abortion – women's alliances were significantly weakened and legislation was not enacted (Alatorre 1999).

The final reason that women's political alliances fail to form around all issues, concerns women's divergent interests and ideas. Some women subscribe to a more conservative or traditional view of women's interests. In this view, gender equality is desirable, as long as it doesn't question women's roles as wives, mothers and homemakers. According to a contrasting feminist position, the precondition to equal opportunities is the questioning and restructuring of traditional gender roles. There is enough compatibility between these two visions to permit the formation of political alliances around issues like domestic violence, equal treatment in the workplace, and protection of children. The two visions diverge most radically in issues surrounding reproduction. It is most difficult to form alliances of women to push for family planning programmes and for a liberalisation of laws punishing abortion.

It is rare to find women politicians who openly identify as feminists, although there are important exceptions. The label 'feminist' carries a negative social stigma in Latin America because it is associated with a denial of sex difference and a rejection of femininity. Many women politicians avoid associating themselves with feminism because they believe it limits their political opportunities. As one Argentine politician said, 'I make claims as a feminist, but I don't publicly identify as one because it would isolate me... In very male political parties, gaining access to decision-making positions as a feminist is impossible. One can practice politics with feminist principles... but astutely and surreptitiously.'[20]

A common saying in Latin America goes 'cuerpo de mujer no garantiza conciencia de género' ('being a woman does not guarantee having a gender conscience'). For those concerned about outcomes favourable to women's rights, what seems to matter the most is a 'conciencia de género' (gender conscience), and not a 'cuerpo de mujer' (being a woman). Limited comparative evidence suggests that the existence of broad political alliances joining women in politics and women in society, not a quota, is the most effective guarantee of a conciencia de género.[21]

Quotas as symbol

The final argument in favour of quotas focuses on the symbolic or cultural dimension. Quota laws help to educate the public about gender equality, introduce new items on the policy agenda and legitimise women's political leadership. In short, quotas help make culture more egalitarian and democratic. As Mexican Senator Amalia García puts it: 'The challenge of the minimum percentage [quota] is not its application as obligatory but rather to transform the collective conscience, the culture of both men and women' (Rodríguez 1998: 14). Camacho *et al.* (1997: 93–4) add that 'Quotas benefit all of society... [quotas] have deepened societal understanding of discrimination and clarified the need to seek alternatives to change the present reality.'

There is plentiful evidence to suggest that quota law proposals have succeeded in making gender parity in decision-making a national issue. By introducing quota bills in the national legislature, women legislators forced their male counterparts to formulate and defend opinions about gender equality. In many countries, media coverage surrounding the quotas stimulated debates about the history of women's leadership and introduced affirmative action in other areas. In Brazil, congresswoman Marta Suplicy proposed that ballots be gender neutral,[22] that campaign literature feature women and men in equal proportions, that official agencies gather data about the sex of candidates, and that a fixed proportion of party funds be allocated to finance women's political campaigns (Suplicy 1997). Quota proposals have served an important agenda-setting function among educated elites; as the Argentine experience shows, the national law spurred discussion about the adoption of quotas in other decision-making arenas.

On the other hand, most of the population remains ignorant about quotas. According to an opinion survey of 1850 Peruvians, conducted in late 1997 and early 1998, 75 per cent of the population is unaware of the existence of a quota law. Nonetheless, the vast majority of those polled in Lima declared that in politics, women are more honest than men, more concerned with poor people, better administrators, and less authoritarian (Blondet 1998).

Conclusion

In theory, the requirement that women comprise 20 to 40 per cent of political party candidates in national elections demands a radical sacrifice from male politicians and a dramatic restructuring of intra-party politics. The relatively speedy enactment of quota laws in many countries therefore gives reason to pause. Why would male politicians forfeit their historic monopoly on power without a prolonged and vicious struggle?

As we have shown in this chapter, factors such as the nature of the party list, the existence of a placement mandate, district magnitude, and good-faith party compliance determine whether quotas increase women's presence in parliament. Quota laws have achieved only limited success because of a failure to address all of these issues. As a result, male politicians have made few sacrifices on behalf of the quota. With the exception of Argentina, quotas have been a relatively painless way to pay lip service to women's rights without suffering the consequences.

Still, the enactment of quota laws in 12 Latin American countries is of tremendous symbolic importance. Since women gained the right to vote in the 1930s, 1940s and 1950s, no policy measure has stimulated such an intense debate about gender equality in politics and decision-making. The quota movement of the 1990s reflects the growth and strength of women's movements, the leadership of women politicians, and the influence of international norms and agreements pertaining to gender equality. Through their advocacy on behalf of quotas, women activists are forging fresh notions of equality, democratic legitimacy and women's citizenship.

When quotas work, women have an equal chance to participate. Preliminary data suggests that the presence of more women in power produces spillover effects and introduces new items to the policy agenda. Yet, significant policy changes have been brought about by women's political alliances in countries without quota laws. Broad-based political alliances, not quotas, are what it takes to produce legislative action benefiting all women.

The quota debate pushed Latin American societies to confront gender inequality in the public sphere, but much work remains to be done to make quotas a truly effective policy tool for improving women's representation in decision-making. Laws adopted in 12 countries represent advances in women's rights, but in many cases quota laws lacked teeth. Quotas reflect the tendency of Latin American governments to grant citizens formal rights before modifying the institutional contexts where these rights are enforced. The lesson of quotas is that rights matter most when institutions change to make rights effective.

Notes

1 The Latin American average was calculated based on data from 18 countries found at: Inter-Parliamentary Union <http://www.ipu.org/wmn-e/classif.htm>.
2 Quota legislation was enacted by the Colombian Congress in 1999. As this chapter was going to press, the Constitutional Court verified the constitutionality of the legislation. As the exact details of the implementation of the law remain unclear, we do not include it in our subsequent discussion. The first congressional election under this new legislation will take place in 2002.
3 Interview with Senator María de los Angeles Moreno, Mexico City, 30 January 1998.
4 Personal communication with Mala Htun, 12 February 1998.
5 Interview with Marta Suplicy, Brasília, 7 August 1997.
6 In Argentina, the support of President Carlos Menem was decisive in passing the quota law. Although the law enjoyed the support of women from all major political parties, it was unlikely to be approved because of male resistance. Last-minute persuasion by President Menem and his Interior Minister, José Luis Manzano, was decisive in swinging the congressional vote in favour of quotas (Durrieu 1999).
7 Following adoption of the quota, women's presence in the Ecuadoran Chamber of Deputies jumped by 13 percentage points. However, the gain in women's representation is largely attributable to voters' lack of familiarity with the new electoral system, not to the success of the quota. Instead of utilising the preference aspect of Ecuador's block voting method, voters tended to vote for a party's entire slate of candidates, a behaviour encouraged by the parties which strategically placed their most popular candidates at the

top, middle, and bottom of their respective lists. For example, in the province of Guayas where 18 deputies were elected, the Partido Social Cristiano won twelve seats with a mere 29 per cent of the overall vote, while two other parties each won 25 per cent of the vote but only three seats each. We thank Andrés Mejía Acosta for providing data and information on the 1998 Ecuadoran elections.

8   The one exception is Ecuador, which currently employs the block vote for the election of its provincial deputies. It is likely though that Ecuador will modify its electoral system, adopting one of the more common proportional representation allocation methods, prior to its next scheduled legislative election in 2002.

9   Some systems also permit voters to cast a vote for the entire list.

10 As indicated in Table 2.1, a large proportion of legislators in Bolivia (Chamber of Deputies), Mexico (Chamber of Deputies), Panama and Venezuela (Chamber of Deputies) are elected from single-member districts, where the quota law does not apply.

11 The implementation of the Argentine Ley de Cupos is regulated by Executive Decree 379/93 (as this chapter went to press in December 2000, a new, more progressive, decree was being drafted). Although the Ley de Cupos currently applies only to the election of the national Chamber of Deputies, starting in 2001 (when senators will be directly elected) it will apply to national Senate elections.

12 The Brazilian electoral law requires parties to reserve candidate slots for women, but does not require parties to actually fill these slots with women candidates. If a party fails to find women candidates to complete its list it may still contest the election. A failure to present the maximum number of candidates is unlikely to adversely affect the parties, as they are allowed to present a number of candidates in excess of the number of legislators being elected from the district (1.5 times as many for parties, and twice as many for coalitions of parties).

13 Parties that voluntarily adopted a women's quota include: Brazil's Partido dos Trabalhadores (30 per cent); Chile's Partido Socialista (30 per cent), Partido por la Democracia (40 per cent), and Partido Demócrata Cristiana (20 per cent); Costa Rica's Partido Unidad Social Cristiana (40 per cent); El Salvador's Frente Farabundo Martí para la Liberación Nacional (35 per cent); Mexico's Partido de la Revolución Democrática (30 per cent) and Partido Revolucionario Institucional (30 per cent); Nicaragua's Frente Sandinista de Liberación Nacional (30 per cent); Paraguay's Asociación Nacional Republicana (20 per cent); and Venezuela's Acción Democrática (20 per cent).

14 The relatively large number of FMLN and FSLN women deputies elected is due not only to the quota rules, but also to the relatively high level of women's participation within the FMLN and FSLN as well as the parties' historic commitment to the election of women.

15 Legislators make requests to the leader of their party's congressional delegation regarding which committees they want to serve on. While legislators do not always receive assignments on their preferred committees, with the exception of assignments on the most prominent committees (e.g., Budget, Constitutional Affairs, Foreign Affairs), legislators generally obtain assignments on the committees they requested.

16   Men and women did not differ significantly in the overall number of bills they presented. During this period women on average presented 3.6 bills while men presented 4.2.
17   The reproductive health bill, however, died in the Senate, where women occupy a mere 3 per cent of the seats. Women's high presence in the City of Buenos Aires Constituent Assembly was also responsible for the progressive character of the city's constitution. Among other things, the Constitution of the City of Buenos Aires recognises the 'right to be different', and proclaims that 'sexual and reproductive rights' are 'basic human rights' (Rodríguez 1997).
18   Article 40 of the 1991 Constitution also states that 'The authorities will guarantee the adequate and effective participation of women in the decision-making levels of Public Administration.'
19   Interview with Deputy Elisa Carrió, Buenos Aires, 4 August 1998.
20   Interview with the City of Buenos Aires Councillor Marta Oyhanarte, Buenos Aires, 31 July 1998.
21   For discussion of the importance of multi-sectoral women's political alliances in advancing women's interests in Latin American politics, see Alvarez (1990), Friedman (1997) and Stevenson (1999).
22   Instead of relying on the 'false gender neutrality' of 'governador', 'senador', or 'deputado' (Brazilian Portuguese for 'governor', 'senator', and 'deputy'), Suplicy proposed that ballots make reference to 'governador/governadora', 'senador/senadora', and 'deputado/deputada'.

Bibliography

Alatorre, Anna-Lizbeth (1999) 'Parties, gender, and democratization: the causes and consequences of women's participation in the Mexican Congress' BA thesis, Harvard University

Alvarez, Sonia E. (1990) *Engendering Democracy in Brazil: Women's Movements in Transition Politics*, Princeton: Princeton University Press

Blondet, Cecilia (1998) 'El poder político en la mira de las mujeres' in *Poder político con perfume de mujer: Las cuotas en el Perú*, Lima: PROMUJER, 49–66

Camacho Granados, Rosalia, Silvia Lara Povedano and Ester Serrano Madrigal (1997) *Las cuotas mínimas de participación de las mujeres: Un mecanismo de acción Afirmativa*, San José: CMF

Caul, Miki (1999) 'Women's representation in Parliament: the role of political parties' *Party Politics*, 5(1) 79–98

Crisp, Brian, Maria Escobar-Lemmon, Bradford S. Jones, Mark P. Jones and Michelle Taylor-Robinson (n.d.) 'Variation in legislative entrepreneurship in presidential systems: evidence from six Latin American democracies' unpublished manuscript

Dahlerup, Drude (1998) 'Using quotas to increase women's political representation' in Azza Karam (ed.) *Women in Parliament: Beyond the Numbers*, Stockholm: International IDEA, 91–106

Dodson, Deborah L. and Susan J. Carroll (1991) *Reshaping the Agenda: Women in State Legislatures*, New Brunswick: Center for the American Woman and Politics

Durrieu, Marcela (1999) *Se dice de nosotras*, Buenos Aires: Catálogos Editora

Friedman, Elisabeth (1997) *Unfinished Transitions: Gendered Political Opportunities and Women's Organizing in Latin American Democratization*, Ph.D. dissertation, Stanford University

Htun, Mala (1998) 'Women's political participation, representation and leadership in Latin America', Women's Leadership Conference of the Americas issue brief, inter-American dialogue/International Center for Research on Women, September

Htun, Mala (1999) 'Women's rights and opportunities in Latin America: problems and prospects' in Richard Feinberg and Robin Rosenberg (eds) *Civil Society and the Summit of the Americas*, Miami: North-South Center Press, 535–51

Htun, Mala (n.d.) 'Women, the law, and the judiciary in Latin America', unpublished manuscript

Inter-Parliamentary Union (1995) 'Women in parliaments 1945–1995: a world statistical survey', Reports and Documents Series, no. 23, Geneva: Inter-Parliamentary Union

Inter-Parliamentary Union (1997) 'Men and women in politics, democracy still in the making: a world comparative study', Reports and Documents Series, no. 28, Geneva: Inter-Parliamentary Union

Jones, Mark P. (1997) 'Legislator gender and legislator policy priorities in the Argentine Chamber of Deputies and the United States House of Representatives' *Policy Studies Journal*, 25(4) 613–29

Jones, Mark P. (1998) 'Explaining the high level of discipline in the Argentine Congress' presented at the 1998 Congress of the Latin American Studies Association, Chicago, Illinois

Luciak, Ilja A. (1997) 'Women and electoral politics on the Left: a comparison of El Salvador and Nicaragua' presented at the 1997 Congress of the Latin American Studies Association, Guadalajara, Mexico

Molinelli, N. Guillermo (1994) 'Argentina: the (no) ceteris paribus case' in Wilma Rule and Joseph F. Zimmerman (eds) *Electoral Systems in Comparative Perspective: Their Impact on Women and Minorities*, Westport: Greenwood Press, 197–202

Morgan, Marta I. (1992) 'Constitution-making in a time of cholera: women and the 1991 Colombian Constitution' *Yale Journal of Law and Feminism*, 4 (2) 353–413

PROMUJER (1998) *Poder político con perfume de mujer: Las cuotas en el Perú*, Lima: PROMUJER

Rodríguez, Marcela (1997) 'La situación legal de los derechos reproductivos y sexuales en Argentina' in *Nuestros cuerpos, nuestras vidas: Propuestas para la promoción de los derechos sexuales y reproductivos*, Buenos Aires: Foro por los Derechos Reproductivos, 29–42

Rodríguez, Victoria (1998) 'The emerging role of women in Mexican political life' in Victoria Rodríguez (ed.) *Women's Participation in Mexican Political Life*, Boulder, Colo.: Westview Press, 1–20

Staudt, Kathleen (1998) 'Women in politics: Mexico in global perspective' in Victoria Rodríguez (ed.) *Women's Participation in Mexican Political Life*, Boulder, Colo.: Westview Press, 23–40

Stevenson, Linda S. (1999) 'Gender politics in the Mexican democratization process' in Jorge Domínguez and Alejandro Poiré (eds) *Towards Mexico's Democratization*, New York: Routledge, 57–87

Suplicy, Marta (1996) 'Ações afirmativas e novas paradigmas nas esferas de poder' *Estudos Feministas*, June

Suplicy, Marta (1997) 'Constitucionalidade e necessidade das cotas' *Gazeta Mercantil*, 2 July

Suplicy, Marta (n.d.) 'Mulheres e cotas' unpublished manuscript

3
Getting Rights for Those without Representation: the Success of Conjunctural Coalition-building in Venezuela

Elisabeth Jay Friedman

Introduction

In 1990, the Venezuelan Congress passed a reform of the Organic Labour Law that, among other provisions, gave women workers equal rights with men and improved the rights of working mothers. This striking combination of equality and protectionism for women cannot be credited to the usual sponsors of legislative reform. Instead of relying on one of the then dominant political parties or the good auspices of the powerful executive branch, women came together in a 'conjunctural' coalition to lobby for the reform.[1] To establish and/or improve their rights they united across political arenas at a particular time around a particular set of issues, without demanding ongoing organisational or ideological coherence, and achieved their goal. But that goal was dependent on another crucial strategy: the use of a rights discourse that emphasised the familial and social benefits made possible by simultaneously asserting women's equality with, and difference from, men.

The use of national-level coalitions for the advancement of women's rights has become a common strategy across Latin America, given particular national and international opportunities. During the democratisation process in Chile and El Salvador, for example, women sought to assert a wide range of demands. In Chile the National Coalition of Women for Democracy (Concertación Nacional de Mujeres por la Democracia: CNMD) was created in 1989 as an autonomous women's coalition in support of the centre-left Coalition of Parties for Democracy (Concertación de Partidos por la Democracia), which won the first democratic elections in Chile following the Pinochet dictatorship.

Drawing together party members, women from nongovernmental organisations (NGOs) and feminists, the CNMD sought to raise gender issues in the transition to democracy. It proposed gender-specific government policies and the promotion of women within political parties. It clearly influenced government policy: 'most of the gender-specific policies implemented by the democratic government between 1990 and 1994 were initially proposed by the CNMD' (Frohmann and Valdés 1995: 288). Moreover, in the 1989 presidential campaign all political parties, even those outside the coalition, included gender-specific proposals in their platforms and at least discussed the need for female leadership (ibid. 287–9).

After finding themselves largely excluded from the peace process that initiated the transition to democracy in El Salvador, women formed the 'Mujeres '94' coalition. Its purpose was to use the opportunity of the 1994 elections as a means to raise gender consciousness in the new democracy. It had three plans of action: 1) to develop a women's political platform and publicise which parties (if any) responded to their demands; 2) to support female candidates who promoted the platform; and 3) to help register the thousands of unregistered voters, estimated to be 75 per cent female. The coalition's efforts resulted in an improved record of registered female voters, although turnout was disappointing as a whole. On the municipal and national levels the proportion of women elected did not improve. However, the government and opposition coalition signed a document on International Women's Day promising to implement a minimum set of women's demands regardless of the outcome of the election (Saint-Germain 1997). The coalition was active again in 1997, when members continued to work during the elections to promote a women's initiative for equality in political participation (Luciak 1998).

In Brazil, the preparations for the 1995 Fourth World Conference on Women in Beijing sparked the formation of the Union of Brazilian Women for Beijing '95 (Articulacão de Mulheres Brasileiras), which assembled nearly 100 representatives of women's groups to 'bring Beijing home to Brazil'. It organised a series of preparatory conferences and meetings in 25 of Brazil's 26 states, seeking to capitalise on the international attention to gender inequality by raising awareness at the national level. Hundreds of organisations participated in this process. Although the Union was criticised for its centralisation and seeming elitism, it did attempt to engage women at the local level around their particular issues as well as to influence the government efforts around Beijing (Alvarez 1997).

These examples show that coalitions have provided the means for effective mediation among women to articulate a set of gender-specific demands at the national level, particularly when women face a history of political exclusion. But the strategy of uniting women across ideological, organisational and socioeconomic differences is also useful for specific goals. In contrast to the more platform-oriented coalitions, much of the coalition-building in Venezuela has been focused on gaining legal rights.[2] Its success reveals several factors that may be crucial considerations for such achievement in contexts where women may not have equal access to traditional representational channels.[3]

To begin with, the Labour Law reform coalition drew on past experience with rights advocacy. Most recently, on 6 July 1982, the Venezuelan Congress passed a reform of the Civil Code, formerly one of the three most discriminatory in Latin America, to ensure women's and men's equal legal rights within the family and children's equal rights regardless of their parents' marital status.[4] Eight previous attempts at reform since 1970 had failed to bring results. Thus instead of relying on the traditional state- or party-backed methods for achieving legal change, the reform proponents drew together a coalition of women working inside and outside of the state. First, a professional women's organisation (the Venezuelan Federation of Women Lawyers – Federación Venezolana de Abogadas: FEVA), and then the head of the national women's agency, Mercedes Pulido de Briceño, took the lead. They built an alliance that relied upon women's capacity for autonomous organising across partisan differences and political arenas, using an explicitly nonfeminist, pro-family rhetorical strategy.

The development of this strategy was provoked by the reform opposition, conservative congressmen and lawyers who saw the reform as a radical feminist challenge to the sanctity and stability of the family. In response, instead of focusing on how the reform would give women and men equal rights, reform proponents promoted the reform as one that would foster democracy in the most fundamental building block of society, the family. This strategy neatly sidestepped the contentious debate over the structure of gender relations within the family by focusing instead on the societal value of democracy. The result was a reform of the Civil Code supported by women from a spectrum of civil society groups and legislators from every political party.

Some aspects of coalition-building were developed and/or improved following the Civil Code reform. The Labour Law reform proponents exploited changing national, international and regional opportunities for women. On the domestic front, more autonomous civil society-based organisations were taking advantage of the relatively stable political environment of a consolidated regime, and beginning to challenge the party-permeated politics of Venezuela. Internationally, the 1985 Nairobi meeting to close the UN Decade on Women (1975–85) promoted and legitimised national discussion of women's issues. Many governments felt obliged to give at least rhetorical support to women's rights and advocates made good use of the opportunity to prepare both governmental and nongovernmental documents assessing women's status. Regional and international networks blossomed under these auspicious circumstances.

By the time they started working on labour legislation, women themselves had improved their capacity for effective action. The new head of the national women's agency, Virginia Olivo de Celli, cooperated closely with leaders of a newly constituted umbrella organisation, the Coordinating Committee of Women's Nongovernmental Organisations (Coordinadora de Organizaciones No-Gubernamentales de Mujeres: CONG). This latter group was quite heterogeneous, bringing together representatives of professional and grassroots groups inspired by their successful collaboration around the Civil Code reform.

Women's cooperation was anchored by their transformation of representational mechanisms. In and outside of the state, women developed organisations that were strikingly different from the traditional models of Venezuelan political representation, which were reliant on hierarchical and usually partisan control over centralised structures. In contrast, the two organisations upon which the reform of the Labour Law would depend, the national women's agency and the CONG, were largely independent from particular parties and relatively decentralised. Their membership was 'mixed', that is, drawn from different parties as well as from independents, and included well-connected political leaders. The organisations were linked together through a set of commissions that assisted in the coordination of women's mobilisation without leading to state cooptation of civil society groups. During the reform process, the new institutional resource in the legislative branch of a bicameral commission on women's rights helped generate further support.

In order to promote women's workplace rights, reformers used a rhetorical strategy that built upon past success by emphasising the family-friendly aspects of the new legislation. But in a new twist, they focused on the 'social function of maternity' as the underlying justification for gender-sensitive workplace legislation. They clearly differentiated this social function of women – or the rights of mothers – from the equal rights of female and male workers, promoting the recognition of both women's difference from and their equality with men.[5]

Finally, reform proponents publicised a personal tragedy that they saw as clearly linked to the need for reform. At a crucial juncture in reform organising, October 1985, a pregnant employee of the Labour Ministry who had been delaying her inadequate maternity leave died from complications linked to work-related stress. Her case became a *cause célèbre* of the reform movement and a sympathetic media brought it to the attention of national decision-makers.

Despite the success women achieved through coalition-building, the coalition was not fully representative of women from all classes. Like earlier efforts, it was composed principally of, and was certainly led by, professionals, union women and middle-class political activists, resulting in low-income women's demands being sidelined. This dominance of more elite women was reflected in the reformed law. It did not extend equal rights to those women who worked in the home, whether their own or someone else's. Some of the reform leaders were not willing to acknowledge legally the work of the women who made it possible for these very leaders to have full-time careers by carrying out their families' domestic chores.

Civil society organises

It is widely recognised that the global call put out to women's organisations to prepare reports on the status of women for Nairobi sparked the creation of the first Venezuelan umbrella organisation for women's NGOs (CONG 1988b, García and Rosillo 1992). On 22, March 1985, five NGOs that had interacted during the Civil Code reform sponsored a meeting to discuss plans for the Nairobi NGO forum, to be held close to the time of the government conference.[6] But the 20 groups that attended this historic meeting decided to go beyond Nairobi-oriented efforts. They established the CONG, a nonpartisan, civil society-based women's rights association.

The CONG was the first Venezuelan organisation to bring together feminist and nonfeminist women's groups on an ongoing basis. Its official statutes proclaimed its commitment to the principle of 'unity within diversity': its stated purpose was to assemble groups working to end legal, economic, social, political and cultural discrimination against women and to promote women's full participation in national life. All types of associations were welcomed, including social, political, economic, labour, religious, professional, cultural, neighbourhood and housewife groups.[7] This diversity led to – and was dependent on – the development of the CONG's alternative structure.

The innovative structure largely responsible for the CONG's foundation and successes was developed in direct response to the way in which Venezuelan parties had coopted almost every sector of civil society while marginalising and separating women. Nora Castañeda, a CONG member, gave the example of how parties essentially created their own unions, which were then bound to the parties through their labour bureaux. But at the same time, parties had done very little for women, because the women's bureau did not function as well as the others.[8] Instead of promoting women's interests in the party, these bureaux mainly took on infrastructural tasks that mirrored the housekeeping duties of women in the private sphere (Friedman 1998). Meanwhile, partisan rivalries kept women from uniting outside of party structures. Thus the CONG founders sought to construct an organisation that would address women's concerns without imposing a 'party line'.

Due to the influence of the dominant channels of representation, however, a new structure had to be carefully negotiated between those who rejected traditional structures altogether and those still working within them. After considerable debate, the feminists convinced the other members that a very different structure would be more conducive to the CONG's goal: bringing together women's organisations to exchange information and work on common projects without interference in the specific workings of any member group.[9]

As a result, the CONG statutes called for decentralisation and nonhierarchical decision-making, with each member group being autonomous. All decisions were to be based on the consensus of the group representatives who attended bimonthly meetings. The coordination of the CONG was to be done by a three-person council that rotated among the groups every six months and was elected by direct and open election.

The rejection of traditional organising had an impact not only on the structure of the CONG, but also on its membership and leadership. Many CONG members feared that, as had happened in the past, party women would try to colonise the group on behalf of their party. The extent to which partisan loyalties were embedded in Venezuelan society could not be ignored; however, it was soon recognised that many of the NGO affiliates were also active in parties. Moreover, those women who were party activists made no attempts to take over the CONG. Finally it was decided that members could join as representatives of the nondominant parties. The leadership council generally represented the three different types of activists who made up the CONG: feminists or professionals, party activists and grassroots organisers.

A contributing factor to early group unity was, paradoxically, a lack of funding. This was yet another element which differentiated the CONG from traditional interest-group organising, often predicated on support from particular parties. The CONG's resources were always strained. Dues came in sporadically and outside support was minimal. Several CONG members were able to go to the Nairobi meeting only when Fidel Castro chartered a plane from Cuba to Kenya to ferry 100 Latin American activists. However, the lack of funding was not seen as an obstacle. The CONG met in a donated space and members shared infrastructural duties. Furthermore the lack of resources prevented schisms around distribution issues. Castañeda noted how surprised a few CONG members were to find out at the regional feminist meeting in Argentina (1990) that conflict had arisen between professional feminists running NGOs and the women in whose name they supposedly raised funds. In contrast, CONG members saw that their lack of outside funding protected them from such infighting.[10]

The decision of the CONG member groups to focus on women specifically, across ideological and programmatic differences, had several results. Members began to analyse discrimination in their personal and professional lives;[11] the CONG as a whole sponsored a multi-issue event 'Women Take Over the Cultural Centre!' in March 1986; and members began to rely on gender solidarity in several campaigns. But the largest of these were dependent on collaboration with the state women's agency, the National Women's Office.

Solidifying state action for women[12]

Civil society was not the only arena affected by preparations for Nairobi. With a change of administration in 1984, incoming Social Democratic president Jaime Lusinchi closed down his Christian Democrat predecessor's Ministry for the Participation of Women in Development (Ministerio para la Participación de la Mujer en el Desarrollo). This action shut off the crucial channel to the state women relied upon in the Civil Code reform. But a pivotal activist within the state, Virginia Olivo de Celli, ensured that this key factor for women's mobilisation would not be abandoned. In order to justify maintaining a national women's agency, she relied on the legitimacy provided by international attention to women's issues during the UN Decade on Women. As the then head of the Family Department of the Youth Ministry, she attended a 1984 women's meeting of the Socialist International at which she heard of the need for a state women's agency. After discussions with collaborators on the Civil Code reform confirmed the key role the now defunct women's agency had played, she was determined to maintain this resource for women in the executive branch. Olivo de Celli established the National Women's Office (Oficina Nacional de la Mujer: ONM) within the Youth Ministry in 1984, using two justifications: the recommendation of the Organisation of American States' Interamerican Women's Commission that every member state have a national women's agency, and secondly the need to coordinate a report for the Nairobi conference.

Olivo de Celli was well positioned for her activism on women's behalf. She was politically connected through her prominent Social Democrat family and, ironically, did not have a history of visible women's activism. Her lack of previous involvement in women's issues allowed her to serve as a nonthreatening outer representation for women's transformative actions within the state, while simultaneously making her dependent on encouraging collaborative work. To facilitate collaboration, she took on as the direct head of the ONM Rosa Paredes, a well-known activist on women's issues, particularly those of low-income women.

Olivo de Celli's need for advice and the obvious success of collaborative efforts around reforming the Civil Code led to a significant difference in organisation between the ONM and the previous women's agency. The ONM went one step beyond the frequent nongovernmental consultations to incorporate explicitly women from outside the government within its structure. The first description of the ONM's functions included interaction with several NGOs mentioned by name; not coincidentally several of the key players in the Civil Code reform (Ministerio de la Juventud 1984: 50). Members of these and other groups were to be incorporated into the work of the office through the mechanism of voluntary advisory commissions. Commission membership ranged across parties and philosophies: the official swearing-in ceremony included Social Democrats, Christian Democrats, Socialists, Communists and even the most radical feminists.

As Olivo de Celli was promoted through the executive branch she took the office with her. When she was made the Minister of the Family in 1987, she converted the ONM into its own department, the Department for Women's Advancement (Dirección General Sectorial de Promoción a la Mujer or Directorate). By this time 170 women were participating in the commissions, and state women's offices were operating in 17 of 22 states (Ministerio de la Familia 1987: 60). Policy design, not execution, was the limited prerogative of the women's agency.

However, the commissions' input spurred a notable transformation in the interests expressed through the agency's policy-making. From a focus on women's contribution to development and their needs as mothers, policies gradually shifted to promoting women's legal rights and improving their economic and social status.

State–civil society relations and results

The institutionalisation of women's representation through the ONM/Directorate resulted in a modification of the traditional methods of state-based interest mediation. These methods had been based on the incorporation of the major players in interest group politics, such as capital and labour, directly into the state.[13] In contrast, the women's advisory commissions formed a decentralised network with autonomy in its decision-making and represented a wide range of women. Instead of privately reconciling class interests through the state by striking bargains over economic resources, the ONM/Directorate and its commissions became motors for public campaigns on women's issues.

The collaborative model of the ONM/Directorate proved so successful that at the UNICEF-sponsored regional meeting 'State and Civil Society Joining Forces to Support Women' (Caracas, 15–17 August 1988) the Venezuelan experience was used as a model of successful cooperation (Rocha Sánchez 1991). But the model was also dependent on its other half: the increasingly organised women in NGOs whose input was central to developing more explicitly women-focused policies. Many women from the CONG sat on the state commissions and took an active part in much of the ONM/Directorate's work.

Despite its close relationship with the state agency, the CONG membership did not consider its practice of autonomous decision-making compromised. Moreover, the lack of financial ties between the CONG and the state agency kept the type of clientelistic relationship that often results in the political subordination of the constituencies of state agencies to dominant political interests from developing. At the 1988 UNICEF meeting, CONG members explained that they had no definitive methodology for their work with the agency. Much as they interacted in their internal process, they cooperated with the agency around conjunctural issues. This method was the only one possible due to the heterogeneity of political outlooks represented in the CONG and the state administration (Rocha Sánchez 1991: 42–3).

Instead of leading to political subordination, the cooperation between the two organisations undergirded three successful campaigns against gender discrimination. The campaign to free Inés María Marcano (1987), a young single mother unjustly imprisoned for child abandonment, was largely an effort of the CONG membership in conjunction with women from the marginal neighbourhoods, but it also relied upon sympathetic actors in the Directorate (CONG 1988c). The United Women Leaders' movement (1987–88), which sought to improve women's positions on party electoral lists, was coordinated by the Directorate with the help of CONG members and elite party women. Finally, the successful fight to reform discriminatory aspects of the Labour Law (1985–90) drew on the entire spectrum of women activists, from union members to politicians to feminists.[14]

Reforming the Labour Law

The ONM began work on the reform early in its tenure. In the evaluations undertaken for Nairobi, the need for reforms in the Labour Law, as well as the Penal Code, surfaced with vigour. In one of the first uses of the advisory commissions, Olivo de Celli called together women from parties and civil society to discuss the reforms in February 1985, and the ONM submitted a proposal for reform of the Penal Code to Congress in late 1985. But the proposal was quickly dismissed. Among other reformed articles was the liberalisation of abortion restrictions, which would have decriminalised abortion in the cases not only of risk to the mother's life, but also if the pregnancy were the result of rape or incest, or if the foetus were badly malformed (Sgambatti 1992: 81, 85). The abortion debate provoked severe dissension among the mainly male legislators, who put aside the women's proposal.

The dismissal of the Penal Code reform illustrates the problem women faced in altering discriminatory legislation. Anything that could seen as a radical departure from traditional gender relations, such as increasing women's control over reproduction, was politically too sensitive. Supporting maternity was more popular than controlling it, as was evidenced by the family-focus of the Civil Code reform. Thus, it is not surprising that women promoted the reform of the Labour Law as protection for the mothers of future generations of Venezuelans. But in doing so they also made an important departure: this protection was justified in a way that recognised that not all women workers were working mothers, and that motherhood had a function for society as a whole beyond family boundaries. In this way reform proponents managed to simultaneously promote gender difference and gender equality.

The ONM found highly placed allies in its quest to reform the Labour Law. Ex-president Rafael Caldera, a Christian Democrat and the co-author of the original 1936 legislation, headed a bicameral congressional commission already working on a comprehensive reform. The preparations for the 1985 UN women's conference in Nairobi helped extend this effort, in the form of the Congressional Commission to Evaluate the Decade on Women. Under the guidance of Social Democratic congress-woman Paulina Gamus, the Commission took up the reform of the Labour Law as a priority for women. These efforts were united in a Commission workshop in early May attended by those already working on the reform: the ONM, CONG members, the Labour Ministry, and the influential business organisation FEDECAMARAS (the Venezuelan Federation of Chambers of Commerce and Production). Those present at this workshop agreed that there were two types of discrimination to be addressed in the Labour Law. Women workers were still excluded from certain positions due to antiquated protective legislation (such as limitations on nightwork), but working mothers needed increased workplace rights (such as the provision of onsite nurseries for the infants of women who were breastfeeding). This differentiation challenged the automatic association of women with motherhood. The protective clauses were rejected on the grounds that working women should have the same rights as working men. The increased rights were solicited on the basis of the central importance of healthy maternity to family and social life. In promoting these various demands supporters cited their inclusion in international agreements such as the UN Convention to Eliminate All Forms of Discrimination Against Women, which Venezuela had ratified in 1982 (Comisión Especial n.d.: 5–1.).

But in the general agreement over changes to be made in the Labour Law, one point of contention stood out: that of which classes of women would have full rights. Whether to extend workplace rights to paid domestic workers was fiercely debated at the workshop. Some congress-women and FEVA lawyers spoke against their inclusion, while the ONM and CONG members fought for it (*Ultimas Notícias*, 5 May 1985). Shortly after the workshop the CONG sent a letter to Olivo de Celli to clarify that as an organisation, it supported the equality of home- with work-place-based workers. The ONM was in agreement; its director, Rosa Paredes, understood the need for domestic workers' rights from her experience organising women in marginal neighbourhoods. The debate pointed to the conflicting interests within the coalition. Those opposed to including paid domestic workers were not willing to compromise their class privilege and acknowledge that their ability to lead professional lives was based on the potential exploitation of other women. Those for inclusion insisted that all women deserved equal rights at the workplace, irrespective of the impact on particular classes.[15]

To ensure representation of nongovernmental women's perspectives in the reform, the CONG held a three-day meeting to analyse the government proposals. Members found few disagreements with the proposals from the ONM and the Decade Commission. But as explained by CONG member organisation All (Women) Together (Todas Juntas), Caldera's version, which already had been introduced into Congress in August 1985, was problematic. It left in place too many outdated protections, did not strengthen the enforcement of workplace nurseries for workers' children, and paid little attention to the situation of domestic workers (*Revista SIC* 49: 484:159–60.).

As in the case of the Civil Code, lawyer and judge Yolanda Poleo de Baez authored the final proposals that the CONG agreed to support. To end discrimination against women workers, she proposed eliminating sex-specific employment advertising, banning pregnancy tests for female applicants and prohibiting any other sex-specific limitations on employment. In supposedly neutral but gender-freighted provisions, she sought flexible and shorter workdays (which would make women's balancing of home and work obligations easier), an end to the law whereby one spouse (usually the husband) could ask the other (usually the wife) to give up her job on the grounds of it being 'prejudicial to the family', and, finally, a limitation on workers' early liquidation of their severance benefits to 50 per cent without the consent of their spouses, to guard against the loss of housewives' communal property.

In order to clarify that the rights she sought to expand in the reform were to protect maternity (or parenthood) and not women *per se*, Poleo de Baez proposed changing the section entitled 'Women and Minors' to 'Protection of Maternity and the Family'. Within it she argued for an expansion of pre- and postnatal leave from 12 to 18 weeks, and the adoption of a maternity exemption protecting pregnant women and new mothers from being fired. The demand for the exemption was based on a legal exemption that protected union organisers from being fired during union drives and while serving in union positions. If firing procedures were started for some severe violation of workplace conduct, they had to be carefully monitored by a state labour inspector. In a sense, the application of these conditions to pregnant women protected the 'union' being formed between mother and child.

To help new mothers Poleo de Baez suggested a six-hour workday for nursing mothers, the expansion of workplace nurseries into childcare centres for the children of male and female workers,[16] and fines, closure, or jail for owners who did not protect pregnant women and provide onsite childcare. The reform also asked for obligatory social security for housewives; and finally, it stipulated equal rights for paid domestic workers, including set hours, vacation time, and social security, as well as social security for home-based and pieceworkers (*La Mala Vida*, March 1986: 3).

Shortly after the CONG workshops, a tragic incident gave the reform movement a powerful case around which to mobilise support for their cause. Cípriana Velásquez was a pregnant office worker in, of all places, the Labour Ministry. She had been working as close as possible to the end of her term in order to save her six week prenatal leave to add to her six-week postnatal leave; a strategy used by many women who wanted more than a month and a half to spend with their newborns. However, upon receiving a memo in late October stating that the procedure for firing her was underway due to several unexplained absences, Velásquez went home, became hysterical and, despite a recent bill of good health, went into shock. She died shortly after.

No sooner had her death made a banner headline in the major daily *El Nacional* on 31 October 1986, than the CONG started organising. They united women's efforts across separate arenas to bring the individual tragedy and its social meaning to the public's attention. The following day a congresswoman demanded a full investigation of the case in Congress. The matter was taken up the Committee on Social Affairs within the week. Meanwhile the current president of FEVA gave a press release decrying the case as one more result of a faulty Labour Law. CONG members from the Central University quickly established the Cípriana Velásquez Committee, bringing together academics, staff and students. The Committee immediately made a public demand for the firing of Cípriana's supervisor, who under the current law had been responsible for giving at least three verbal warnings to her employee before beginning firing procedures. Women from the major labour con-federation, the CTV, used the case to highlight the need for a maternity exemption: it would have granted Cípriana, as a pregnant worker, an exemption from being fired. On 6 November women from the CTV, the Cípriana Velásquez Committee and two feminist organisations staged a protest outside of the Labour Ministry and Congress to demand the immediate reform of the Labour Law, especially the protection of pregnant women, longer maternity leave and onsite daycare. This protest set off others in cities in the interior (*El Nacional*, 31 Oct.–6 Nov. 1985).

At the Caracas-based protest, the CONG began a petition drive in honour of Cípriana to introduce their version of the reformed Labour Law into Congress.[17] As with a similar petition drive for the Civil Code reform, it raised awareness of the issues throughout the country. Six months after the Labour Law petition was begun 20 000 signatures were delivered to Congress (8 April 1986). Outside, the 8 March theatre group, which had been started in 1983 to publicise the Civil Code reform, performed a new piece about the issues at stake in the Labour Law reform. CONG members passed out leaflets claiming that 'the Venezuelan State should recognise maternity not as a particular and private problem of a woman and her family, but as a social and public problem which requires State policies' (CONG n.d.). As a result of the petition drive, the CONG-sponsored reforms joined those already under discussion in Congress.

Work slowed during the 1987–88 electoral season. When Caldera introduced the reform for congressional consideration in August 1988, he sat on the fence when it came to women's demands, simultaneously warning that the 'overprotection' of women might make employers opt for men and acknowledging that 'women have been the sector most interested' in the reform (*El Nacional*, 8 April 1988). In June 1989 the debate started to heat up again and the coalition was ready. The CONG and women from the major labour confederations declared the establishment of a united front to fight for their reforms, helped by two new state organisations for women's issues: the latest version of the executive-branch women's agency and one in Congress.

By this time the national agency for women had taken on yet another form with the change of administration in 1989. Under pressure from female party activists, the reelected Social Democratic president, Carlos Andrés Pérez, reestablished the Presidential Women's Advisory Commission (Comisión Femenina Asesora de la Presidencia: COFEAPRE) from his previous term in office (1974–78). Although linked with the new administration, COFEAPRE continued the reform campaign of the Directorate and made its support public. In its press releases, COFEAPRE affirmed the separation of women's equal work conditions from protection of the 'social function' of maternity and called on international norms in support of it:

> We support the proposal of the Labour Law in all its parts, because it constitutes a significant advance in Venezuelan labour legislation... Chapter Seven [on maternity and family protection] deserves special attention because it considers maternity as a social function,

contains dispositions which protect it and achieves the objective of the principles contained in our Magna Carta and the UN Convention on the Elimination of All Forms of Discrimination Against Women, so that women might exercise their right to employment in conditions of equality, might have access to all the economic activities and enjoy the social benefits for their condition of female worker, such as the maternity exemption. (*El Nacional*, 7 August 1989)

During the course of the debates, Congress also instituted a new mechanism for women's representation in the legislature which congresswomen put at the service of the reform effort. The idea for the Bicameral Commission for Women's Rights (Comisión Bicameral de Derechos de la Mujer) started in the wake of the furore over the death of Cípriana Velásquez, when congresswomen proposed a specific commission to oversee women's rights issues.[18] Officially convened in June 1989, by mid-1990 the Commission was sponsoring a series of forums to keep discussion of the reform alive in state legislatures and city halls across the country.

Meanwhile women outside the government teamed up with a congressional representative to ensure the continued effectiveness of the women's coalition. Amarilis Valor, a member of the CTV and recently elected congressional deputy, brought together female party leaders and CONG members in regular meetings on the reform. She reported on what was being discussed in Congress and all would plan what she would say on the House floor.[19]

One of Valor's speeches underscored both this concerted consultation and the lessons women had learned from prior mobilisation: speak of the family, but make sure everyone knows that united women are seeking their rights. Her speech began: 'Notice, citizens, that we are not talking about women. We are speaking without bias about the Law which protects families.' Yet despite her universalistic rhetoric, throughout the rest of her speech Valor continually mentioned the range of women consulted on the bill and women's refusal to let it get dismissed, as had happened in the early stages of the Civil Code reform (*Diario de Debates*, 4 July 1989: 33). To make sure the message got through, every time Valor spoke in Congress, CONG activists demonstrated outside for the reform. Occasionally they took their protest inside, opening up a big banner in the House balcony declaring 'we women want the reform of the Labour Law NOW' when debate was particularly intense.[20]

The opposition to the Labour Law grew fiercest towards the end of the deliberations. The main opponent was the business organisation

FEDECAMARAS, despite its earlier support of reform efforts. It was generally against the law's increase in worker benefits and protections at a time of changing economic conditions,[21] but the section protecting maternity came under particular attack. According to FEDECAMARAS, the maternity exemption would only result in employer reluctance to hire women. Moreover, small businesses would go under if they had to provide the level of childcare specified in the law. That sort of social service, business argued, was the duty of the state.

In response to the opposition, women turned again to appeals based on the family-oriented nature of maternity protection. In the closing congressional debates on the reform, congresswomen took the floor to defend the different provisions of the section on 'Maternity and the Family'. A Social Democrat argued:

> It is not women we are protecting in a special manner by considering them inferior to men, they are equal to men, they have the same rights and duties in that which does not have to do with the function of maternity; when women are mothers, it is their children whom we ought to protect, and that has been the intention of this Chapter which refers to maternity and to the family. (Ibid., *Diario de Debates*, 8)

Because the Labour Law was not only concerned with women, the reform coalition was far from alone in its advocacy. It took advantage of the opportunity afforded by the broader reform debate to advance women's rights. Being on the side of the workers was a claim all parties in Venezuela had made at some point in their history, generating a great deal of political support for the reform. Party objections to FEDECAMARAS's accusations of political interference in the economy reached a peak when the Senate passed a resolution stating that it had been offended by the way in which the business community had publicly disparaged the Congress (*El Nacional*, 16 November 1990). The reform passed 27 November 1990.

Results of the reform

The new Labour Law included many of the original proposals generated by the ONM and the CONG. From the removal of discriminatory articles to the newly entitled chapter 'Of the Labour Protection of Maternity and the Family', the reform made clear that no differences were to be permitted that denied working women's equal rights with men, only those that allowed them to combine work and motherhood. Thus, discrimination on the basis of sex, in employment advertising and work conditions (for example mandatory pregnancy testing) was banned, and neither spouse could now ask the other to give up their job on the basis of family needs. Simultaneously, the special maternity dispensations were explicitly labelled as nondiscriminatory. Pregnant women were exempted without penalty from work that might harm their pregnancies and granted 18 weeks of maternity leave, compensated for by Social Security. The maternity exemption was included, protecting women's employment while they were pregnant and for one year following birth (or adoption). Breastfeeding women were given the right to two half-hour breaks to nurse their children at onsite nurseries, or two one-hour breaks if their children were at home. Finally, employers with more than 20 workers had to supply a childcare centre, or make provisions for childcare, for all of their employees (male and female) with children under six.

But because the predominately upper-class women who had led the reform campaign could not agree to protect low-income women's rights, class-based discrimination remained in the final document. Paid domestic workers were not given equal rights. Although these workers continued to be legally entitled to one day off a week, ten hours of rest a day, 15 days paid vacation a year and yearly bonuses, they were not given health care benefits or social security. Pieceworkers and outworkers were also denied these benefits.

Two years after the law's passage, business continued to object to it – and the coalition of women continued to support their victory. In November 1992, a business lawyer brought a claim to the Supreme Court to annul the daycare provisions in the Labour Law and its enabling legislation. His argument was that the extension of these provisions went against the original spirit of the law, which was only to provide a place for women to nurse infants, not to supply daycare for the young children of workers of both sexes. The coalition partners reunited to fight the claim, filing a brief that explained that the intent of the reform was to bring the law up to date, not violate its spirit, by protecting all workers' children (García Prince *et al.* 1993).

The implementation of the Labour Law revealed a gap between *de jure* and *de facto* rights for women. Following the Supreme Court suit, a few of the enabling provisions were nullified, making it easier for businesses to pay parents directly to provide for their own childcare – the preferred solution of those businesses that complied with the law.[22] Moreover, the sanctions put in place for the many businesses that violated the provisions were not as serious as the activists had asked for. Violators of any dispositions of the maternity section were fined between one and four times the minimum wage. Finally, the growing informal labour sector – where many of the poorest worked – could not be forced to comply with any legislation.

Conclusion

Although implementation would turn out to be a problem, the movement to reform the Labour Law demonstrated the potential of women's coalition-building for achieving their rights. This particular coalition was dependent on women's organisational innovations. The women's agency in the state provided a forum for the expression of demands by a range of women, and helped advance these demands through the mechanism of its advisory commissions. Meanwhile the decentralised, non-hierarchical CONG significantly altered the traditional model of interest organisations in civil society; it united women around issues of common concern and maintained access to the state. Both organisations took advantage of the presence of international processes directed at women.

These organisational innovations were bolstered by innovations in political discourse. Without abandoning appeals that asserted women's rights claims as essential to a healthy family life, Labour Law reform proponents combined demands for women's equal and different rights. Moreover, as the 'democratising' Civil Code proponents had before them, they argued that women's rights had social, and not merely individual, benefits.

Built by women who as a group shared a common experience of marginalisation or exclusion from traditional politics, the model of organising that was responsible for the successful reform had little to do with the dominant model of representation through highly centralised, hierarchical and partisan structures. In contrast, organising in loose-knit coalitions around a specific issue allowed women to work together despite their many differences – the very differences that would most likely have destroyed a highly organised women's group. Long-time activist Esperanza Vera described how Venezuelan women had developed this 'intermediary form' of organisation through experience:

> It is as though reality is showing us that women, through this method of not being organised in the traditional manner but being unified around something which interests us, are creating something like a different form of collective action ... Even if it might not be

exactly the same as the organisations that we know... it's a way to avoid the frictions. And to avoid the differences, because the differences exist. If we are all together in an organisation that has requirements like the traditional ones, these differences will come into conflict every day. Meanwhile as we are we only unite when there is agreement... It's a good strategy, but [rather than coming from theory] it has arisen from the activism itself.[23]

One product of such a contingent form of organising was compromise, leaving out the more radical demands that presented too strong a challenge to the gender or class *status quo*. But considering the nature of Venezuelan political society, the coalition model was remarkable. Through it, a politically excluded group demanded and achieved rights formerly denied to them.[24]

Notes

1 The concept of conjunctural coalition-building comes from Sonia Alvarez's work on the Brazilian women's movement; see Alvarez (1990: 237). Previous versions of this chapter were presented at the Latin American Studies Association Meeting, 24–6 September 1998, Chicago, Il. and the Columbia University Institute for Latin American and Iberian Studies Faculty Seminar, 1 February 1999; some of the work also appears in Friedman (2000). Field research was made possible in large part by a Fulbright Fellowship. The author would like to thank the interviewees for their kind cooperation, and the editors for their helpful comments.

2 For examples of historical conjunctural coalition-building, see Friedman (2000: ch. 2, 3).

3 In the Venezuelan case, these traditional channels include the historically powerful political parties, the state executive branch, and party-dominated organisations of central interest groups. Until recently, partisan rivalry and party dominance of civil society was a defining feature of Venezuelan political life. Parties participated in the founding of the central associations of major interest groups, which were also incorporated into party structure through secretariats or sectoral bureaux; see Powell (1971), Coppedge (1994: esp. 31–5). Recent developments, particularly the decline in the political legitimacy and power of the traditionally dominant parties (the Social Democrats and the Christian Democrats) and the reconfiguration of the party system, may well change these dynamics in the future. Details of how these representational channels excluded women are discussed later in the chapter (see also Friedman 1998).

4 For a more complete discussion of the reform of the Civil Code, see Prince de Kew (1990), Friedman (2000: ch. 4), Friedman (1993).

5   The debate over strategies emphasising equality or difference in women's rights struggles has a long history in Latin America; see Miller (1991: ch. 4), Lavrin (1995).

6   The NGOs were FEVA, the women's department of the Communist union federation, the feminist journalist group 'Women and Communication', the women's studies programme at the Central University of Venezuela, and the feminist publication *La Mala Vida*.

7   The first NGOs organising the CONG were feminist, professional, popular, labour, and solidarity. When it was officially constituted, partisan, religious and health groups also joined (CONG 1988a). Because the CONG saw itself in opposition to mainstream politics, the dominant centrist parties, the Social Democrats and Christian Democrats, were excluded.

8   Interview with Castañeda, 30 August 1994, Caracas.

9   Interview with CONG founding member Fernando Aranguren, 23 April 1994, Caracas.

10   Interview, 30 August 1994.

11   Interview with CONG member Benita Finol, 26 July 1994, Caracas; cf. García Guadilla (1993).

12   Much of the information for this section comes from an interview with the head of the women's agency, Virginia Olivo de Celli (6 June 1994, Caracas) as well as from the annual reports of the Youth Ministry and Family Ministry (1984–88).

13   For a discussion of this 'semi-corporatist' network, see Crisp, Levine and Rey (1995).

14   The other campaigns are described in Friedman (2000: ch. 5).

15   Elsa Chaney (1979), and Elsa Chaney and Mary García Castro (1989) have further explored the impact of the class divide between female employers and domestic employees on solidarity in Latin American women's organising.

16   In the original 1936 Labour Law all businesses with more than 30 employees were supposed to provide nurseries where nursing mothers could breastfeed during the workday. The reform sought to have all businesses with more than 20 employees provide daycare for both female and male employees' children under six years old.

17   Article 165 of the Venezuelan Constitution stipulates that one of the five ways a law can be directly introduced in Congress is through a popular initiative signed by 20 000 citizens. The Civil Code reform coalition was the first group to ever use this mechanism.

18   Interview with Senator Ixora Rojas, 9 September 1994, Caracas.

19   Interview with Amarilis Valor, 1 August 1994, Caracas.

20   Interview with Benita Finol, 26 July 1994.

21   Accusing the reform of 'populism', business leaders claimed that the reform would drive up business costs on the order of 30 per cent, increase inflation and consumer costs, discourage foreign investment, hurt efforts at privatisation and generally derail new economic efforts (*El Nacional* Oct.–Nov. 1990).

22   Despite the failure of the demand for annulment as a whole, onsite daycare continues to be insufficiently provided. Its implementation, though called for regularly by women's and children's advocates, has largely taken a back seat to a national homebased daycare programme.

23 Interview with Esperanza Vera, 13 July 1994, Caracas.
24 The coalition strategy for achieving gender-sensitive legal reform seems to be continuing in Venezuela, currently focused on constitutional reform (Mérola 1999). It has also been used effectively elsewhere in Latin America, for example in the establishment and implementation of quotas for women's representation on party lists in Argentina (Jones 1996: 78–80) and the passage of a gender equality law in Costa Rica (Saint-Germain and Morgan 1991).

Bibliography

Alvarez, S. E. (1990) *Engendering Democracy in Brazil*, Princeton, NJ: Princeton University Press

Alvarez, S. E. (1998) 'Latin American feminisms "go global": trends of the 1990s and challenges for the new millenium' in S. E. Alvarez, E. Dagnino and A. Escobar (eds) *Cultures of Politics/Politics of Cultures: Re-visioning Latin American Social Movements*, Boulder, Colo.: Westview Press, 293–324

Chaney, E. (1979) *Supermadre: Women in Politics in Latin America*, Austin, Tex.: University of Texas Press

Chaney, E. M. and M. G. Castro (1989) *Muchachas No More: Household Workers in Latin America and the Caribbean*, Philadelphia, Pa.: Temple University Press

Comisión Especial de la Camara de Diputados del Congreso de la República de Venezuela para Evaluar el Decenio de la Mujer (n.d.) *Informe*, Caracas

CONG (Coordinadora de Organizaciones No-Gubernamentales de Mujeres) (1988a) *Estatutos*, Caracas

CONG (1988b) *CONG*, Caracas: CONG

CONG (1988c) *La Mujer y La lucha Solidaria: En el caso de Inés María Marcano, Una en un millón*, Caracas: CONG

CONG (nd) 'Defendamos Nuestros Derechos en el Trabajo', Caracas

Coppedge, M. (1994) *Strong Parties and Lame Ducks: Presidential Partyarchy and Factionalism in Venezuela*, Stanford, Calif.: Stanford University Press

Crisp, B. F., D. H. Levine and J. C. Rey (1995) 'The Legitimacy Problem' in J. McCoy *et al.* (eds) *Venezuelan Democracy Under Stress*, New Brunswick, NJ: Transaction Publishers, 139–70

Friedman, E. (1993) '¿Democracia en la Casa? A Study of the Venezuelan Civil Code' *Americas & Latinas: A Journal of Women and Gender*, 1 (1) 16–22

Friedman, E. (1998) 'Paradoxes of gendered political opportunity in the Venezuelan transition to democracy' in *Latin American Research Review*, 33 (3) 87–156

Friedman, E. (2000) *Unfinished Transitions: Women and the Gendered Development of Democracy in Venezuela 1936–1996*, University Park, Pa.: Penn University Press

Frohmann, A. and T. Valdés (1995) 'Democracy in the country and in the home: the women's movement in Chile' in A. Basu (ed.) *The Challenge of Local Feminisms: Women's Movements in Global Perspective*, Boulder, Colo.: Westview, Press, 276–301

García, C. T. and C. Rosillo (1992) 'Conquistando nuevos espacios: la investigacion y las organizaciones de mujeres' in *FEMENTUM: Revista Venezolana de Sociologia y Antropologia*, 2 (4) 3–17

García Guadilla, M. (1993) 'Ecología: women, politics and environment in Venezuela' in S. A. Radcliffe and S. Westwood (eds) *Viva: Women and Popular Protest in Latin America*, London: Routledge, 65–87

García Prince, E. and associates (6 July 1993) 'Amicus brief to Supreme Court', Caracas: photocopy in author's possession

Jones, M. (1996) 'Increasing women's representation via gender quotas: the Argentine ley de cupos' *Women & Politics*, 16 (4) 75–99

Lavrin, A. (1995) *Women, Feminism and Social Change in Argentina, Chile, and Uruguay, 1890–1940*, Lincoln, Nebr.: University of Nebraska Press

Luciak, I. A. (1998) 'Gender equality and electoral politics on the Left: a comparison of El Salvador and Nicaragua' *Journal of InterAmerican Studies and World Affairs*, 40 (1) 39–66

Mérola, G. (1999) 'Por Una Nueva Constitución' *Fempress* 209, online at <http://www.fempress.cl/209/temas2.html>

Miller, F. (1991) *Latin American Women and the Search for Social Justice*, Hanover, NH: University Press of New England

Ministerio de la Familia (various) *Memoria y Cuenta*, Caracas

Ministerio de la Juventud (various) *Memoria y Cuenta*, Caracas

Powell, J. D. (1971) *Political Mobilization of the Venezuelan Peasant*, Cambridge, Mass.: Harvard University Press

Prince de Kew, C. (1990) *Reforma Parcial del Código Civil: Analisis de una política pública*, Caracas: Coediciones Universidad Simón Bolívar Congreso de la República

Rocha Sánchez, L. (1991) *Estado Y Sociedad Civil Conjugando Esfuerzos En Apoyo A La Mujer*, Bogotá: UNICEF

Saint-Germain, M. A. (1997) 'Mujeres '94: democratic transition and the women's movement in El Salvador' in *Women & Politics*, 18 (2) 75–99

Saint-Germain, M. A. and M. I. Morgan (1991) 'Equality: Costa Rican women demand "The real thing"' in *Women & Politics*, 11 (3) 23–75

Sgambatti, S. (1992) 'Legislación Penal' in COFEAPRE (ed.) *II Congreso Venezolano de la Mujer*, Caracas: COFEAPRE, I, 81–5

4

Taking the Law into their Own Hands: Women, Legal Reform and Legal Literacy in Brazil

Fiona Macaulay

Introduction

This chapter examines the way in which women in Latin America have taken an increasingly proactive and transformative approach to the legal apparatus of their respective countries over the last two decades. This development reflects growing international attention to legislation and access to the justice system as tools for improving women's full enjoyment of citizenship. The chapter begins by surveying how women have historically been marginalised from the justice system and denied adequate protection of their rights. The way in which women across the region have begun to challenge and overturn antiquated and discriminatory laws and practices is then analysed in the context of global trends. Finally, the chapter looks at women's legal aid and legal literacy projects in Latin America, in particular one run by Themis, a Brazilian NGO that trains grassroots outreach workers who in turn assist working-class women in accessing the justice system. It is a project which seeks to extend citizenship beyond the letter of the law and secures for women positive rights as well as redress when their rights are violated. It has also led to reconsideration of certain discriminatory aspects of the local criminal justice system, and to reforms of such practices.

Women's access to the legal system

For many Latin Americans justice remains a distant concept, as they are effectively denied access to the system. The courts are often overloaded, understaffed and sometimes corrupt, biased or subject to political influence and interference. The continent has a highly sophisticated and well-established legal system. Nonetheless, many of the numerous new laws and constitutional guarantees enacted in the twentieth century remain a dead letter because of the lack of effective remedies and anti-remedies,[1] and the structural flaws in the institutions of the justice system. To take just one measure of access: the number of judges employed per capita in Latin America, compared to the USA and western European countries, is very low. In 1996, Brazil employed 8600 judges, for a total population of 172 million. Some six million court cases are underway at any given moment, making 700 court cases per judge. Each case gives rise, on average, to three appeals, adding some 18 million appeals to an already overburdened system. The 5895 judges working in the lower courts (of whom only 20 per cent are women) represent one judge per 26 400 inhabitants.[2] This compares very unfavourably to one per 3500 population in Germany, or one per 9000 in the USA. The negative consequences of such paltry access to justice are varied: individuals or communities may take the law into their own hands, indulging in extra-systemic violence such as lynchings, death squads or revenge killings (Huggins 1991). The creation of such an 'uncivil society' deepens the existing 'unrule of law' in these neighbourhoods (Méndez et al., 1999). The shortage of judges, prosecutors and legal aid lawyers may result in unfair trials of criminal defendants.[3] Many crimes go unreported, unrecorded, uninvestigated and unprosecuted. Crimes against women, such as sexual or domestic violence, are still less likely to reach a court of law due a number of additional factors outlined below.

Women's access to legal defence of their rights is even more restricted than that of men in the region. First, a number of laws remain on the statute books that discriminate against women, even though these laws are now at odds with both the provisions of the international conventions and agreements signed by the respective countries, as well as the principles set out in their modernised or revised national constitutions. Second, women suffer a number of specific abuses of their rights related to the prevailing gender roles in Latin American society, for example domestic and sexual violence, as well as abuses related to the denial of reproductive rights. Third, certain sectors of women, for example indigenous or rural women, suffer diminished access to the protection potentially afforded by the criminal justice system by virtue of language differences, higher levels of illiteracy than their male peers, and geographical distance from services such as women's police stations, which tend overwhelmingly to be located in heavily urbanised areas.

Public services, in this case state judicial institutions, are rarely sensitive to the needs of the consumer, still less to those of the female client, and to her different time and space patterns (Rose 1993). Restricted opening hours may deter working women who struggle with the demands of their double shift. The United Nations (UN) Special Rapporteur on Violence against Women has criticised the fact that women's police stations in Brazil generally operate during normal working hours, whereas most assaults on women occur at nights and at weekends (ECOSOC 1997: 14). They are also understaffed, with an average of 24 officers compared to around 60 in ordinary police stations. A woman reporting sexual assault or domestic violence is then obliged to travel across town to have her injuries examined by a police forensic doctor, at the separate Legal Medical Institute (Instituto Médico-Legal: IML), and return with the report. In addition, services are often located in the most inappropriate places: the women's police station in Rio de Janeiro is located directly above a high-security prison holding 600 men convicted of homicide and drugs offences (ECOSOC 1997).

Women's lower incomes in relation to men also constitute a serious barrier in a region in which there are chronic shortages of public prosecutors and legal aid lawyers available to bring state prosecutions for gender-based violations, or to offer legal assistance in bringing a private case, whether in relation to domestic violence or alimony payments. Women are most likely to need, or seek, legal assistance for family-related matters, such as birth certificates, child custody, maintenance, separation and divorce and complaints of sexual assault or domestic violence. An analysis of over 15 000 enquiries in the early 1990s to Chile's newly established network of women's legal advice centres (Centros de Información de los Derechos de la Mujer: CIDEM) shows that the clients most commonly sought information on family related issues (53.4 per cent), followed by domestic violence (14.7 per cent), and housing (10.1 per cent) (SERNAM 1994a, 1994b). Their concerns also varied depending on their marital and financial status. Single, separated or widowed women were more likely than married women to seek advice on their and their children's rights. Married women, on the other hand, made proportionately more enquiries about domestic violence and household issues. Widows constituted the group of women most concerned with housing rights and state benefits.[4] In the case of domestic violence, a combination of factors – women's ignorance of their rights, institutional shortcomings, lack of resources and social prejudice – has resulted in an extremely low prosecution rate of offenders. In Brazil, it is estimated that only 2 per cent of male perpetrators end up serving a sentence (ECOSOC 1997).

Finally, the effective defence of women's rights is undermined by the still-prevalent gender prejudices embedded in the institutions of the justice system, and expressed by its agents, namely by judges, police, and prosecutors, particularly in relation to the more 'taboo' and 'private' areas of sexuality, reproductive choice, and sexual and domestic violence (Cadernos CEPIA 1994, 1995). This has given rise to anomalous situations in which the customary application of the law is at odds with the letter and spirit of the existing legislation. It was noted in Brazil in the 1980s, for instance, that men who murdered their wives or partners whom they believed to have committed adultery were routinely acquitted. Juries in these homicide cases were swayed by the defence lawyers' invocation of the 'honour defence'; that is, that the accused had acted justifiably in order to redress damage done to his personal 'honour'. Such a defence does not exist under Brazilian law[5] and in 1991 the highest criminal court (Superior Tribunal de Justiça: STJ) overturned a decision by the lower courts and ordered a retrial in one such case, following a women's movement campaign (Americas Watch 1991). Subsequent awareness-raising among the judiciary has decreased the use of such a defence, but not eliminated it,[6] in part because the decisions of the STJ are not binding on lower courts.[7]

Similarly, in most countries in Latin America abortion, although criminalised, is nonetheless permitted in certain circumstances, namely following rape or incest or in order to preserve the mother's life.[8] In reality, very few public hospitals provide such a service, as doctors refuse either on the basis of their own moral judgements, or out of a fear of possible prosecution. Often, the bureaucratic steps involved in procuring authorisation are labyrinthine, painfully slow, or biased against the woman. For example, in Nicaragua a woman is allowed an abortion only with the permission of her husband or a near relative, and after the request has been considered by a panel composed of three suitably qualified people, most often men. In many countries, judges, prosecutors or police officials have complete discretion to decide on the veracity of a woman's claim of having been assaulted, quite independently of any criminal charges being brought and proven against the assailant. In Brazil doctors will not act without a police report and police medical examination, although neither is required by law. Article 128 of the 1940 Brazilian Penal Code defined the conditions for legal abortion and this law should, in theory, be auto-applicable; that is, it does not require supplementary legislation in order to be put into effect. In practice, however, the women's movement has had to campaign for additional enforcement measures. In 1989 the city of São Paulo, under the woman mayor Luisa Erundina of the left-wing Workers' Party (Partido dos Trabalhadores) passed a municipal ordinance requiring a large public city hospital to provide legal abortions. By 1999 at least 13 hospitals in seven states had followed suit.[9] A bill put forward by two federal deputies, Eduardo Jorge and Sandra Starling, both of the Workers' Party, to enforce the law nationwide had not been passed by early 2000, although the Ministry of Health had by then committed itself to establishing uniform internal guidelines committing public health services to providing legal abortion.

The judiciary is by nature a conservative body, slow to reform its practices and values. In Brazil, where there is far less political interference in the judiciary than in other parts of Latin America, federal officials told the UN Special Rapporteur that they did not have the powers to train judges with respect to domestic violence for fear of compromising the independence of the judiciary. Clearly, reform initiatives have to come from within the institution and, as we shall see later, local initiatives in conjunction with civil society have led to greater debate around issues of gender and justice. It is possible, although not a given, that higher representation for women within the justice system may gradually eradicate such discriminatory practices. Whilst women's presence in the judiciary in Latin America is not as low as in other continents, nevertheless they entered late (after the 1940s), are barely visible at the top of the hierarchy, and tend to be clustered either in the lowest ranks or in certain fields such as small claims and family courts, or else serve as Justices of the Peace (Valdés and Gómariz 1995: 167–8). Women are virtually non-existent in the Supreme Court (federal or national level), constitute around 20 per cent in the Court of Appeals (at state level) and 45 per cent in the lower trial courts (local courts).[10] In Brazil women have 34 per cent representation in the labour courts, 18 per cent in civil courts and 15 per cent in the federal courts, whilst the first woman was appointed to the Supreme Court only in 1999.[11]

Women's rights in the international arena

The above discussion highlights the complex relationship between the legislative process, that is, the drafting and approval of gender-sensitive rather than discriminatory legislation, on the one hand, and the often glaring disparity between the letter and the application of the law, on the other. It is this implementation gap that is being increasingly being addressed throughout the region via women's legal aid and legal literacy projects. The heightened concern of the Latin American women's movement with both the letter and the application of the law following two decades of evolving debate in the international arena is evident in the conclusions of the Third and Fourth World Conferences on Women (Nairobi in 1985 and Beijing in 1995) and in the two most important international instruments on women: the 1979 United Nations Convention on the Elimination of all forms of Discrimination against Women, CEDAW, and the 1994 Inter-American Convention on the Prevention, Punishment and Eradication of Violence Against Women, known as the Belém do Pará Convention. Although the 16 key articles of the CEDAW frequently recommend legislative reform as a means of combating discrimination, the proposals remain generic and vague. Only article 15 addresses the law as such, and mentions only women's right to equality before the law and to the choice of domicile. The Nairobi Forward-Looking Strategies for the Advancement of Women continue to place more emphasis on social and economic issues than on legal strategies for enhancing women's status. Sixteen paragraphs of a 372-paragraph document address constitutional and legal measures: several emphasise the need for more research in this area, as well as the establishment of working groups to eliminate 'discriminatory practices'. However, paragraph 75 does recommend in-service training for the judiciary and paralegal professionals regarding the progress made on women's rights in international conventions and in national constitutions and laws. It also urges the recruitment and training of more women in the legal field.

The perception of the law as both an obstacle to, and an instrument for, social change and gender equality underwent a sea change after the 1993 United Nations Conference on Human Rights in Vienna. In Latin America this conference coincided with the transition to, and consolidation of, democracy in several countries. In this process the new political authorities increasingly adopted the discourse of rights current among the social movements and opposition political forces prior to the transition. Civil liberties and *de jure* rights acquired a greater importance in the aftermath of decades of authoritarian rule and the suspension of the most fundamental guarantees. The Belém do Pará Convention, which addresses one specific gender-based rights violation, goes into much greater detail as to the state's obligations to provide *effective* redress, not just through the introduction of new legislation, but also by paying attention to the institutions and mechanisms of the justice system, to their efficacy in protecting rights and to their accessibility. The Convention refers explicitly to the state's responsibility to exercise 'due diligence' in order to prevent, investigate and punish violence against women. It thus invokes the operational, rather than normative or discursive, elements of the criminal justice system. State's parties are urged to establish fair and effective legal procedures, including protection orders, swift trials and 'effective access' to redress for female victims of violence. The text reflects the frustration experienced throughout the region by women's groups concerned with sexual and domestic violence, for although some countries have criminalised such acts, access to justice has been stymied by lack of resources, and by sclerotic and ineffective legal procedures.

The Platform for Action that resulted from the 1995 Beijing Conference took its lead from the Vienna Conference and the philosophical assertion that women's rights *are* human rights. Strategic Objective One dealing with the Human Rights of Women tackles in unprecedented depth the practical obstacles facing women in securing these hard-won rights. It criticises the gap between the existence of rights and their effective enjoyment and blames this, at national level, on the lack of government commitment and resources, and weak enforcement of family, civil, penal, labour and commercial codes and laws. In addition, 'overly complex administrative procedures, lack of awareness within the judicial process and inadequate monitoring... coupled with the under-representation of women in the justice system, inadequate information on existing rights and persistent attitudes and practices perpetuate women's *de facto* inequality' (paragraphs 217 and 219). Paragraph 227 identifies the lack of information as a key obstacle to women's enjoyment of their human rights and identifies *legal literacy* and *empowerment* of women in relation to their rights as major tools: 'Achieving legal literacy' is included as one of the key strategic objectives. A number of important legal literacy programmes around the world predate the Beijing conference (Schuler and Kadirgamar-Rajasingham 1992). However, the Platform for Action gives this strategy a vital global dimension and foregrounds the crucial and dynamic interplay between changes in the normative text of laws, the democratisation of information about, and access to, the justice system, and the introduction of tangible improvements in the application of the law. In short, the better women understand their rights as currently enshrined under national laws, and the more they are empowered to demand those rights, the greater will be their awareness of the shortcomings of both the legislation and the justice system. As a consequence, pressure from below for real changes to both will grow ever more powerful. Legal literacy should not be understood merely as a means of passing on apparently neutral information about the legal system to passive recipients, but rather as a process by which individual and collective consciousness is transformed, often leading to eventual changes in the letter and application of the law. Reforms to the law in Latin America, as we shall see, have been wrought in part as a result of women's changing consciousness in different political conjunctures, and in different phases of women's movement organisation.

Women and legal reform in Latin America

Laws codify and legitimise women's status in society and the gender roles allocated to each sex. The law both reflects social attitudes towards women and contributes to the construction of those beliefs and prejudices. Therefore a change in the law not only entails a modification, in practical terms, of the rights available to women, but also signals a symbolic shift. Sometimes changes in the law lag far behind those in social attitudes and sometimes the opposite is true. The 1982 Law of Nurturing introduced in Nicaragua (Collinson 1990: 111), or the clause inserted in the Goiás state constitution in Brazil in 1989, both of which require men to share equally in childcare and housework, are purely declaratory and symbolic, effectively unenforceable and very distant from public consciousness. The sexual division of labour in Cuba remains virtually untouched by years of official revolutionary rhetoric and by the 1975 Family Code (Molyneux 2000). Nonetheless, legal change which may be spearheaded by a small group of reformers can stimulate important public debate, especially if it airs a hitherto taboo subject such as reproductive rights. In some cases, for example legislation on domestic violence, the spirit and logic of new laws can pull prevailing opinion along in its wake, and a new public consensus can be created. The 1980s and 1990s have seen widespread debate across Latin America about gender-related reforms to national and subnational level constitutions, as well as to the civil and penal codes.[12]

In Latin America during the colonial period and for most of the nineteenth century, men held parental authority (*patria potestad*) over children and rights over women. The emergence of liberalism in the nineteenth century brought a reworking of the regulatory framework which had protected and restricted women. Reforms enacted in the later post-independence period were, however, of mixed impact on women (Dore 2000). On the one hand, women's individual rights were expanded. Women were protected from male violence and Mexico's Civil Codes of 1870 and 1884 extended parental authority to widows and single mothers.[13] In several countries, unmarried women were released from parental authority and the age of majority was lowered. On the other hand, women's property-owning rights were eroded and civil codes in the region legalised adultery for men and criminalised it for women (Lavrin 1995). This latter inequality was being removed from the statute books in the last decade of the twentieth century.

Towards the end of the nineteenth century, women came to act as the protagonists rather than as the objects of legal reform. Women began to organise to improve working conditions, changes to family and property law, female suffrage and demand access to the labour market, the professions and higher education institutions (Miller 1991). Increased secularisation led Mexico to legalise divorce on the grounds of mutual incompatibility in the Civil Code of 1884. Absolute divorce was permitted in Uruguay in 1913 and in Mexico in 1914. Brazil's 1943 Consolidated Labour Laws (Consolidação das Leis Trabalhistas: CLT) passed under President Vargas provided for workplace crèches and outlawed sexual discrimination in the workplace. Women's demands that the state dismantle patriarchal privilege were, however, met only very slowly, and many of the issues on the agenda of these 'first wave' feminists remained unresolved, reappearing on the platform of the contemporary women's movement. For example, the provisions of the CLT were never enforced, and the Brazilian women's movement in the 1990s had to fight for additional legislation to operationalise laws already on the statute books, such as that providing for legal abortion.

Transitions from authoritarian rule or from civil conflict to elected governments in the 1980s and 1990s, combined with increased emphasis on women's rights in transnational arenas, focused the attention of women's movements in Latin America ever more on the institutional and legal arena (Jaquette 1994). National and regional networks formed, functioning as an invaluable forum for exchange and cross-fertilisation of ideas, often prompted by the process of consultation and debate that preceded and accompanied the UN Nairobi, Vienna and Beijing conferences. The Latin American and Caribbean Committee for the Defence of Women's Rights (Comité de America Latina y el Caribe para la Defensa de los Derechos de la Mujer: CLADEM) was founded in 1987 in Costa Rica following the Nairobi conference. With national groups in 17 countries in the region, it has in part been responsible for the establishment of legal literacy programmes in the region, as it publicised the Peruvian experience (see below). Some national women's NGOs, such as the Feminist Research and Advisory Centre (Centro Feminista de Estudos e Assessoria: CFEMEA) in Brazil, have very effectively spearheaded lobbying efforts to change domestic legislation (Macaulay 2000).

One of the markers of regime transition is frequently the drafting of a new constitution, signalling a symbolic discursive and normative break with the preceding regime and its values.[14] As a text which sets out the definition of citizenship, the relationship between state and citizen, and the boundaries between private and public spheres – all of which are underpinned by gendered conceptions – they have been a focus of women's mobilisation to insert articles which explicitly outlaw sexual discrimination and extend women's rights.[15] Some constitutions (Guatemala, Mexico, Paraguay) advocate the equality of men and women, whilst others (Colombia, Honduras, Panama, Peru) explicitly forbid sex discrimination.[16] The Paraguayan Constitution of 1992, reflecting the organised lobbying of the women's movement, outlines the state's specific responsibility to eradicate discrimination.[17] Others have continued to use the generic term 'men'.[18] In May 1999, after a long battle between the political right and the women's ministry (Servicio Nacional de la Mujer – SERNAM), article one of Chile's 1980 Constitution was changed from 'All men are born free and equal in dignity and rights'[19] to 'all people are born free',[20] adding for good measure 'Men and women are equal in the eyes of the law'.[21] The process of women's mobilisation and public debate around the drafting of a new constitution often marks a high point of networking and common cause amongst women's groups. In Nicaragua, during the grassroots consultations (*cabildos abiertos*) held nation-wide in 1985 and 1986 prior to the approval of the 1987 constitution, women managed to insert more than ten articles on women's rights (Collinson 1990: 112). In Brazil, the women's movement elected a number of feminists to the Constituent Assembly of 1986–88 in order to ensure women's input, and they scored significant victories as a result, such as the extension of social security provisions to women previously excluded, and a legally enforceable statement of equality (Verucci 1991).

Constitutional reform, however, has also resulted in a degree of anti-feminist backlash, particularly over the controversial topic of reproductive rights. In a number of countries attempts have been made to nullify existing provision for legal abortion by changing the text of the constitution, adding the words 'from the moment of conception' to the article guaranteeing the right to life. This was mooted during the failed constitutional revision of the mid-1990s in Brazil, whilst President Menem attempted to change the Argentine Constitution in 1993 and later in 1999 article 15 of the Civil Code to this effect. In 1999 the state assembly in Nuevo León in Mexico approved such an alteration to the state constitution, in contradiction to national legislation.[22]

Some of the most discriminatory legislation on the statute books, and the subject of feminist campaigns, concerns women's sexual rights and physical integrity.[23] All penal codes with the exception of Cuba and Nicaragua until recently considered the social reputation of the female victim to constitute a key definition of certain crimes and to determine their punishment. The crimes of infanticide and abortion *honoris causa* carried lighter sentences if the woman committed them in order to conceal her dishonour. In the penal codes of a number of countries, rape may still be punished less severely if the victim is not an 'honest woman' or is a prostitute. No penal code classified rape in marriage as a crime (Valdés and Gómariz 1995: 149) until 1998 when the Chilean senate approved a bill criminalising rape, including rape in marriage. In the same year Nicaragua was one of the last countries in the region to decriminalise adultery. Prior to this, a woman could be accused on the strength of her husband's word alone. Men, on the other hand, could only be accused of the lesser crime of 'concubinage' (*amancebamiento*) which required witnesses as well as additional evidence of 'scandalous' behaviour. The honour of the woman is such a defining feature of these penal codes that several still allow for charges to be dropped if the offender in crimes with a sexual connotation (rape, statutory rape, abduction) marries the victim. El Salvador repealed such a provision in 1996 whilst Peru was scandalised in 1998 by a gang-rape case in which one of the attackers sought to take advantage of this loophole. Under these codes, the violation was committed not against the woman's individual bodily integrity or inalienable rights, but rather against the woman's honour *as a collective good*. As a result, sexual assault tended to be categorised as a violation of 'public morality' or 'decency'. Reforms to the penal code to establish sexual violence as a crime against the person have been passed in Argentina and Chile, and are pending elsewhere (Brazil, Ecuador).

Domestic violence has also been the subject of much new legislation. In the 1990s Chile, Costa Rica, Ecuador, Nicaragua, Venezuela, Puerto Rico and Peru introduced it into the penal code as a specific crime, whereas before only generic charges such as 'bodily harm' could be brought.[24] Legal procedures have also been altered in favour of the victim. Prior to the 1998 criminal procedures code, in El Salvador the victim's testimony was inadmissible in cases of sexual or domestic violence, although the victim was most likely to be the only witness. A number of other initiatives, such as women's police stations, women's refuges, fast-track family courts and restraining orders have also increased in practical terms women's protection and redress. However, as this is a relatively new area, both the law and judicial mechanisms are still evolving.

Family relationships are governed mainly by Civil Codes. Women generally have full legal capacity, except in matters of marital property which is still the subject of legislation in Chile and Brazil. Most laws accord children equal rights, but Chile continued to distinguish between 'legitimate', 'illegitimate' and 'natural' children until 1998 when a new law gave all children equal legal status.[25] Chile is also the only country which does not allow divorce and subsequent remarriage (*divorcio vincular*), resorting instead to a specious piece of legal trickery, 'annulment', according to which the marriage never actually took place due to a procedural 'error'. So controversial is this subject that a bill to rectify the situation has been submitted by a group of legislators rather than by the centre-left Concertación government in conjunction with SERNAM which together have submitted most other bills affecting the family or gender relations since 1990. In June 1999, the UN Committee on the Elimination of Discrimination against Women, when considering Chile's Third Periodic Report on the country's implementation of its commitments under the CEDAW, criticised Chile for its slowness in tackling both divorce and reproductive rights,[26] two controversial areas in which the Christian Democrat dominated government is extremely sensitive to pressure by the Catholic church.

Most constitutions guarantee the basic right to work although only Cuba's and Peru's refer to women's specific equality in this respect. They also establish equal pay for equal work without distinction of sex. The relevant legislation of most allows for maternity and even paternity leave, and frequently requires workplaces with over a certain number of employees to provide a daycare centre, although this is rarely complied with (Valdés and Gómariz 1995: 154). However, employers often oblige would-be women employees to take a pregnancy test or to provide a certificate of sterilisation. This practice was finally made illegal in Chile in 1998,[27] and has been the subject of both state and municipal legislation in Brazil.

Legal aid and legal literacy

Legislative reform may have accelerated in the last decade, but multiple obstacles still undermine women's effective access to the justice system. Chief among these is women's lack of knowledge of their rights and of the mechanisms of the law. The need highlighted in the Beijing Platform for Action for legal literacy programmes and democratisation of information and empowerment, particularly for low-income and marginalised women, has been taken up by a number of organisations in the region. Responses tend to fall into two main categories. On the one hand, a number of national Women's Ministries or official bodies have set up legal aid and information offices, employing professionals. In 1983 – a decade before the Beijing Conference – the Sandinista government's women's organisation, AMNLAE (Asociación de Mujeres Nicaragüenses Luisa Amanda Espinoza) set up in Nicaragua the first women's legal aid office (Oficina Legal de la Mujer: OLM) in Managua, followed in 1985 by others in Estelí, León, Granada and Masaya. The bulk of casework tended to concentrate on domestic violence, child maintenance and custody, whilst the lawyers and social workers employed in the centres offered counselling and reconciliation work. This was groundbreaking work, and the professionals soon perceived the need for training and awareness raising with the police and judiciary, as well as for radical changes to the law, for which the OLM lobbied vigorously until AMNLAE moved to tone down the OLM's politics (Collinson 1990: 149). In Chile, following the return to democracy in 1989, SERNAM set up women's legal advice offices in every region. Analysis of the needs of the users, noted earlier, then provided valuable information to SERNAM as to the priority areas for legal reform.

The other response has consisted of grassroots initiatives involving volunteer, community-based outreach workers and originated in feminist groups or NGOs, in emulation of programmes adopted in countries as diverse as the Philippines, Uganda and India. These 'paralegals' (*promotoras legales* in Peru, *monitoras* in Chile and *promotoras legales populares* in Brazil) carry out educational and consciousness-raising work with working class women about their rights and about how they can access the institutional arena in order to make those abstract rights a reality (Schuler and Kadirgamar-Rajasingham 1992).

In Latin America, the idea of training legal outreach workers first started in Peru in the 1980s at the Flora Tristán women's centre (Themis 1998c). It was, however, forced to suspend its project due to the Sendero Luminoso guerrilla movement's hostility to any form of community organising it did not control. The Manuela Ramos centre also started working, albeit with no legal background, with low-income women and indigenous groups around the Glass of Milk (Vaso de Leche) project. Meanwhile, other initiatives sprang up in Chile, Costa Rica, Rosario in Argentina and Cochabamba in Bolivia. However, the most enduring and arguably successful project in Latin America has been that set up by Themis, a feminist NGO in Porto Alegre, the capital city of the southern

Brazilian state of Rio Grande do Sul. It is this experience which I now examine.

Themis

Named after the Greek goddess of justice, Themis (Legal Assistance and Gender Studies) was founded in 1993 with the aim of bridging the gap between gender perspectives and feminist concerns on the one hand, and the mechanisms and institutions of the law, on the other. The women's movement in Brazil has been active since the 1970s, emerging as part of the opposition to military rule, then taking advantage of the new democratic conjuncture to achieve some notable advances in social policy regarding gender relations (Alvarez 1990). The first women's police stations in the continent, now much copied, were set up in the mid-1980s. The debate generated by the 1986–88 Constituent Assembly underscored the inadequacy and discriminatory nature of current legislation with respect to women's legal status, and brought home to the eventual founders of Themis the urgent need for the women's movement to intervene more proactively in legal arenas. A feminist lawyer, Denise Dora, who founded and coordinated Themis until 1999, came into contact with CLADEM's Women's Legal Training project (Capacitación Jurídica a las Mujeres) and the Peruvian experience through an Inter-American Institute of Human Rights course in Costa Rica in 1990. In the run-up to the 1993 Vienna Conference, a preparatory meeting of Latin American feminists in Costa Rica in December 1992 raised gender and justice, particularly issues of access, as an important theme. Denise Dora and a group of feminists, including three lawyers, further identified the need for a women's NGO in the south of Brazil: hitherto the better known women's NGOs had been based in São Paulo, Rio de Janeiro and Recife. They also believed it should be dedicated to legal issues: existing women's NGOs or government advisory bodies tended to concentrate on health and reproductive rights. Themis promotes and defends women's rights principally through its Access to Justice Programme which works in three main areas: democratisation of information and the periodic publication of new feminist writing on legal issues (Campos 1999, Dora and Silveira 1998, Dora 1997), a training programme for paralegals, and a feminist-legal training programme for legal professionals and feminist activists.

The organisation publishes regular twice-yearly summaries of women's issues as they have appeared in the media for justice system professionals (judges, prosecutors, legal aid lawyers, law lecturers), as well as for those bodies and individuals making public policies. Subjects to date have included domestic violence, abortion, sexual violence and sexual rights. In this respect Themis is akin to CFEMEA. However, where CFEMEA concentrates on the preparation, debate and approval of new, gender-related legislation and thus concentrates its efforts on the legislature, Themis concentrates on the application of existing law. Its publications are also intended to further debate within the feminist community and legal profession on key issues. A recent collection of essays (Campos 1999) challenges an alleged overemphasis on criminalisation as a solution to sexual and domestic violence.

The paralegal programme was adapted from the Peruvian model to Brazil, and began in 1993 when Themis trained 20 paralegals recruited from low-income women in the Porto Alegre metropolitan area in the basic precepts of law, the Brazilian justice system, constitutional rights and human rights, violence against women, sexual and reproductive rights, racial discrimination and workplace discrimination. Their methodology has evolved over time, shifting from purely legal issues to addressing the gulf between the letter of the law and women's lived experiences, using specific problems as the starting point for seeking viable legal solutions. Eventually, the course content broadened to cover other issues such as income generation, and now comprises a mixture of lectures and discussions[28] offered on a *pro bono* basis by judges, prosecutors and legal professionals, combined with onsite visits to key institutions of the criminal justice system, such as police stations, courts, and the IML (Themis 1998a). Contact between the trainee paralegals and officials in the system ensures some degree of mutual trust as well as a personal point of contact once the paralegals begin working in their communities and advising local women through the six Women's Information Service offices (Serviço de Informação à Mulher: SIM) based in low-income neighbourhoods of Porto Alegre and in the town of Canoas.

The SIMs, first set up in 1996, offer a walk-in information service where local women can get advice on domestic violence, sexual assault, racial and workplace discrimination, paternity suits and family-related matters. They do not, however, deal with matters related to separation and divorce, such as alimony and child maintenance. This is a strategic choice determined by relatively limited resources and their identification of their priority areas as 'controversial' ones in which there is little support available within the mainstream justice system, and to which Themis can bring more 'value added' as a feminist organisation in challenging existing prejudices within the general population and among justice system professionals. Over six years Themis and the

SIMs have assisted 5000 women, and over 300 cases have resulted in civil or criminal court cases, of which 65 per cent concern sexual or domestic violence.[29]

The paralegals themselves offer advice and sometimes material assistance, may accompany the woman to the police station, IML or courts and, where necessary, refer the clients to Themis lawyers who will then assist in the prosecution of, for example, a violent partner or assailant. With one cohort a year since 1993, by early 2000 Themis had trained over 200 paralegals, generally recruited by word of mouth through the friends and relatives of other trainees.[30] The trainees have a better than average level of education and a high level of community involvement in their neighbourhood.[31] The personal links and individual aspirations increase the motivation of the trainees, whilst their visibility in their community gives them a greater degree of acceptability and status. One paralegal in Restinga, Marlene Salete da Silveira Pinto, commented that, when they went to the courts or police station to put a case, they were treated as equals (Themis 1998b: 39). A number have gone on to be elected to positions in the community, for example as members of the statutory local Children's Guardianship Councils (Conselhos Tutelares), or as community delegates to the city's participatory budget discussions. The training course is provided free of charge whilst the SIMs cover women's travel and other expenses and compensate them for loss for earnings for the time they spend working as volunteers. For most, however, the benefits of working as paralegals are more intangible. Their experiences improve self-esteem and confidence, and they learn skills such as basic accounting, fundraising and office management which are easily transferable to the workplace and offer access to better-paid jobs.[32] The SIMs are housed for free in premises lent by community organisations, such as the church, or by state or municipal government entities. Although Themis could have opted for renting accommodation, their preference has been for community partnerships which add legitimacy, increase the profile of the SIM and reinforce the paralegals' self-image as providers of an important local service.[33] I witnessed a group of experienced paralegals negotiating with the local military police commander and civil police chief for use of a police-run community centre.[34] In particular they were obliged to explain their motives for this voluntary work, and to clarify that they did not, and could not, substitute the police's work in tackling violence in an area of high drug-related crime, although they would form an important axis between the community and police.

Themis's programme is notable for its horizontal and democratic structure. The paralegals have discretion to adjust their priorities to local needs. In one case a paralegal helped families involved in a land occupation to engage in a community arbitration process which resulted in the squatters deciding to prioritise women-headed households when allocating the land. The SIM offices form a community network, and the paralegals have their own self-help, support and discussion group, quite autonomous of Themis. Several of the more experienced paralegals have also set up their own community initiatives, and in April 1999, the SIM in Restinga voted to become an NGO independent of Themis (Themis 1998b) and to focus their work on teenage pregnancy and income generation. Having identified unemployment as a key concern among women in her neighbourhood, one paralegal left to set up a woman-run recycling depot. Others have become trainers on the courses for new trainees.

The third plank of Themis' work is that of awareness-raising and debate with professionals in the justice system who have come to appreciate the paralegals' role as intermediaries between the local population and the public institutions. A local judge in Canoas observed how few cases of domestic violence ever reached his court and approached Themis for assistance. In 1999 a number of local groups, including the chamber of commerce, town council and bar association, clubbed together to send 32 local women on Themis' training programme.[35] They now work closely with the courts, liaising with court officials and accompanying women to the hearings. This informal role as a court assistant will be formalised and supported by the Ministry of Justice in 2000.

Themis has received considerable public recognition, enabling it to consolidate institutionally. It has received several awards: in 1996 it won the Ministry of Justice's National Human Rights prize for NGOs; in 1997 it was awarded a prize by the state Legislative Assembly; in 1998 it won a prize from a popular women's magazine, *Claudia*. Themis has also consolidated its position as the leading local and national NGO. It engaged in a number of activities: it coordinated the group representing women and NGOs from Rio Grande do Sul (Articulação Gaúcha de Mulheres) during the preparatory process for the Beijing Conference; organised the regional meeting to debate and draw up the National Human Rights Programme which was approved in May 1996; ran courses on accessing the Inter-American Court of Human Rights in conjunction with Human Rights Watch; and set up a training course for female candidates to city councillor in the municipal elections of 1996 (in which a quota of 20 per cent women on every party list was introduced for the first time) in association with the Brazilian Institute of Municipal Administration

(Instituto Brasileiro de Administração Municipal). In 1997 it was contracted by the Ministry of Justice to write the country's first periodic report on progress in implementing the CEDAW. Themis also has plans to expand horizontally, that is, to set up more SIMs in cities throughout the state. Themis' paralegal scheme has already been successfully copied by a women's group in São Paulo (União de Mulheres de São Paulo, 1997), whilst the Ministry of Justice and UNDP is funding Themis to replicate its experience in other states by collaborating with NGOs working on a range of rights: children, the Black community, sexual minorities and women.[36] Eventually they want to set up a permanent legal literacy school focused primarily on the methodology of training and outreach.[37]

Themis's experience in running a legal literacy programme highlights the dynamic relationship, noted above, between women's increased knowledge of their rights and of the mechanisms of the law, and eventual campaigns to change both the law and the institutions of the justice system. In Rio Grande do Sul, the activities of the SIMs and the paralegals have stimulated debates about reform, for example, as to the relocation of the IML within the police stations, the establishment of a gender unit within the judicial apparatus and whether specialist women's police stations should be replaced by women's units in every station.

Conclusion

Legal reform in Latin America in relation to gender equity has been a dynamic process over the last one hundred years, as both political elites and women's movements in the region have responded to globally evolving notions of equality, citizenship and subjecthood. Particular historic moments have stimulated spurts in new legislation and revised rights. The late nineteenth century saw concern with women's education. The first decades of the centuries brought secularisation and reforms such as divorce laws in some countries. The immediate post-World War II period saw the spread of female suffrage across the continent. The most recent political conjuncture, that of democratisation, has been accompanied by the accelerated concern of national and regional women's movements to eradicate archaic and discriminatory legislation, especially in regard to the private sphere, that is, in family relations, sexuality and reproductive rights. Women's groups have also recognised that, just as the welcome return to democracy did not necessarily or automatically increase women's representation in political life, so too changes in the letter of the law do not inexorably lead to their *de facto* application. Women have begun to demand modifications to the very institutions which administer political representation and the law, and to seek greater access through alternative channels. In the political sphere this includes the quotas for women on party electoral lists or for internal party positions now in operation in a number of countries. In the ambit of justice and law, legal literacy and legal aid projects such as Themis have both expanded access, especially for low-income women, through knowledge-sharing and advocacy, and encouraged certain practical initiatives within the justice system to respond to women's needs, for example women's police stations and fast-track family courts.

While the many deficiencies of the justice institutions of newly democratised countries in Latin America have prompted some groups and individuals to 'take the law in their own hands' in violent and extra-systemic ways, these feminist initiatives to change the law, to educate women about their rights, and to challenge and demand access to justice system services and institutions have served to strengthen local civil society and render it less 'uncivil'. In the long run, such a strategy legitimises the bodies inevitably charged with upholding the rule of law and bolsters democratic rights and values. By engaging with the legal system, women's groups hope not merely to gain new rights as citizens, but also to have them honoured in practice. Reform of the justice system institutions within a democratic society is now on the agenda for the twenty-first century. Groups such as Themis and its 200 trained paralegals contribute to the creation of a 'usable' state in Latin America, one capable of delivering on its promises of equality and citizens' rights.

Notes

1 Remedies are actions (injunctions, damages or restitution) which a court may take to enforce a ruling. Anti-remedies are actions to force a remedy or correct an inadequate one.
2 *Veja* 11 Dec. 1996. Information supplied by the Supremo Tribunal Federal (Supreme Court) and Associação dos Magistrados Brasileiros (Association of Brazilian Judges).
3 In Brazil most pre-trial detainees cannot afford a private lawyer, and often wait for several years to be allocated one of the few state-funded legal aid lawyers. This shortage also affects their enjoyment of their legal rights once convicted, such as parole and transfer to a lighter prison regime (Amnesty International 1999, Human Rights Watch 1998).

4   Housing prompted 22.7 per cent and state benefits 20.7 per cent of widows' enquiries, compared to 12.8 per cent and 4.2 per cent respectively for married women (SERNAM 1994a, 1994b).

5   The Brazilian Penal Code abolished this defence in 1830.

6   A few years later, the STJ contradicted its first decision, upholding a jury's acquittal of a wife murderer, arguing that the jury's decision was sovereign and reflected public opinion and the community's social values. The use of the honour defence appears to have crept back in (interview with Denise Dora 18 July 2000).

7   Brazil is rare among federal systems in that the Supreme Court does not set precedents to be followed by lower courts.

8   The exceptions are Chile, which banned abortion under any circumstances in1989, one of the final decisions of the Pinochet government, and Colombia which did so in 1980.

9   *Fêmea* 6 (63), April 1998. Of the 26 state constitutions drawn up in 1989, eight refer to the state's obligation to provide legal abortion via the public health service. The city of São Paulo includes this provision in its Lei Orgânica Municipal, and Law 1042 passed in 1987 does the same for the city of Rio de Janeiro. (Pitanguy and Sarmento Garbayo 1995). However, the state constitution of Espírito Santo contradicts the penal code and outlaws abortion altogether. As all the states in the Brazilian federation are subject to the same criminal law, this declaration is merely rhetorical, and has no legal force (Informe Nacional de Brasil: Investigación sobre 'El tratamiento legal del aborto en América Latina y el Caribe', CLADEM website www.derechos.org/cladem/aborto). This website contains studies of the legal and practical issues concerning abortion in 14 Latin American countries as well as a comparative summary.

10   Under socialist governments women have fared better. For example, in the 1980s in Nicaragua women came to comprise 33.6 per cent of the 'people's judges' (Valdés and Gómariz 1995). In Cuba by 1993 women comprised 39.3 per cent of professional judges, 60.4 per cent of lay judges and held 32.1 per cent of senior management posts in the judiciary (FLACSO website www.eurosur.org/FLACSO/mujeres/cuba/portada.htm).

11   Although there has been a certain 'feminisation' of the lower echelons of the justice system, female judges and lawyers tend not to be in criminal practice.

12   See Inter-American Commission on Human Rights (1998) for examples of recent changes to the Civil Codes, as well as policies to combat violence against women.

13   It was not until the 1928 Civil Code, which incorporated the 1917 Law of Family Relations, that married women were accorded parental authority as it removed the requirement for women to obey their husbands (Varley 2000: 242).

14   With the election of a new and controversial Constituent Assembly, women's groups in Venezuela mobilised in 1999 to take part in a revision of the existing Constitution (*Mujer/Fempress* 209, 211, 213).

15   Article 16 of the 1860 and 1994 Argentine Constitutions only forbids privilege or distinction on the basis of social class 'La Nación Argentina no admite prerrogativas de sangre, ni de nacimiento: no hay en ella fueros personales ni títulos de nobleza' ('The Argentine Nation does now allow any prerogatives on the basis of blood, or of birth; there are no personal privileges or titles of

nobility'). Article 37 of the 1994 Constitution further guarantees women real equal opportunities in access to elected office and party position via quota systems. Note: all translations here are by the author.

16 For an up-to-date comparison of constitutions in the region see the website www.georgetown.edu/pdba/Comp/comparative.

17 Article 48 'De la igualdad de derechos del hombre e de la mujer... El Estado promoverá las condiciones y creará los mecanismos adecuados para que la igualdad sea real y efectiva, allanando los obstáculos qu impidan o dificultan su ejercicio y facilitando la participación de la mujer en todos los ámbitos de la vida nacional.' ('On equal rights for men and women... the state will promote the conditions and create appropriate mechanisms to ensure that equality is real and effective, removing obstacles which impede or hinder the exercise of that equality and facilitating women's participation in all aspects of national life.')

18 Chile and Costa Rica's 1949 Constitutions read 'Todo hombre es libre en la República...' ('All men are free in the Republic'). In the late nineteenth century women in Mexico, Chile and Brazil had already challenged the use of the generic term 'men' in their bid to exercise the franchise. In each case it was ruled that the term 'men' did *not* in fact include women who were then explicitly excluded from voting.

19 'Los hombres nacen libres e iguales en dignidad y derechos' ('Men are born free and equal in dignity and rights').

20 'Las personas nacen libres' ('People are born free').

21 'Los hombres y mujeres son iguales ante la ley' ('Men and women are equal before the law').

22 Meanwhile, the authorities in Mexico City had been actually extending the legal grounds for termination.

23 Information regarding the passage of gender-related legislation may be found in the monthly regional publication *Mujer/Fempress* which is the source for the data in this section, unless otherwise stated. Individual references have been omitted for reasons of space.

24 Paraguay and Brazil were still debating such a reform as of early 2000.

25 The law was sanctioned by President Frei on 13 October 1998 (*La Tercera* 14 October 1998). Nicaragua gave all children equal rights and established equal obligations for parents in 1982 (Collinson 1990: 111).

26 See the Committee's press releases on their website www.un.org/News/Press/dosc/1999/19990622.wom1144 and 1145.

27 The original bill was submitted by the government on 28 November 1995.

28 The classes are designed for maximum interaction and student input, in order to retain those who might have had a negative experience of formal school education.

29 Data from Denise Dora and internal Themis information.

30 One cohort consisted of a woman and her two aunts, another three who brought their adult daughters, two pairs of sisters, 13 employees of three daycare centres and nine women who knew each other from Catholic church activities (Themis 1998c).

31 Three anthropologists accompanied the third cohort of paralegals trained by Themis. See their report dealing with the profile of the women and their relationship with the local community (Themis 1998c).

32 Author's interview with paralegals in Morro Santa Cruz in June 1999.
33 Denise Dora felt that, when SIMs ran in trouble, the women kept going because of a sense of obligation to the community generated by these partnerships.
34 Morro da Cruz, June 1999.
35 *Diário de Canoas* 24 August 1999.
36 The project was put into effect in seven states in 1999.
37 This will be supported by UNESCO and by an internationally acclaimed local literacy project GEEMPA.

Bibliography

Alvarez, S. (1990) *Engendering Democracy in Brazil: Women's Movements in Transition Politics*, Princeton: Princeton University Press

Americas Watch (1991) *Criminal Injustice: Violence against Women in Brazil*, New York: Human Rights Watch

Amnesty International (1999) *'No One Here Sleeps Safely': Human Rights Violations against Detainees*, London: Amnesty International

Cadernos CEPIA (1994) *Violência contra a mulher a cidadania: Uma avaliação das políticas públicas*, CEPIA: Rio de Janeiro

Cadernos CEPIA (1995) *O judiciário e a violência contra a mulher: A ordem legal e a (des)ordem familiar*, CEPIA: Rio de Janeiro

Campos, C. (ed.) (1999) *Criminologia e Feminismo*, Porto Alegre: Editora Sulina

Collinson, H. (ed.) (1990) *Women and Revolution in Nicaragua*, London: Zed Books

Dora, D. (ed.) (1997) *Feminino, Masculino: Igualdade e Diferença na Justiça*, Porto Alegre: Editora Sulina

Dora, D. and D. Silveira (1998) *Direitos Humanos, Etica e Direitos Reproductivos*, Porto Alegre: Themis

Dore, E. (2000) 'One step forward. Two steps back: Gender and the state in Latin America's long nineteenth century' in E. Dore and M. Molyneux (eds) *The Hidden Histories of Gender and the State in Latin America*, Chapel Hill, NC.: Duke University Press

Dore, E. and M. Molyneux (eds) (2000) *The Hidden Histories of Gender and the State in Latin America*, Durham, NC: Duke University Press

ECOSOC (United Nations Economic and Social Council) (1997) 'Report on the mission of the special rapporteur to Brazil on the issue of domestic violence' 15–26 July 1996

Huggins, Martha K. (ed.) (1991) *Vigilantism and the State in Modern Latin America: Essays on Extra-Legal Violence*, New York: Praeger

Human Rights Watch (1998) *Behind Bars in Brazil*, New York: Human Rights Watch

Inter-American Commission on Human Rights (1998) *Report of the Inter-American Commission on Human Rights on the Status of Women in the Americas*, Washington, DC: IACHR

Jaquette, J. (1994) *The Women's Movement in Latin America: Participation and Democracy*, Boulder, Colo.: Westview Press

Lavrin, A. (1995) *Women, Feminism and Social Change in Argentina, Chile and Uruguay, 1890–1940*, Lincoln: University of Nebraska Press

Macaulay, F. (2000) 'Getting gender on the policy agenda: a study of a Brazilian feminist lobby group' in E. Dore and M. Molyneux (eds) *The Hidden Histories of Gender and the State in Latin America*, Durham NC: Duke University Press

Méndez, Juan, G. O'Donnell and P. S. Pinheiro (eds) (1999) *The (Un)Rule of Law and the Underprivileged in Latin America* Notre Dame: University of Notre Dame Press

Miller, F. (1991) *Latin American Women and the Search for Social Justice*, Hanover, NH: University Press of New England

Molyneux, M. (2000) 'State, gender and institutional change: the Federación de Mujeres Cubanas' in E. Dore and M. Molyneux (eds) *The Hidden Histories of Gender and the State in Latin America*, Durham, NC: Duke University Press

Pitanguy, J. and L. Sarmento Garbayo (1995) *A Implementação do Aborto Legal no Serviço Público de Saúde*, Rio de Janeiro: CEPIA

Rose, G. (1993) *Feminism and Geography: The Limits of Geographical Knowledge*, London: Polity Press

Schuler, M. and Kadirgamar-Rajasingham, S. (1992) *Legal Literacy: A Tool for Women's Empowerment*, New York: OEF International and UNIFEM

SERNAM (1994a) *Necesidades de Información de las Mujeres*, Santiago: SERNAM

SERNAM (1994b) *Análisis de las Fichas de Consulta en los Centros de Información de los Derechos de la Mujer*, Santiago: SERNAM

Themis (1998a) *A Experencia das Promotoras Legais Populares*, Porto Alegre: Themis

Themis (1998b) *Gênero e Justiça*, Porto Alegre: Themis

Themis (1998c) *Programas de Capacitação Legal*, Porto Alegre: Themis

União de Mulheres de São Paulo (1997) *Promotoras Legais Populares: A experiência de São Paulo*, São Paulo: União de Mulheres de São Paulo

Valdés, T. and E. Gómariz (1995) *Latin America Women: Compared Figures*, Madrid and Santiago: Instituto de la Mujer and FLACSO

Varley, A. (2000) 'Women and the home in Mexican family law' in E. Dore and M. Molyneux (eds) *The Hidden Histories of Gender and the State in Latin America*, Chapel Hill, NC.: Duke University Press

Verucci, F. (1991) 'Women and the new Brazilian constitution' *Feminist Studies*, 17 (3) 551–67

5
In Pursuit of the Right to be Free from Violence: the Women's Movement and State Accountability in Uruguay

Niki Johnson

In the 1980s and 1990s domestic violence became a focal point in the agenda of Latin American women's movements. Multidimensional national and regional campaigns were carried out which included research, awareness-raising and service provision as well as lobbying the state. Women's movements' demands for greater state accountability were backed by international legal definitions of domestic violence as a violation of women's human rights and norms outlining states' duties to protect women's right to be free from violence. By the end of the twentieth century, women's movements throughout Latin America had successfully transformed what had previously been considered a private, personal problem into a public, political issue. In addition, in many countries outdated legislation had been reformed and new legal measures had been introduced.[1]

This chapter reviews the campaign against domestic violence of the Uruguayan women's movement. Uruguay stands out in the region for its early concession of political (1932) and civil (1946) equality to women, as well as a series of laws passed in the first three decades of the twentieth century on divorce, maternity leave and women's labour and education rights.[2] These women-friendly policies formed part of a development project premised on an interventionist role for the state, not simply in terms of economic participation and regulation, but also of welfare provision and policies to tackle social inequalities. However, following the achievement of formal citizenship, the question of women's rights disappeared from the political agenda. Consequently it proved difficult for the second wave women's movement, which emerged in the early 1980s, to persuade the political establishment that specific measures were required to ensure substantive equality for women and to tackle previously invisible issues, such as domestic violence. In addition, in the post-dictatorship period the predominance of neoliberal ideas advocating a reduced role for the state meant that governments were reluctant to regulate the private sphere. This chapter examines the strategies developed by the Uruguayan women's movement to overcome these obstacles and to achieve legal recognition of the specific gendered dimension of domestic violence, along with greater state accountability for prevention and protection. The analysis explores how the campaign was affected by the changing nature of the relationship between the movement and the state, and also by the interaction between the national campaign and regional and international developments.

Making the invisible visible

By the time domestic violence was placed on the political agenda in Uruguay, participants at the first Latin American and Caribbean Feminist Encounter (Bogota 1981) had designated 25 November as International Day Against Violence Against Women (Ortiz 1997: 18).[3] In international arenas it was also beginning to be recognised as a matter requiring attention. At the closing conference of the UN Decade for Women in Nairobi in 1985, violence against women was identified as an impediment to peace. In the same year the UN General Assembly passed a resolution urging member states to implement preventive measures, review legal procedures and provide services to victims (Fitzpatrick 1994: 536).

In Uruguay the issue was pursued by women who were beginning to engage in gender-based activism in political parties and autonomous women's groups within the context of the transition from military dictatorship during 1984–5. One of the proposed measures drawn up by the Women's Committee of the left-wing Broad Front for its 1984 election manifesto was the penalisation of all forms of violence against women and children and the creation of help centres for victims.[4] The specific problem of domestic violence was raised by the Working Group on Women's Status, a coordinating body of female representatives from all political parties and women's social organisations who had fought successfully to be included in the National Consensus-Building Forum (CONAPRO).[5] The Working Group recommended that violence against women in the home be analysed 'from a social and political perspective' and that the government promote research and set up preventive and awareness-raising programmes.[6] However, despite being approved by CONAPRO's executive body, the proposals met the same fate as the majority of the CONAPRO agreements – they were not followed up by the Colorado Party government that took power in March 1985.

In the face of this inaction, the priority of the women's movement in the first post-dictatorship administration (1985–90) was to break the traditional taboo surrounding the subject of violence against women. The recently established feminist press and feminist journalists writing in mainstream newspapers highlighted how domestic violence was made invisible by the fact that society at large – including legal and political establishments, and in particular the media – regarded it as an example of deviant behaviour. In contrast, feminist analyses saw it as a structural problem, linked to the wider question of gendered power relations.[7] As in other Latin American countries emerging from authoritarian rule, the need for an urgent response to domestic abuse was incorporated in the demand for a truly democratic society to be constructed in the aftermath of years of repression, encapsulated in the slogan 'democracy in the country and in the home'.

The lack of reliable statistics on domestic violence prompted feminist organisations to carry out research and hold awareness-raising workshops. Some women's groups began providing support services for victims, including self-help projects, legal and medical advice, therapy and aftercare.[8] In 1988 the first women's organisation to specialise in domestic violence – SOS Woman – was founded and was joined later by other specialist NGOs. Their work ranged from treating child, as well as women, victims of domestic abuse to rehabilitation programmes for male abusers.[9] From 1987 public events were organised to mark 25 November, and one-off demonstrations were held on several occasions to protest against the state's failure to protect abused women who were assaulted or murdered by former partners.[10]

The first state responses

Until the early 1990s most feminist organisations prioritised grassroots mobilisation over lobbying, and their attitude towards national government tended to be denunciatory, criticising the lack of effective action on gender issues. However, CONAMU (Uruguayan National Council of Women), the liberal feminist organisation, pursued a policy of negotiation and collaboration with the state, resulting in the first official steps to tackle the problem of domestic violence. In February 1988 CONAMU set up a multidisciplinary research team working with NGOs and government bodies to visit the first women's police station in the region, established in São Paulo, Brazil, in 1985. CONAMU then success-fully lobbied the Ministry of the Interior for a women's police station, which opened in Montevideo in November 1988. The women's movement welcomed this as a step in the right direction, but doubts were voiced regarding the police station's effectiveness since it was not allocated a separate budget and organisations working with victims of domestic violence considered that its staff had not received proper training.[11] To further the campaign, in October 1988 CONAMU organised a joint seminar on domestic violence with the National Women's Institute, and in 1989 set up the Help Centre for Abused Women in a collaborative project with the Ministry of Public Health.

The National Women's Institute was founded in 1987 by the Colorado Party government, with a remit to design, coordinate and monitor policy on women. After the National Party took office in 1990 it did not function for two years and was recreated as the National Institute for the Family and Women (INFM) in 1992. From the start it designated domestic violence a priority area, with activities including seminars, training for police officers and members of the judiciary, the creation of women's rights centres across the country and a Centre for the Prevention of Domestic Violence and Victim Support in Montevideo. Again, these measures were criticised by the women's movement for being inadequate in scope and lacking proper backing. It is true that the institute was limited in what it could do in practical terms because it had no budget allocation until 1995, when the Colorado Party took power again, and did not have the status of a ministry, which meant that it had insufficient political weight in its dealings with other state bodies. However, its work was also characterised by a lack of continuity, with changes in personnel and renegotiation of agreements with other authorities at each consecutive changeover in administration. This meant that basic training on gender issues had to be repeated for new staff and the completion of crucial projects – such as a women's refuge – was delayed.[12] The original National Women's Institute had functioned as an interministerial council, but this structure was subsequently aban-doned, hampering the elaboration of an integrated, cross-sector policy on domestic violence. In addition, the council had included two repre-sentatives from women's organisations, whereas during the following two terms the INFM was marked by a reluctance to work with the women's movement, primarily for ideological reasons since members of a number of NGOs had links with the left.[13]

The 1990s: networks, regionalisation and specialisation

By the beginning of the 1990s, regular contact had been established between women's movements across Latin America and the Caribbean through the Feminist Encounters encouraging an exchange of experiences.[14] Transnational initiatives were also emerging to exchange information and mount regional campaigns on a range of gender issues.[15] In 1988 Isis International, a women's documentation and communication centre based in Santiago, Chile, launched a research project funded by the UN Development Fund for Women to gather information about the incidence of gender-based violence in the region and the organisations working on the issue (Isis Internacional 1990). The process and results of this project brought together women's groups from different countries and in November 1989 the Southern Cone Network against Domestic Violence was set up by NGOs in Argentina, Chile and Uruguay. At the Fifth Feminist Encounter in 1990 members of this network promoted the idea of a wider coordinating structure to cover the whole region, and in 1992 the first meeting of the Latin American and Caribbean Feminist Network against Violence towards Women took place (Red Feminista 1996, Ortiz 1997).[16] During this meeting an international petition to the UN was circulated, which provided links to women's movements' campaigns against violence outside the region. The petition requested that women's human rights and gender-based violence be placed on the agenda of the World Conference on Human Rights to be held in Vienna the following year (Paredes 1993: 91).

In Uruguay the early 1990s were characterised by a generalised drop in political and social activism, economic recession and more stringent structural adjustment measures. At the same time a process of 'NGOisation' began in the women's movement, with an increasing number of organisations receiving international funding (Alvarez 1998: 306–8). Internal restructuring took place and project work and provision of services started to take priority over mobilisation and movement-wide coordination. The resulting fragmentation of the women's movement was accentuated by the dissolution of the two existing movement-wide coordinating bodies.[17] Meanwhile, the institutional response to the problem of domestic violence remained inadequate, and NGOs providing services for abused women found themselves unable to meet the growing demand. The development of new issue-based forms of coordination, drawing on the positive example set by the regional networks, was seen as a possible way of overcoming these obstacles.

In November 1992 eight women's organisations founded the Uruguayan Network against Domestic and Sexual Violence (RUVDS), as a means of sharing experiences of working with victims of domestic violence and pooling resources in the organisation of awareness-raising campaigns. The RUVDS also maintained links to regional developments through its participation in the Latin American Network Against Violence. The following month Feminist Space was formed as 'a forum for reflection and action' by 60 feminists, both activists from a range of organisations and individuals participating on an *ad hoc* basis.[18] Domestic violence was designated a priority concern, and a lobbying strategy was developed to 'take advantage of all the openings provided by the legal system to exert pressure and introduce issues on to the agenda'.[19] In 1993 members of Feminist Space formed the Interdisciplinary Group on Violence Against Women with experts from outside the women's movement.[20] The group was conceived of as a specialist research and lobbying organisation, whose objectives included:

> the detection of failures or lack of responses in the intervening systems; the formulation of public policy proposals... participation in the drafting of a legal framework to promote articulation between the actions of civil society and those carried out by state institutions.
> (Beñarán *et al.* 1997: 13)

A primary aim of these three new organisations was to develop strategies to press for greater state accountability in the prevention of domestic violence and the protection of its victims; a goal that became particularly urgent in the second half of the 1990s when international funding for NGOs began to dry up. The elaboration of new strategies was facilitated by the increased knowledge generated by national and regional networking, and was grounded in a rights-based discourse influenced by advances in international law and feminist theory.

Arguing for domestic violence as a human rights question

The definition of domestic violence as a human rights violation was linked to the global campaign by women's movements to 'engender' human rights and the law.[21] The language and concept of universal human rights had originally come under attack from feminist academics in the North for ignoring the fact that 'many violations of women's human rights are distinctly connected to being female' (Bunch 1990: 486, cf. Binion 1995). An important victory in the struggle to achieve international institutional recognition of this reality was the declaration made at the Vienna Conference that women's human rights are 'an inalienable, integral and indivisible part of universal human rights' (cited in Amnesty International 1995: 13).

Between 1990 and 1993 increasing concern over the issue of domestic violence was shown in international arenas (Heise *et al.* 1994: 1172). In January 1992 the UN Committee on the Elimination of Discrimination Against Women issued General Recommendation 19. This identified gender-based violence as 'a form of discrimination which seriously inhibits women's ability to enjoy rights and freedoms on a basis of equality with men' (cited in Fitzpatrick 1994: 534). Six months after the Vienna Conference, the UN General Assembly issued the Declaration on the Elimination of Violence against Women which defined such violence in broad terms, signalling its basis in unequal gendered relations of power and situating it clearly within the area of human rights (Carrillo 1997: 7–8). In March of the following year the UN Commission on Human Rights appointed a Special Rapporteur on violence against women. The UN's recommendations were restated in the accords signed at the Fourth UN World Conference on Women in Beijing (1995), and at regional level in the 1994 Belem do Pará Inter-American Convention on the Prevention, Punishment and Eradication of Violence Against Women. To publicise this international recognition of women's human rights and condemnation of gender-based violence, the global and Latin American women's movements organised human rights 'tribunals' where cases of violations of women's rights were presented and judged.[22]

Following the international feminist position that domestic violence should be considered a human rights violation (see Romany 1994, Carrillo 1991), Uruguayan activists regarded the right to be free from violence as a right with social, economic and political dimensions, in that it affects women's enjoyment of all their other rights. The RUVDS referred to violence against women as a 'scourge that infringes women's human rights and individual liberties, restricting the full exercise of their citizenship',[23] an analysis clearly paralleling CEDAW's Recommendation 19. Feminist Space argued that the gender-specific, structural nature of domestic violence made it a human rights issue *per se*: 'our aim is that violence against women be understood as a global political problem... We consider this kind of violence to be systemic in nature, which is what forces us to see it as a question of human rights.'[24] Feminist Space sought to achieve greater legitimacy for this conception of domestic violence by insisting on the 'responsibility of human rights organisations to include violence against women in their campaigns'.[25] However, this argument alone did not provide sufficient theoretical justification to support feminist groups' claim that the state was accountable for what were private acts of violence, not abuses perpetrated by state agents.[26]

Conceptions of the state's role

Despite the long tradition of state intervention in Uruguay, the constitutional foundation of the state is liberal democratic. Liberal democracies have at their centre a paradigm of state–civil society relations that establishes a theoretical separation between the 'private/personal' and the 'public/political' spheres. By locating family relations in the former, the model rejects the classification of domestic violence as a political issue and thus refuses to see it as a valid area for state intervention (see Chinkin 1995: 24, Eisler 1987: 291–6). Although in practice gender relations and family life are widely regulated by the state, politicians in liberal democracies have always been reluctant to be seen to be 'meddling' in the private sphere. After the experience of state invasion of all areas of private life during the period of military rule in Uruguay (1973–85), this non-interventionist stance was taken by parties right across the political spectrum. The Broad Front refused to include in its 1984 electoral manifesto the Women's Committee's demand for 'democracy in the home', arguing that 'the Broad Front could be accused of trying to intervene in the domestic sphere or interfere in the privacy of the home' (Rodríguez Villamil 1986: 15).

The notion of a restricted sphere of action for the state was shored up by the neoliberal ideology and policies adopted during the last three decades of the twentieth century, paralleling the pattern in other Latin American countries. The economic crisis that had begun in the late 1950s was blamed on an inefficient and bloated state. From the early 1960s, and most systematically under the National Party administration (1990–95), structural adjustment programmes were implemented to reduce national spending, privatise public services and limit state regulation of the economy and social inequalities (Finch 1998). As a result, demands for greater state intervention and provision of services – central elements of the women's movement's campaign on domestic violence – met with considerable resistance.

In their challenge to the political establishment's resistance to treat domestic abuse as a human rights issue, Uruguayan feminists drew on

CEDAW's Recommendation 19, arguing that the state could be considered to be condoning such violence if its agents did not make a sufficient effort to eliminate or prevent it.[27] By monitoring the way cases were dealt with by state actors, Feminist Space identified instances of state complicity 'on the basis of omission on the part of members of the police force, either because they trivialise the risk that women face, or regard these incidents as minor offences, or unconsciously legitimise this kind of male violence' (Dufau 1993: 2). The Interdisciplinary Group further reasoned that since the state had the monopoly on punitive action this imposed on it the obligation to provide the victim with the same guarantees under the law that were afforded to the accused (Dufau 1993: 110). In other words, they claimed that domestic violence could be regarded as a human rights violation – and the state held accountable for it – since the legal system systematically discriminated against victims by not guaranteeing their right to equal and effective access to redress (cf. Romany 1994: 105, Thomas and Beasley 1993: 43).

Making the state accountable

In order to influence the policy-making process, the RUVDS, Feminist Space and the Interdisciplinary Group targeted individual ministries directly rather than channelling their demands through the INFM, because they considered the latter to be ineffective. The presence of an increasing number of 'femocrats' in ministries facilitated participation by the women's groups not only in the implementation of projects, but also in policy design.[28] In 1995 the Minister of the Interior invited all three organisations to contribute their views on possible legislation on domestic violence (see below). The following year the RUVDS and the Interdisciplinary Group proposed a comprehensive project to tackle domestic abuse involving both state and civil society actors that won the backing of the female director of the National Crime Prevention Office, Graciela López Machín. Implemented by the Ministry of the Interior and funded by the Inter-American Development Bank (IDB), the project included training for the police and teachers, a public awareness campaign, the financing of nine NGO-run projects and the creation of a national database (Dufau 1999). In March 1998 an honorary Inter-ministerial Committee to Formulate a National Plan for the Prevention, Detection and Treatment of Domestic Violence was created, to which the RUVDS was invited to nominate three delegates.[29] The main focus of its work in the first year was the drafting of a comprehensive bill for presentation to parliament (see below).

Uruguayan feminists also made use of international mechanisms in an attempt to establish a legal precedent defining the state's obligation to provide adequate protection for abused women. In September 1993 Feminist Space, backed by the Uruguayan Institute of Legal and Social Studies (IELSUR), presented the first claim against a government for failure to protect the human rights of a victim of domestic violence under the provisions of the Inter-American Human Rights Convention.[30] The case concerned a woman who was killed by her ex-partner despite making three statements to the police that he was threatening to do so. Feminist Space argued that the Uruguayan government had failed in its duty under the convention to guarantee the victim's rights to life (art. 4), protection of the family (art. 17), equal protection before the law (art. 24) and judicial protection (art. 25.2). It also documented other cases to demonstrate that this was not an isolated incident, but part of a systematic violation of women's human rights.[31] In its defence, the Uruguayan government argued that the accused was not a state agent and that the state had fulfilled its obligations by prosecuting and sentencing him after the murder.[32] Feminist Space responded with the state complicity argument that '[t]he responsibility of the State does not only apply when a public employee commits a criminal offence, but also when their lack of action or negligence provokes an action that causes harm',[33] but no further proceedings were instigated. Although this case did not have the desired outcome, it represented an important attempt to transform international conventions from symbolic state rhetoric into an instrument for change.

Women as subjects of rights and the biases of the law

Uruguay has a strong legalistic tradition, accordingly an important aim of the women's movement's campaign was to promote the construction of a legal framework governing domestic violence. The Interdisciplinary Group supported the criminalisation of domestic violence, but did not regard it as a sufficient response on its own:

> [O]ur approach divides the problem into four broad and closely related areas: values, formal and informal education, the media, etc.; preventive and protective measures; criminalisation; and rehabilitation measures. It implies the need to consider what is most appropriate in each area, and the links between them; some will be measures which should be enacted as laws, not all of them prohibitory.
>
> (Dufau 1993: 3)

Furthermore, laws were regarded as serving a purpose, but only if women were active subjects of their rights: 'None of [the legal instruments which we women have at our disposal to defend and assert our rights] will be of use if first we are not conscious of the fact that those rights pertain to us and are unswerving in our will to assert them' (Anández n.d.: 36; see also Beñarán *et al.* 1993: 1).

In order for women to know and claim their rights, it was necessary for those rights to be defined in law. This meant recognition of the specificity of gender-based violence and identification of the preventive, punitive and protective duties of the state. In legal terms domestic violence remained invisible in Uruguay until 1995 because it was not a statutory offence. As such incidents were treated as common crimes of violence, according to the seriousness of the injuries sustained (Beñarán *et al.* 1997: 8). In addition, the law determined that certain violent offences would be prosecuted only at the instance of the injured party. Those supporting changes in the law – including important figures in the judiciary – [34] argued that this requirement ignored the psychological state of victims, who might not press charges for fear of reprisals (Balbela de Delgue 1991: 76, Langón Cuñarro 1988: 75).

The law also failed to provide adequate protection for victims after they had made their statement to the police. Under the Constitution the home is 'an inviolable sanctuary' which the police can only enter during the day and with court authorisation (Art. 11), and the presumption of innocence means that the accused cannot be detained. Respect for these rights meant that in domestic violence cases the victim was left without legal recourse to protection: 'these... advances in the defence of the rights of the accused create an *imbalance* between those rights and the possibility of rapid and effective action in the case of crimes committed within the home' (Balbela de Delgue 1991: 76, original emphasis). In other words, the specificities of gender-based crimes challenged the supposedly neutral and objective foundations of the law and advocates of reform argued that the gender-blindness of the legal system needed to be overcome if women's rights were to be properly protected.

Another discriminatory feature of existing legislation derived from the fact that women had not originally been defined in law as subjects of rights, because of the ideological configuration of society into public and private spheres, and women's relegation to the latter. In Uruguay's Penal and Civil Codes women were conceived of as equivalents of minors whose sexuality and reproductive capacity were strictly controlled. Neither the granting of civil equality to women in 1946 nor the ratification in 1981 of the CEDAW was accompanied by a comprehensive overhaul of the Codes (Dufau 1991); although by the 1990s some discriminatory articles had been removed and others had fallen into disuse. As a result, the legal right protected in many norms governing sexual offences remained, not the woman's right to sexual self-determination and reproductive autonomy, or bodily integrity and personal security, but archaic concepts such as family honour or chastity. In addition, despite enjoying one of the longest democratic traditions in Latin America, a legacy of the twelve-year period of military dictatorship was that the efficacy of the rule of law was undermined and existing legislation was not always enforced.[35] Uruguayan feminists working on domestic violence did not, however, reject the potential of the law as an instrument for the protection of women's rights – a position taken by some feminists in the North (see Smart 1989, MacKinnon 1987).

Protecting women's rights in national legislation

As part of its campaign to bring the state to account, Feminist Space sought to establish the legislature's general responsibility to address the question of violence against women. The case studies showing examples of state complicity were presented to the Chamber of Representatives' Human Rights Committee, chosen 'for its specific jurisdiction and because its members are the most direct representatives of the citizen body' (Dufau 1993: 2). Feminist Space highlighted the duties of the legislature towards those who had elected it and the 'supervisory function over other state powers assigned to it under the Constitution'. This function, feminists argued, included guaranteeing 'full respect for the human rights recognised in the Constitution and national legislation, and in the international agreements and conventions ratified by the country' (Dufau 1994: 118). The Human Rights Committee made public statements expressing its commitment to tackling the problem of domestic violence but in practice the legislative process was slow and problematic.

In the 1990s eight bills concerning domestic violence were presented to the Uruguayan parliament, three of which were passed, although two were not implemented (see Table 5.1). The first three bills were presented during the period, at the start of the decade, when the women's movement was fragmented and lobbying was not a priority. This did not mean, however, that the movement was entirely marginalised from the process. The Institute for the Prevention of Domestic Violence and Rehabilitation of Victims (IPRE) bill (CRR588/90) was presented by a

Table 5.1   Bills on domestic violence presented to the Uruguayan Parliament, 1990–99

Date	Bill number and description[1]	Status[1]
29/08/90	CRR588/90 Institute for the Prevention of Domestic Violence and Rehabilitation of Victims (IPRE).	Passed in modified form as art. 102 of National Audit Law 16.462, 11/1/94. Not implemented.
13/11/91	CRR1635/91 Criminalisation of sexual and domestic violence.	Shelved.
11/12/91	CRR1718/91–CSS997/92 Office for the Defence of the Rights of Victims of Sexual and Domestic Violence (Defence Office).	CRR passed CSS shelved. Re-presented as CRR101/95.
31/03/95	CRR101/95–CSS274/95 Defence Office (re-presentation of CRR1718/91).	CRR passed. CSS shelved.
04/04/95	CRR124/95–CSS192/95 Public security. Art. 14: criminalisation of domestic violence.	Law 16.707, 12/07/95.
15/08/95	CSS242/95–CRR622/95 Belem do Pará Convention ratification.	Law 16.735, 05/01/96. Partially implemented.
04/06/96	CRR1034/96 Penal Code reform. Art. 7: domestic violence.	Shelved.
16/03/99	CRR3358/99 Detection and prevention of domestic violence and victim support.	Shelved.

[1]CRR = Chamber of Representatives; CSS = Senate.
Sources: Own compilation from parliamentary *Diario de Sesiones* and computing services data.

female Communist Party deputy, Carmen Beramendi, who had links to the party's women's committee and the NGO Woman Now. She also sought advice from feminist activists in drafting the bill. In contrast, the first bill for the criminalisation of domestic violence (CRR1635/91) and the two bills to establish the Defence Office for the Defence of the Rights of Victims of Sexual and Domestic Violence (CRR1718/91–CSS997/92 and CRR101/95-CSS274/95) were presented by a male deputy from the Broad Front, Daniel Díaz Maynard. His legislative record showed a consistent concern to eliminate the discriminatory norms remaining in Uruguay's codes, but he did not seek advice on or approval for his legislative proposals from the women's movement.[36] However, the parliamentary committees studying the IPRE project and the first Defence Office bill interviewed members of women's NGOs as part of the scrutiny process.[37] In the second half of the decade, the women's movement became more proactive in its monitoring of the legislative process. The RUVDS, Feminist Space and Interdisciplinary Group requested interviews to discuss the 1995 Defence Office bill, and lobbied for the ratification of the Belem do Pará Convention (bill CSS242/95–CRR622/95), as well as drafting the article on domestic violence for the 1995 bill on public security (CRR124/95–CSS192/95). The wide-ranging 1999 bill (CRR3358/99) was drawn up by the Interministerial Committee, on which the RUVDS had representation, and was based on the multidisciplinary approach that had been promoted by the women's movement.

In spite of mounting pressure from the movement and the increasing openness to the issue shown by the political establishment in the 1990s, there remained serious obstacles to the construction of a legal framework governing domestic abuse. The first criminalisation bill contained radical proposals emphasising the rights of the victim in rape and domestic violence cases, including the presumption of guilt against the husband or partner when offences occurred within the home and allowing the judge to convict when hard evidence was lacking.[38] Although these proposals are clearly problematic, the fact that the bill was shelved without even being discussed at the committee stage illustrates the level of institutional resistance to recognising the inadequacy of existing norms for dealing with gender-specific crimes.

Similarly, the women's organisations' draft of the article criminalising domestic violence in the public security bill was incorporated verbatim, except for one small, but significant, change. Where the draft specified women as the passive subjects of the crime, the law enacted did not identify the sex of the victim; instead, a sub-clause established an increase in the penalty when the victim was a woman. Therefore, the Interdisciplinary Group argued, the basic definition of the crime could only refer to two situations: female aggressor–male victim and male aggressor–male victim. As a result, the law did not reflect the lived reality of domestic violence – that the majority of victims are women – and maintained the androcentric conception of human rights (Beñarán *et al.* 1997: 122).

Attempts to define the state's responsibilities in the areas of prevention, and protection and rehabilitation of victims, were impeded by the complex nature of the problem, which allows for multiple possible responses requiring coordination between state actors in a wide range of policy-making and law enforcement bodies.[39] The IPRE bill was finally passed after four years, but the original project was much reduced in scope, and transferred from the Supreme Court of Justice to the Ministry for Education and Culture: a location that would give it far less status. The bill to establish the Defence Office (Defensoría) was passed by the lower house twice but shelved by the Senate (see Table 5.1), owing to unresolved questions concerning which state body should have ultimate jurisdiction and bear the budgetary costs – no small matter at a time of reductions in public spending. The nomination of the Interministerial Committee to draft the 1999 bill, which covered conceptual definitions, procedures, jurisdictions and interinstitutional coordination, represented an attempt to overcome such impediments in the preliminary stages.[40] Even so, the bill was automatically shelved at the end of the legislative period (February 2000) without reaching discussion in parliament, indicating that domestic violence was still not regarded as a priority issue.

Nor did the obstacles end with the passing of bills. The Ministry of Education and Culture never carried out the IPRE project, despite lobbying by Feminist Space. Similarly, the Belem do Pará Convention was ratified by parliament in 1995 (Law 16.735), but there was no systematic implementation of its many recommendations. The criminalisation of domestic violence in Law 16.707 was an important advance in that it became a legally defined crime and judges were allowed to initiate proceedings in these cases. However, judges' unfamiliarity with the issue[41] led to difficulties in applying the law – in particular in interpreting the clause that specified that the violence or threats should be 'repeated over a period of time'. Bill CRR1034/96 proposed the elimination of the problematic clause, a solution rejected by the Interdisciplinary Group and RUVDS, which argued that it would undermine the conceptual specificity of the offence that distinguished it from other crimes of violence.[42] In their view, the solution lay in adequate training for the judiciary, not in modifications to the law's wording.

Conclusions

By the end of the 1990s clear advances had been made by the Uruguayan women's movement in its campaign to defend women's right to be free from violence. Domestic abuse was included in the Penal Code as a statutory offence and the implementation of projects in various state agencies and ministries indicated that it was no longer considered an individual, private issue. In addition, women's organisations specialising in domestic violence had achieved a degree of legitimacy as interlocutors in the eyes of some state actors. Despite these gains, the movement's campaign to make the state accountable had not been entirely effective.

The impediments to the enactment of the more complex legislative initiatives presented in the 1990s indicate that in such cases lobbying through established channels can have only a limited effect. It may be that constructing alliances with key actors in the legislature – as had been achieved with some femocrats – would improve the chances of such projects being passed, by ensuring that they are promoted from within. This may be more possible in the 2000–2005 term with the increased number of female deputies elected in the November 1999 elections.[43] On 8 March 2000 a group of these new MPs demonstrated their willingness to engage in cross-party promotion of legislative initiatives by jointly re-presenting the bills on gender issues – including the one on domestic violence – that had not been dealt with in the previous term.

The fact that the only major state project in relation to domestic violence to be implemented was financed by the IDB, signals the danger that policies to tackle domestic violence will rely on the continued availability of external funding. In order to avoid this dependence, key instances and arenas of decision-making on the state budget must be targeted to press for the allocation of permanent funds to tackle the problem.[44] Furthermore, the women's movement was unable to broaden the state's policy focus, which was mainly limited to punitive aspects involving the judiciary and police. Despite the movement's emphasis on the importance of education, it did not carry out a concerted campaign to get the issue of domestic violence included in the education reform programme initiated in 1995.

Lobbying has not only begun to occupy much of the women's movement's time and human resources, but the activity itself is usually regarded as the domain of experts. This, together with the focus on service provision, which runs the risk of turning women into passive clients, has reduced its potential as a mass-based, transformatory movement empowering women to claim actively their rights. A final challenge facing the Uruguayan women's movement is to broaden the debate and situate its demands relating to domestic violence within an integrated campaign on sexual and reproductive rights.[45] By the end of the 1990s, issues such as the decriminalisation of abortion had not achieved the same level of legitimacy in the political agenda as violence against women. Unless women's rights to sexual autonomy, reproductive self-determination and bodily integrity are respected in relation to the whole range of women's life experiences, the concept of women's human rights is seriously weakened and the gains made in the campaign against domestic violence could come under threat.

Notes

1 By the end of the 1990s laws on domestic violence had been passed in Puerto Rico (1989), Costa Rica (1990, chapter 4 of the Law Promoting Social Equality for Women, and 1996), Peru (1993, 1997), Chile (1994), Argentina (1994), Uruguay (1995), Ecuador (1995), Bolivia (1995), Mexico (1996), Colombia (1996), Dominican Republic (1997).

2 This legislation was based on the philosophy of 'compensatory feminism', which aimed to redress the unequal balance of power between men and women by forms of special protection or positive discrimination (Vaz Ferreira 1945).

3 In Brazil (Pitanguy 1995), Mexico (Duarte and González 1994) and Argentina (Chejter 1995) feminist organisations began campaigning on violence against women in the 1970s and early 1980s.

4 Broad Front 1984 election document, 'A las Mujeres Uruguayas'.

5 Concertación Nacional Programática. CONAPRO was a forum of representatives from political parties and civil society organisations whose aim was to ensure a smooth transition from military rule by building consensus around a minimum platform for the new government.

6 CONAPRO, 'Documento Aprobado por la Mesa Ejecutiva de la Concertación Nacional Programática en el Día 14 de Febrero de 1985. Tema: Orden Jurídico', Part III: 'Autoritarismo y Violencia'.

7 For example, Ofelia Machado Bonet, articles in *El Día* cultural supplement (6 Aug. 1985 and 12 July 1986); *Cotidiano Mujer*, Epoca I, 17 (May 1987), 21 (Sep. 1987), Epoca II, 6 (Nov. 1991); the weekly women's supplement *La República de las Mujeres* (first published August 1988), which includes a monthly summary of violent crimes against women.

8 Montevideo-based groups included the Uruguayan National Council of Women, Uruguayan Women's Plenary, Woman Now, La Unión Women's House, Women and Society Institute; outside Montevideo, the Paulina Luisi Movement, based in Melo, Cerro Largo.

9 In Montevideo the specialist groups New Moon and Maia Woman were founded; outside Montevideo SOS Paysandú and Life Group (Salto); for child victims, Rainbow; and for male abusers Corners and Rebirth.

10 These women include Flor de Lys Rodríguez, murdered on 12 November 1989; Silvia Mabel Ferreira, critically wounded on 2 October 1991; Silvia Rodríguez Richieri, murdered on 26 March 1993.

11 'Mujer Ahora', *Cotidiano Mujer*, Epoca II, 6 (Nov. 1991): 18.

12 The refuge was originally proposed by the INFM in 1992, but it was not until 1998 that the project was initiated in an agreement with an existing church-run shelter for women.

13 In contrast, a more fluid working relationship developed between the NGO community and the Women's Commission that was created in 1991 in the municipal government of Montevideo (Intendencia Municipal de Montevideo, IMM). This was facilitated partly by their closer ideological affiliation – the capital's government was controlled by the Broad Front from 1990 – but more importantly by the fact that the women's movement had formal representation on the Commission's council to define policy directions and monitor programmes. In 1992 a help-line for victims of domestic violence was set up jointly by the Commission and the Uruguayan Women's Plenary (IMM Comisión de la Mujer/PLEMUU, 1995). The Women and Society Institute helped the Commission set up women's advice centres in outlying sectors of the capital and provided awareness-raising and training on domestic violence in the IMM's health, citizen action and educational programmes (Mazzotti 1996). The fact that the Broad Front remained in power for consecutive administrations (1990–95 and 1995–2000) also allowed the Women's Commission to develop a greater degree of continuity in its work than the INFM.

14 After the first in 1981, Feminist Encounters took place in Peru, 1983; Brazil, 1985; Mexico, 1987; Argentina, 1990. The latter was organised jointly by Uruguayan and Argentinian feminists. For accounts of these and later Encounters (El Salvador, 1993; Chile, 1996), see Sternbach *et al.* (1992) and Alvarez (1998).

15 For example, the Latin American and Caribbean Women's Health Network and the Latin American and Caribbean Committee for the Defence of Women's Rights (CLADEM).

16 Henceforth Latin American Violence Network.

17 The Women's Consensus-Building Forum (Concertación de Mujeres) and the Women's Coordination. As well as a lack of time and resources to devote to movement-building, internal divisions had arisen from the conflicting positions adopted by movement members *vis-à-vis* the December 1986 law granting the military immunity for human rights abuses and the subsequent campaign for a referendum to overturn the law.

18 Feminist Space document (11 April 1993).

19 Interview with Graciela Dufau (16 June 1997).

20 Its members included lawyers, a sociologist, a psychiatrist and a psychologist, who was also a serving police officer.

21 For an example of this campaign in Latin America, see CLADEM (n.d.).

22 'Tribunals' were held at the global NGO Forums in Vienna and Huairou (parallel to the Beijing Conference), and at the regional Sixth Feminist Encounter in Chile.

23 RUVDS press release, *La República de las Mujeres* (1 Dec. 1996).

24 Feminist Space letter to Chamber of Representatives' Human Rights Committee (23 April 1993).

25 Feminist Space press release, *La República* (25 Feb. 1993). While mainstream and motherist human rights groups supported the women's movement's protests, they did not work on the issue themselves. This distance between women's and human rights movements has been signalled by several authors

as an important obstacle to the promotion of women's rights as human rights (Thomas 1993: 87–8; Thomas and Beasley 1993: 57–8; Bunch 1990: 488).

26 For analyses of whether the claim for domestic violence to be regarded as a human rights abuse is reconcilable with current conceptions of human rights and the parameters of international law see Thomas and Beasley (1993), Copelon (1994) and Roth (1994).

27 Analyses of this state complicity argument can be found in Roth (1994: 330) and Romany (1994: 100–1).

28 For example, the Interdisciplinary Group helped draft a new domestic violence report form for the women's police station, and member organisations of the RUVDS ran awareness-raising courses in police stations in the interior.

29 This Inter-ministerial Committee also had delegates from the Ministry of the Interior, the Ministry for Education and Culture, the Ministry of Public Health, the National Crime Prevention Office, the women's police station and the INFM.

30 Interview with Gabriel Dufau (16 June 1997) and interview with Nea Filgueira (15 Aug. 1997).

31 IELSUR letter to Inter-American Human Rights Committee (21 Aug. 1995).

32 Inter-American Human Rights Committee letter to IELSUR (14 July 1995).

33 IELSUR letter, op.cit.

34 For example, Minister of the Supreme Court of Justice, Dra Jacinta Balbela de Delgue and Attorney-General Dr Miguel Langón Cuñarro.

35 For example, Law 16.045 on equal opportunities and treatment for women at work was passed in 1989 but not implemented by the Labour Ministry – headed for the first time in Uruguay's history by a woman, Ana Lía Piñeyrúa, – until 1997.

36 When challenged on this matter by movement representatives, he replied that he was under no constitutional obligation to consult them. Chamber of Representatives' Human Rights Committee, Record of Meeting 1137 (17 Sep. 1992): 4.

37 They were invited in their capacity as representatives of the IMM Women's Commission.

38 *Diario de Sesiones de la Cámara de Representantes*, 2235 (13 Nov. 1991): 154–5.

39 The multiplicity of approaches is illustrated by the varying nature of legislation on domestic violence in the region. See Binstock (1999), Gamba *et al.* (1999), and Lamberti (1999).

40 For analyses of the bill, see Dufau (1999: 63–8) and Lamberti (1999: 163–6).

41 There is no trial by jury in Uruguay.

42 Beñarán *et al.* (1997: 124–7); RUVDS cited in *La República de las Mujeres* (24 Nov. 1996): 8.

43 As from 15 February 2000 there are 16 women deputies (12.2 per cent), up from nine (6.9 per cent) in the previous legislature.

44 In particular the National Budget Law, presented in the first year of each new administration, and the Budget and Planning Office, which has exclusive control over the allocation of all state funds. So far, both have been ignored as targets for lobbying by the women's movement.

45 At regional level there have been calls for this. See Red de Salud (1996).

Bibliography

Alvarez, Sonia E. (1998) 'Latin American feminisms "go global": trends of the 1990s and challenges for the new millenium' in Sonia E. Alvarez, Evelina Dagnino and Arturo Escobar (eds), *Cultures of Politics/Politics of Cultures: Revisioning Latin American Social Movements*, Boulder, Colo.: Westview Press

Amnesty International (1995) *Human Rights are Women's Rights*, New York: Amnesty International

Anández, Cecilia (n.d.) *Rompiendo el Círculo*, Montevideo: Casa de la Mujer La Unión

Balbela de Delgue, Jacinta (1991) 'Derechos humanos de la mujer agredida', *Revista Uruguaya de Derecho de Familia*, 4 (5) 73–9

Beñarán, María del Pilar and Graciela Dufau (1993) 'Derechos de las mujeres, derechos humanos: Una puesta en común', unpublished paper presented at round table discussion, GRECMU, Montevideo, 2 December

Beñarán, María del Pilar, Zulma Casanova Damiani, Graciela Dufau Argibay, Clara Fassler, Nea Filgueira and Robert Parrado (1997) *Violencia Doméstica: Un Enfoque Multidisciplinario*, Montevideo: FCU

Binion, Gayle (1995) 'Human rights: A feminist perspective' *Human Rights Quarterly*, 17 509–26

Binstock, Hanna (1999) 'Avances legales en violencia familiar' in S. Larrain, E. Giberti, H. Binstock and E. B. Medina, *Violencia Familiar: Una Aproximación Multidisciplinaria*, Montevideo: Ministerio del Interior, PSC

Bunch, Charlotte (1990) 'Women's rights as human rights: toward a re-vision of human rights' *Human Rights Quarterly*, 12 (4) 486–98

Carrillo, Roxanna (1991) 'Violence against women: an obstacle to development' in *Gender Violence: A Development and Human Rights Issue*, New Brunswick: Center for Women's Global Leadership/Plowshares Press

Carrillo, Roxanna (1997) 'Introducción: Violencia contra las mujeres' in A. M. Brasileiro (ed.) *Las Mujeres Contra la Violencia: Rompiendo el Silencio. Reflexiones sobre la Experiencia en America Latina y el Caribe*, New York: UNIFEM

Chejter, Silvia (1995) *Movimiento Antiviolencia: Aspectos Históricos*, Buenos Aires: CECYM, Violencia contra las Mujeres Informe de Investigación 4

Chinkin, Christine (1995) 'Violence against women: The international legal response' *Gender and Development*, 3 (2) 23–8

CLADEM (n.d.) *Declaration of Human Rights from a Gender Perspective: Contributions to the 50th. Anniversary of the Universal Declaration of Human Rights*, Lima: CLADEM

Constitución de la República Oriental del Uruguay (1997), Montevideo, Cámara de Senadores

Copelon, Rhonda (1994) 'Intimate terror: understanding domestic violence as torture' in J. Cook (ed.) *Human Rights of Women: National and International Perspectives*, Philadelphia: University of Pennsylvania Press

Duarte, Patricia and Gerardo González (1994) *La Lucha contra la Violencia de Género en México: De Nairobi a Beijing, 1985–1995*, Mexico City: COVAC

Dufau, Graciela (1991) *Principales Aspectos del Sistema Normativo Uruguayo en Relación a la Discriminación de la Mujer*, Montevideo: CIEDUR

Dufau, Graciela (1993) 'No hay derecho' *Cotidiano Mujer*, 2 (13) 2–3

Dufau, Graciela (1994) 'Elementos para un diagnóstico sobre la situación de los DDHH de las mujeres uruguayas' in *Las Mujeres y los Derechos Humanos en América Latina*, Lima: Red Entre Mujeres

Dufau, Graciela (1999) 'Violencia doméstica y sexual' in *El Estado Uruguayo y las Mujeres: Monitoreo de Políticas Públicas*, Montevideo: Comisión Nacional de Seguimiento a los Compromisos de Beijing

Eisler, Riane (1987) 'Human rights: toward an integrated theory for action' *Human Rights Quarterly*, 9 (3) 291–6

Finch, Henry (1998) *Towards the New Economic Model: Uruguay 1973–97*, Liverpool: University of Liverpool, Institute of Latin American Studies, research paper 22

Fitzpatrick, Joan (1994) 'The use of international human rights norms to combat violence against women' in Rebecca J. Cook (ed.) *Human Rights of Women: National and International Perspectives*, Philadelphia: University of Pennsylvania Press

Gamba, Susana B., Ana Lía Glas and Lucrecia Ollér (eds) (1999) *Mujeres, Violencia, Mercosur y Después: Nudos Críticos respecto a la Legislación en la Región*, Buenos Aires: Lugar de Mujer

Heise, Lori L., Alanagh Raikes, Charlotte H. Watts and Anthony B. Zwi (1994) 'Violence against women: a neglected public health issue in less developed countries' *Social Science Medicine*, 39 (9) 1165–79

IMM Comisión de la Mujer/PLEMUU (1995) *Un Teléfono que Da que Hablar*, Montevideo: IMM Comisión de la Mujer/PLEMUU

Isis Internacional (1990) *Violencia en contra de la Mujer en América Latina y el Caribe, Información y Políticas: Informe Final*, Santiago de Chile: ISIS International

Lamberti, Silvio (1999) 'Violencia familiar y sistema de justicia. Estado actual de la legislación latinoamericana' in S. Larrain, E. Giberti, H. Binstock and E. B. Medina, *Violencia Familiar: Una Aproximación Multidisciplinaria*, Montevideo: Ministerio del Interior, PSC

Langón Cuñarro, Miguel (1988) 'La mujer víctima de la violencia en el seno del hogar' *Revista Uruguaya de Derecho de Familia*, 2 (2) 70–8

MacKinnon, Catharine A. (1987) *Feminism Unmodified: Discourses on Life and Law*, Cambridge, Mass.: Harvard University Press

Mazzotti, Mariella (1996) 'Aportes para la formulación de políticas municipales de género: La experiencia de la Comisión de la Mujer de la Intendencia Municipal de Montevideo', unpublished paper presented at seminar 'Género y Familia: Políticas Sociales', Red Género y Familia/INFM, Montevideo 14–15 October

Ortiz, Marcela (1997) 'Violencia contra las mujeres: una crisis regional' in A. M. Brasileiro (ed.) *Las mujeres Contra la Violencia: Rompiendo el Silencio. Reflexiones sobre la Experiencia en America Latina y el Caribe*, New York: UNIFEM

Paredes, Ursula (1993) *Violencia Doméstica: Del 'No te metas' a la Crónica Roja*, Montevideo: Mujer Ahora

Pitanguy, Jacqueline (1995) 'Violencia, poder y políticas públicas' in SERNAM (ed.) *Violencia Intrafamiliar y Derechos Humanos*, Santiago, Chile: SERNAM

Red de Salud de las Mujeres Latinoamericanas y del Caribe (1996) *Por el Derecho a Vivir sin Violencia: Acciones y Propuestas desde las Mujeres*, Cuadernos Mujer Salud 1

Red Feminista: Acción a nivel regional (1996) *Por el Derecho a Vivir sin Violencia*, Cuadernos Mujer Salud 1: 77–9

Rodríguez Villamil, Silvia (1986) 'Aproximación a un tema complejo' in *La Mujer Uruguaya Hoy*, Montevideo: PCU

Romany, Celina (1994) 'State responsibility goes private: a feminist critique of the public/private distinction in international human rights law' in Rebecca J. Cook (ed.) *Human Rights of Women: National and International Perspectives*, Phildelphia: University of Pennsylvania Press

Roth, Kenneth (1994) 'Domestic violence as an international human rights issue' in R. J. Cook (ed.) ibid. *Human Rights of Women*

Smart, Carol (1989) *Feminism and the Power of Law*, London: Routledge

Sternbach, Nancy Saporta, Marysa Navarro-Aranguren, Patricia Chuchryk and Sonia E. Alvarez (1992) 'Feminisms in Latin America: from Bogotá to San Bernardo' *Signs: Journal of Women in Culture and Society*, 17 (2) 426–32

Thomas, Dorothy Q. (1993) 'Holding governments accountable by public pressure' in Joanna Kerr (ed.) *Ours by Right: Women's Rights as Human Rights*, London: Zed Books

Thomas, Dorothy Q. and Michele E. Beasley (1993) 'Domestic violence as a human rights issue' *Human Rights Quarterly*, 15 (1) 36–62

Vaz Ferreira, Carlos (1945) *Sobre Feminismo*, Buenos Aires: Editorial Losada

6
Constructing Citizenship in the *Poblaciónes* of Santiago, Chile: the Role of Reproductive and Sexual Rights

Ceri Willmott

Introduction

At a time when there has been a great deal of debate about women's international rights and new areas of rights concerning women have begun to be defined, my aim in this chapter is to consider how such rights operate in specific class and cultural contexts. The area I shall discuss is the *poblaciónes* (low-income settlements) of southern Santiago, Chile. Whilst emphasising the particularity of cultural contexts, I also argue that international rights are applicable across cultural contexts. The process by which women interpret such rights and apply them in their lives illustrates how 'rights' and 'citizenship' can be used as strategic tools in negotiating their position in different contexts.

Chile today presents itself as the *jaguar*[1] of South American countries. It prides itself on its economic success and positions itself as one of the most modern powers in Latin America. In relation to women, it would boast that it has a national agency, SERNAM (Servicio Nacional de la Mujer/National Women's Agency), which deals with women's issues ensuring that women's needs have been taken care of in the transition to, and consolidation of democracy. Yet the reality of women's lives in Chile bears little resemblance to this image. As this chapter illustrates, in terms of women's rights, Chile is one of the more conservative countries in Latin America and, culturally, certain pervasive ideas about women's proper role continue significantly to limit women's ability to exercise their citizenship.[2] Two particular features of Chilean society lie behind this reality. The first is the strength and conservatism of the Catholic Church, which in Chile occupies a particularly dominant cultural position. This has been the case historically and the left has not challenged its position, in part because the Church gained credibility during the dictatorship by setting up the *vicaria*, a bureau to monitor and protest against human rights abuses. The second is the powerful and efficient nature of the state in Chile. From the time of Diego Portales[3] onwards, governments have come and gone, but the state has never collapsed (Góngora 1986).[4] The close relationship between the Catholic Church and the state[5] means that between them they wield a great deal of influence, both politically and ideologically. This has a great impact on women's lives, most notably in the areas of reproduction and sexuality, and has meant that certain notions contained in state and Church discourse are particularly pervasive. These discourses help to position women in a particular way, which, I argue, limit women's ability to put their rights into practice. However, rather than depicting these dominant discourses as totalising, I argue in favour of a more complex picture in which women may be seen, on the one hand, to be complicit in their own subordination by fulfilling the subject positions that these discourses offer, but on the other they also adopt alternative discourses in the negotiation of their daily lives. One example is the new feminist discourse on human rights and the ideas emanating from feminist NGOs, which focus on concepts of freedom and autonomy. Women may be seen to reinterpret these alternative discourses in the course of applying them to their own situations, accepting, rejecting and transforming them in the process. In this way rights discourses may be seen to play a transformative role in the content and practice of citizenship. The extension of the concept of citizenship to incorporate new areas of rights, such as reproductive and sexual rights, creates the potential for women to use these conceptual tools to challenge traditional gender discourses that discriminate against them and inhibit the exercise of their citizenship.

The chapter is based on research carried out in Santiago between January 1995 and January 1997 amongst women's groups in the *poblaciónes* of southern Santiago, including a study of the work of nongovernmental organisations working in this locality, in particular Tierra Nuestra (Our Earth) and Domos. As well as collecting data in the course of participant observation, I constructed life histories of 89 women aged between 15 and 67.[6] These were based on semi-structured interviews and the women interviewed included leaders in the women's organisations, participants in women's groups and women who do not have a history of participation. In addition, I carried out research at the local civil courts in San Miguel, studying 107 cases involving the operation of the new law against domestic violence. The study shows that although

women's experience is situational and specific, in a way that acknowledges the range of cultural, religious, economic and social concerns and
interests that blur theoretical categories, there are many areas of commonality which allow us to see an international dimension to women's
citizenship. [7]

The Chilean state, citizenship and the new discourse of international rights for women

It is the state that continues to prescribe the basis of citizenship, both
through its laws and policies and in terms of the gender discourses that
these embody.[8] In Chile, I argue, the discourses emanating from the
state have tended to be closely interconnected with the gender ideology
promoted by the Catholic Church, forming part of a dominant 'ideological core'[9] which emphasises motherhood as women's 'essential' role.
This high valuation of a self-sacrificing form of motherhood (see Montecino 1991), together with other factors such as female domesticity and
sexual chastity expressed in these discourses contributes to the maintenance of a particular sexual division of roles, which in turn delimits
the categories of male and female citizenship. These ideas and the
images associated with them incorporate what feminists in Chile, both
popular and professional, refer to as the *deber ser* of being a woman,
meaning what one, as a woman, 'ought' to be.

There are many different state institutions in Chile that shape, and are
shaped by, gender relations: the legal system, the education system,
public health and population office to name but a few. These all have
'gendered' policies which reinforce some gender relations whilst challenging others (cf. Fraser 1989). But given the state's multifaceted form,
it is possible to see that while many of the ideas embedded in state
practices are extremely pervasive, the relationship between the state
and gender relations is not fixed and immutable. Discourses are reproduced over time only to the extent that individual men and women
invest in the subject positions that these discourses offer (Moore 1994:
61). Exposure to alternative ideas about gender creates the possibility of
investing in different subject positions and challenging received ideas
about gender. There are spaces for manoeuvre in which individuals and
groups can take an active role in the process of the construction of
gender identities and of citizenship (cf. Waylen 1996: 17). Operating
within these spaces women's and men's multiple activities have a
bottom-up effect on gender, politics and economics, disrupting state
constructions and cultural stereotypes (cf. Peterson 1996, Carroll 1989).

People are both constrained by and able to play with dominant discourses that are around them, as we see below. In particular, discourses centred around international human rights law and local feminist discourses have provided alternative ideas with which to challenge entrenched views about gender which influence women's ability to exercise their rights.[10]

The relationship between state and Church discourses has not remained static. Different governments with different political agendas have resulted in ever-changing tensions and disparities within this set of dominant discourses. Over the last twenty years, and especially since the end of the military dictatorship in 1989 fundamental forms of social and economic restructuring have brought about changes in ideas about gender roles. The process of democratisation and the appearance of new social organisations, as well as the influence of the international community, in particular new international rights directed at women, have all contributed to these changes (Goetz 1995: 45). These processes and the organisations involved in them incorporate new discourses on gender, providing alternative constructions with which individuals can challenge dominant gender ideologies. The state itself has increasingly come under pressure to promote women's interests, such that it now has SERNAM, with the result that the state itself has competing and contradictory discourses within its own structure. The ideas and strategies emanating from SERNAM frequently incorporate views about gender that conflict with the discourses that the state employs in other areas. In this respect, the state may be seen to be negotiating between the two discourses described above: that of the dominant ideological core focused around Catholicism and that of the new discourse of human rights for women.

Nevertheless, change is slow, and the pervasiveness of many stereotypical ideas may be explained both by the close relationship between the Church and the state and the strength of the state. Chile has long been a country with a deep-rooted respect for the rule of law, to the extent that even Pinochet used legal plebiscite, however skewed, to maintain his hold of power. The coalition Concertación government, in power since the demise of Pinochet in 1990, has also reflected this legalistic tradition by abiding by the Pinochet constitution, despite its limitations, and choosing to reform it rather than writing a new constitution. This legalistic approach makes Chile conservative and slow to change. One of Pinochet's last acts was to protect life from the moment of conception by amending the constitution and this change remains in place.[11] Even more unusual is the fact that divorce has *never* been legal in Chile and legislators remain nervous about changing the law, despite the fact that many people acquire dubious annulments to be able to remarry. The Concertación government is a coalition of Christian Democrats and Socialists giving it a centrist complexion. In its early days it set up SERNAM, albeit without ministerial status, to promote women's rights, but the pro-Catholic Christian Democrats reinforce social conservatism, particularly in relation to reproductive rights (Matear 1997: 256). These conservative policies are supported by the Catholic Church. Although the Church was seen as politically progressive in its defence of human rights during the Pinochet dictatorship (Lowden 1993), it remains socially conservative. The Church is not as influential as it once was, but it is still important; something that was reinforced by its human rights activities.

This legalistic tradition also means that Chile engages with international legislation. Like many other countries in the region, Chile has been quick to sign up to the many international declarations and conventions as part of its democratisation process. This has offered many opportunities for feminist and women's NGOs and some members of parliament to use international discourses to extend women's citizenship. But although Chile has signed the declarations of Beijing and Cairo, extending women's sexual and reproductive rights is slow. SERNAM has tended to emphasise women's participation as a neoliberal citizen of the workplace and as a consumer, rather than other aspects of their citizenship (cf. Craske 2000: 50). Less attention has been given to changing reproductive rights, although some movement has been made with a shift in the debate on abortion to place it in the ambit of public health.[12] Nevertheless, by signing international conventions, Chile is committing itself to changing laws to conform with the conventions, however gradual this process may be. Currently an initiative is underway, led by three members of parliament, for a new law in relation to sexual and reproductive rights. The proposed law has stimulated a great deal of debate and has already met with opposition from the Church and right-wing parties. The present head of SERNAM, Adriana Delpiana, recently reaffirmed the position of the socialist President Ricardo Lagos, which is that there will be no change in the law on abortion during this government, but that this did not rule out new legislation concerning adequate education in relation to sexual rights and responsible reproductive health.[13]

The signing of international conventions also serves to reinforce a rights-based discourse, which is used by women to redefine their own sense of their citizenship and subjectivity, as I demonstrate. In Latin American countries, many of which have had the experience of violent and repressive dictatorships, the discourse of citizenship and rights have a lengthy history. In Chile, it has been central to the struggle for democracy and, for the women with whom I worked, the language of 'rights' and especially 'human rights' are a part of everyday life, though not necessarily something they apply to themselves. Using case study materials from workshops I attended concerning sexuality and reproductive rights and interviews with women, I aim to show how the use of these concepts is changing, and how the acquisition of new ideas about rights and autonomy can make a difference to women's lives. Women may be seen to contest dominant local understandings about their rights with alternative discourses, some informed by international human rights. The organisations and workshops that women participate in may be seen as spaces within which women are able to create a 'culture of citizenship' (Jelin and Hershberg 1996: 2).

I use the category 'citizenship' in a broad sense, which emphasises the relationship of the citizen with society as a whole, rather than focusing solely on the individual's relationship with the state (Yuval-Davis 1997: 5). This multi-tiered notion of citizenship advanced by Yuval-Davis (1997), extends the idea of citizenship beyond the relationship between individuals and the state to include their affiliation to dominant or subordinate groups in civil society. I argue that the international level must also be incorporated into this approach. International organisations and collectivities now play a significant role in the construction of citizenship, both in the process of the development of international rights and in their application in different cultural contexts. An important example of this is the new area of reproductive and sexual rights, which was elaborated at Cairo and Beijing. This enables us to see the potential for individuals to make strategic use of rights that reinforce alternative constructions to those that the state may endorse. While it is difficult to measure the effectiveness of human rights pressures, as Jelin points out, in a less visible but equally important sense, the human rights movement is effective when it helps transform the cultural and moral context (Jelin 1996: 72). It is in this sense that human rights play a transformative role in the content and practice of citizenship.

Reproduction: the struggle for bodily integrity

Applying the broad multi-tiered conceptualisation of citizenship outlined above involves examining the cultural factors that influence women's ability to exercise their rights. In the state-endorsed configuration where women's 'proper' role is being a mother, women are positioned as primarily responsible for reproduction, but with no control over it, or by extension over their own bodies. Until recently, the husband's signature was required if a woman wanted to obtain contraceptives and his signature is still required, together with the permission of two doctors, to allow a sterilisation. Chile is one of among only 16 countries worldwide in which abortion is illegal under any circumstance, that is, not even in cases of pregnancy resulting from rape and incest, nor even when the woman's life is endangered (UN 1994). The cultural emphasis on selfless motherhood translates in law into an absolute prohibition against abortion. The message used to justify state intervention is that a pregnant woman is a mother who should think and act foremost to protect the health of the foetus she carries and that she should do so not only to ensure a good future for the foetus, but also for society. When the state regulates women as childbearers it therefore legislates the ideology of motherhood. The legislature's decision to save foetal life by compelling pregnancy, even in cases where such pregnancy might be harmful to the mother, can be interpreted as contrary to a woman's human rights; but it both reflects and enforces prevailing cultural conceptions of women's roles. Clearly, the values represented in law are much broader than the specific laws and judicial decisions that embody them and may be traced back to the dominant ideological core discussed above.

This all has profound significance from the point of view of women's position as political subjects; limiting as it does the most basic right of bodily integrity, it demonstrates that women have a different relationship to the state from men. The full force of each aspect of the dominant ideological core comes into play in the case of abortion. The way in which women talk about abortion also reveals the way in which Catholic discourse, as embodied in the law against abortion, is constitutive of gender. Gisela, a leader in a women's organisation, aged 46 with three children, describes the treatment she received in the Barros Luco hospital where she ended up after becoming infected after her backstreet abortion. Her story reflects that of many others.[14]

A young doctor arrived and asked me what I had done to myself. 'Nothing', I said to him, I already knew that as long as you say nothing they have no way of proving anything, because the woman who carried out the abortion told me. I had already arranged with my sister that if I was kept in hospital she must bring me antibiotics, because if you don't confess to what you have done they don't give you antibiotics. The next day the doctor came again. The tension was terrible; it was torture. The doctor said to me, 'Very well, if you don't tell me what you did to yourself, I am not going to be able to treat you, I'm not going to do anything and you are going to die.' He treated me like an ignorant person. They kept me there until the next day without treating me. I was suffering haemorrhages at brief intervals; the pain in my stomach was terrible. I have a very healthy body, the haemorrhaging stopped at 1 a.m. without the doctor having done a thing. I was lucky.

At 6 a.m. the next day they carried out the *curettage*. I swear that the doctor sought out those shifts to persecute me. I've worked in a hospital and I know a doctor does not work more than two shifts in succession, but this doctor was there three days in a row and each day he came and said to me, 'Tell me.' He would come and take my temperature, which is what the nurses usually do. 'Ah, you still don't have a fever, you still don't have an infection, but it will soon show itself.' He frightened me: 'Because when the infection begins it is going to be a disaster because I won't be able to do anything and you are going to die, so tell me while there is still time, what did you do to yourself? Who did it?' I kept denying everything. He looked at me and said, 'You know that this is a crime? You are going to get infected and you are going to go to prison if you are lucky, because you may well die, so tell me who else helped you.' He kept on and on like this. The day before I was allowed to go home he brought a flask with a foetus in it. He said, 'This is yours,' I knew it wasn't because I had looked at mine so much.[15] Just as well it wasn't otherwise it would have done my head in. I looked at it and looked away and he brought it round to the other side of the bed. The only thing I wanted to do was to cry and cry and to be with someone. I was alone, alone. It was terrible how they treated me. I always say that that doctor tortured me in the name of his precious God...After that experience I began to get involved in the cases of women who wanted to have abortions, in health workshops and so on. Women began to tell me stories about abortions, because in groups women won't say if they have had abortions or if they want to have an abortion. There I began to realise how terrible the problem is.

Gisela's experience illustrates the indirect operation of the law against abortion, which extends beyond the law courts. In this case the woman is not brought before a judge and sentenced to jail but she is nonetheless judged and sentenced, instead by a doctor. Her case also shows the way in which the legal and medical professions become conflated in the process of penalising abortion, reflecting the dominant discourse under-lying them both. The force of this ideology resonates in women's opin-ions about abortion. Thus, Chía, an occasional domestic worker, aged 33, married with six children, who had on one occasion tried unsuccess-fully to provoke an abortion, said she did not believe that there should be a right to abortion:

> Because many women are just irresponsible, it's their problem if they don't look after themselves. In my case it was different because my husband maltreated me to make me lose the baby, as I already had five children and this pregnancy was unwanted...but when the injection didn't work I thought that if I did anything God was going to punish me because it is He who chooses when to take a life away, and I can't take a baby's life away, a human being the same as me.

Dominant gender ideology clearly constrains the strategies that women can adopt to negotiate their lives. But women nevertheless find ways to manoeuvre the best they can in the circumstances. For some women, this means trying to fulfil their understanding of the categories and stereotypes contained in the dominant discourses and use this to wield as much power over their children and spouses as possible within the constraints placed upon them. But the possibilities are limited, and many women express a tremendous sense of powerless-ness in relation to reproduction and consequent anxiety. This stems not just from the practical fact of limited access to contraceptives and adequate support to ensure that they are properly used, but from cul-tural and historical factors which restrict people's awareness about con-traceptives and, especially in the case of younger women, inhibit women from making use of them.

In the face of these realities, many women contest traditional gender ideology, or parts thereof, questioning and challenging their relation-ships at the level of the family, the community and the state. This may involve deciding to use contraceptives in spite of their religious beliefs, in some cases deciding to have children without getting married, some-times deliberately getting pregnant to have something that they feel is 'theirs', working outside of the home in spite of the struggle this usually involves with their husbands, or falsifying documents enabling them to have sterilisations. In the course of negotiating their lives, women, particularly those who have experience of participating in women's organisations and who have therefore had greater exposure to alternative discourses, make strategic use of the concepts of 'citizenship' and 'rights'.

A case in point is abortion. The fact that most women leaders I interviewed and women who have a history of participation in the women's movement believe that there should be a right to safe abortion reflects the influence of alternative discourses in relation to gender and rights. Of the 89 women I interviewed, 62 per cent believed that there should be a broad right to abortion (Willmott 1998: 161). This figure includes participants and leaders in the women's movement as well as nonparticipants.[16] It is also clear that women's views often change over time as a result of experience and through participation in women's organisations. This informs their active construction of themselves as citizens with rights. Whilst participating in the School for Women Leaders organised by the NGO Tierra Nuestra, I was able to witness the process through which a couple of women who had at first been staunchly against abortion on the grounds of their Catholic beliefs, had changed their minds. Yolanda (50 L),[17] who described herself as very religious and against abortion when I first met her, went through a process of change during her time at the School and through participating in the Open Forum for Reproductive and Sexual Rights.[18] Her changed views were demonstrated at a local meeting about parental responsibility where she formed part of the panel, in a powerful and extremely articulate rebuttal of the views of a pastor involved in 'educating' young pregnant women. She emphasised the need for sexual education: 'Sexual education is strictly sanctioned, although in reality sexuality exists and is exercised, and not only for reproductive reasons.' She made use of the concept of citizenship to reinforce her argument that women have the right to exercise control over their own bodies: 'It isn't possible to exercise citizenship in relation to the world if one hasn't learnt to exercise citizenship in one's own life and to decide in relation to one's own body.' In my second interview with her she still said she would not have an abortion herself but felt strongly that each woman had the right to decide for herself in relation to her body, mind and soul, it was not the place of the church or the state to make such decisions. She said that participating with other women had taught her to see things from other women's point of view and not just from her own. She has learnt to analyse the opinions she had and the views she held. Towards the end of this interview she broke down in tears and told me about an abortion that she had had 27 years previously. At the time she already had four children, one of whom had suffered brain damage from meningitis, and had felt so desperate that she took this course of action.

She said that it was her guilt in relation to this abortion that had made her speak out so vehemently against abortion for such a long time and dedicate herself to teaching contraceptive methods. Yolanda's case underlines the power of dominant discourse which is at the root of her sense of guilt about having an abortion, at the same time she exemplifies the way in which an awareness of rights can inform and enable people to challenge traditional ideas about gender and reproduction.

Other women who have participated in women's groups use language that clearly positions abortion as an issue that severely limits women's citizenship. Yamilia (33 L) thinks that some women have abortions when they could have prevented the pregnancy. But she accepts that there are reasons for having an abortion and that doctors take advantage in these situations to treat women badly: 'They punish them and criticise them.' She thought it was unjust that women should be arrested for having abortions. Although she would not have an abortion herself she said that she thought that legalising abortion would make it safer: 'It should be safe like it is for rich women with money up there (in the wealthier districts); they don't have abortions, they have "operations".'

Women's views about the ability to decide in relation to their bodies challenge dominant ideas about selfless motherhood currently embodied in a law which does not allow a woman to have an abortion, even if her own life is in danger. Carmena (65 P) (who herself had four abortions when she was younger) believes that women should have the right to a safe abortion: 'Women should decide in relation to abortion because a woman does not always want to bring up a child.' She says she thinks it is especially important in the case of young women who end up completely ruining their lives and are also unable to provide a child with the care that it needs. In her own case she says that she did not have enough money to bring up a child and she knew that she also was not going to have the support of a partner, 'I was going to have to practically kill myself working to manage.' Juana (39 P) refers to the power of the Catholic Church in relation to abortion and the influence it exerts over government: 'The government decides for me whether I want to have a baby or not.' She referred to the experience of a friend who is plagued with guilt for having had an abortion, because she feels that she has committed a crime and because 'Society takes it upon itself to remind you that you committed a crime.' She sees it as a great injustice that women should be punished for having abortions. These examples clearly show that awareness of reproductive rights informs the way in which women negotiate their lives and position themselves *vis-à-vis* the state and the Church.

Nowhere is the transformative capacity of human rights more apparent than in the discourse and actions of women leaders in the *poblaciónes*. They occupy a pivotal position, influencing women in their communities and representing women's interests at the level of local politics and in national campaigns. Many women leaders have had close involvement with feminist NGOs where they have developed an awareness of gender issues.[19] They make sophisticated analyses of the involvement of the Catholic Church and the state in relation to abortion, which incorporate notions of citizenship and reproductive rights. For Carmen (38 L), the situation with regard to abortion in Chile is a task that the women's movement must continue to work to rectify. Although dismissive of the importance of fighting to change laws in other contexts, she said that in this case it was essential to campaign for such a change in this case. For Luz (39 L) it is essential, that women should have a right to a safe abortion, saying that 'if women followed the precepts of the Church and state we would have all those children, in addition to the ones we already have, and how would we feed them all when the state does not make itself responsible for this situation?' Women leaders have a clear sense of their rights as citizens *vis-à-vis* the state. Manuela (49 L) sees abortion as a decision for each individual woman: 'It is for you decide what to do with your own body, I don't accept other people deciding for me.' For Blanca (37 L), deciding whether to continue a pregnancy is a matter for the individual, not the state: 'The state cannot meddle with each woman's body.' Angela (45 L) recounts how she had a clandestine abortion and almost died as a result. She succinctly sums up her own situation and that of other women in Chile when she asks: 'What citizenship are they talking to me about, if I am not even master of my own body?'

Women's ability to deal effectively with health professionals and other representatives of the state is influenced by their involvement in women's groups and awareness of their rights. Julia (39 P) comments that professionals and officials only respect your rights 'when we women demand them'. She describes having insisted that she be given the contraceptive pill when the professionals at her local clinic wanted to fit her with an IUD (inter-uterine device). Flor (49 P) also says that her work in the women's organisation 'has completely changed my life'. Previously she spent all her time *encerrada* (closed indoors), but not now. Now she has learnt to value herself and make others respect her rights: 'I don't conform anymore, I know how to fight and how to argue, I know about laws, I'm more discerning.' As a result people treat her differently and she sees herself as able to operate more effectively: 'I ask all the questions I want to, even if it annoys them, because I know it's my right to be informed, especially when it comes to my health.' Women also talk about feeling more *parada* (standing upright), feeling more aware and confident when dealing with professionals and officials.

'Body absent, body present': changing ideas about sexuality

> It's bad for women (not to feel sexual pleasure). They get ill. But you have to respond to the traditional marriage. That is what our education, the Church, the system, tell you: that a woman is not a human being and so she cannot feel. If you begin to feel then you are a bad woman. That is how the culture has made you. (Luz (39 L))

The idea that sexuality can be a source of pleasure and satisfaction for women is a relatively new one amongst women *pobladoras*. Women's sexuality, as may be seen in the cases material below, has been closely tied to a powerful discourse that emphasises their maternal role and the denial of sexual feelings or desire. As a result women have seen their sexuality as being at the service of their husband's or partner's pleasure rather than their own, and as being defined by their partner's needs rather than their own. In this sense women's sexuality has been limited to an extension of their maternal role, through which they offer their husbands a further source of nurture and affection. This limited exercise of sexuality also defines women as 'decent' in contrast to 'indecent' women who use their bodies without inhibitions as sexual objects (cf. Lamadrid Alvarez and Muñoz Gouet 1996: 81). For Montecino (1991), women's inhibited sexuality is connected with the attempt to overcome the tension between virginity and motherhood and the opposed poles of Eve and Mary in dominant Catholic discourse. The abnegation of the suffering mother, which serves to resolve these tensions, extends to the denial of sexual pleasure.[20] This denial of sexuality also represents the female counterpart of the male that controls female sexuality in the Mediterranean honour/shame complex, which also forms a part of this discursive matrix.

Against this backdrop, data obtained from interviews with women and from sexuality workshops organised by local women, shows how new ideas about sexuality and sexual rights can be introduced. The data reflect that women are receptive to these new notions. As well as finding them liberating, women are able to connect them with their own experiences and apply them in their personal relationships.

Case studies of workshops concerning sexuality, reproductive and sexual rights

Participating in workshops concerning sexuality, I was able to see how women applied reproductive and sexual rights to their lives, negotiating their meaning in the process. One example was a series of seven workshops given by a *matrona*, or midwife, who is also director of a local clinic in San Joaquín and who had contacts with the Open Forum for Health and Reproductive Rights.[21] There were about 35 participants.

At the first of these workshops the women participants started out expressing the common themes identified above in relation to sexuality, but during the progress of the workshops they began to talk about sexuality in different ways. All the women, when asked to draw themselves on the first day that they menstruated, drew themselves fully clothed. At the second workshop women made collages out of cuttings from magazines to show what they understood sexuality to mean. Many of them selected pictures of babies or pregnant women, which reflected their tendency to see sexuality as inseparable from reproduction. Sexuality is often equated with sexual intercourse with a man in the language women use. One chose a picture of a bride saying that this depicted the beginning of sexuality at the moment of getting married. Others chose images that suggested shame and embarrassment. An image of a woman in a long nightgown, which one woman felt represented the commencement of menstruation, was chosen to express her understanding of sexuality. Underneath the image she had written, 'My first period – a taboo'. Their perceptions often reveal their strong identification as mothers, which permits them to talk in terms of reproduction, but not in terms of sexuality as a notion that embraces pleasure and sensuality. This accords with the argument that the dominant discourse centred on motherhood involves a denial of female sexuality. Typically women selected pictures representing the role of men as *el hombre protector* (man the protector) and of women as *la mujer bonita* (the pretty woman). Many referred to sex as an obligation or referred to mistreatment or aggression, which accords with the high incidence of marital rape.

At a later workshop in the series the *matrona* introduced a list of reproductive and sexual rights produced by the Open Forum for Health and Reproductive Rights. The discussions around each of these rights illustrate the way in which women negotiate the meaning of these rights in applying them to their own situations. All the women said that they could relate to the contents of a right concerning voluntary sexual relations, including in the context of the marriage. Several spoke up about their experiences, saying that they used to or still did have sexual relations when they did not want to. One young woman said that although she felt that it was wrong for her husband to have relations with her when she didn't really want to, she wasn't aware that she had a right not to: 'Things will be different now', she said. When introduced to a reproductive right concerning abortion, Alicia (29 P), having listened carefully to what the *matrona* said, concluded that basically women do not have any right to decide over their bodies. In relation to another right, concerning competent and respectful health personnel, the women were quick to joke about the contents of this right saying ironically that this was, of course, just how things were. They mimicked the way that the personnel actually treat them, telling them to hurry from one queue to another. In relation to being offered information about all the different methods of contraception they joked about being offered 'a Copper T or a T of Copper.' They also recognised the importance of transmitting their newly acquired knowledge to their daughters, even if they felt it was too late to benefit from these rights themselves. María (35 P) observed that although she felt that she had not had the benefit of these kinds of rights, she had daughters and, for this reason, she felt it was important to learn about such things.

At the end of the series of workshops women's notions about sexuality had changed. The women split into groups to evaluate the workshops. In response to the question: what is sexuality? They responded: 'recognition of the body and contact with it'; 'knowing our bodies'; 'I would like to receive more affection from him, but he doesn't respond'; 'it has to do with our bodies and feelings'; 'it is ours', 'it is everything'; 'the recognition of our body'; 'it is everything combined together, a feeling, something physical, psychological and emotional, involving the whole body, skin, smells'; 'it is the personal development of a woman in relation to her sex'; for many it is 'something learnt aged 30 or more'; 'the right to know about your body and to decide in relation to it'; 'affection, kisses, caresses'. Women's awareness about their bodies had also changed, although quite a few still described their bodies in negative terms. Responses to the question: How is your relationship with your body now? included: 'at times my relationship with my body is good, I like myself, but I also feel tired and mistreated'; 'it is good, I look at myself in the mirror and touch all of my body, now I know myself well'; 'I don't feel ashamed [anymore], after this workshop on sexuality I no longer turn off the light'; 'I am aware my body is tired, it aches, I want to be caressed by someone'; 'all my life I have been a *mujer objeto* (an object), now after this workshop I like to look at myself and touch myself.' Women also reported that the workshops made them realise that there was a shared experience amongst them in relation to their bodies and feelings. This is reflected in the tendency to use the second person plural at the end of the workshops: 'We learned to know our bodies and to value ourselves as women' said one group.

Learning to say 'no' is also something women acknowledge in the evaluation of the workshops. One group of women said, 'Before we all found it difficult to say "no" when we did not want to have sexual relations, we felt obliged. But now we say "NO!".'

On another occasion, two women leaders, Elena (49 L) and Rosario (49 L), presented a one-off workshop entitled 'Sexuality as a human right' to a *taller*, women's group of about twenty women. Here, too, women showed themselves to be receptive to notions of reproductive and sexual rights, immediately adapting and applying them to their own lives. A selection of reproductive and sexual rights had been written on pieces of paper and put in a bowl and each woman was asked to choose a right, read it out and explain what she thought it meant. After each woman had done this Elena (49 L) made her a present of that right saying it was 'hers'.

Constanza (39 P) began with: 'The right to exercise sexuality without having genital relations.' Constanza said that this meant that you could have sexual relations in many ways, looking, talking, touching. She said that she and her partner talked and she touched him and he touched her: 'He feels good, we both feel good', she said that she liked this right. Lucía (59 P) read out her right: 'The right to have voluntary sexual relations, including within marriage.' Lucía said that this was now possible, but in her time it wasn't. When Loreto (40 L) asked her if she felt she had the capacity to say 'no' she said that she did now, but that during her marriage she complied with her husband's sexual demands as a duty or obligation. Several women recounted their experiences and said they felt that women were still a long way off from being able to exercise this right, which they believed was very important. Lola (34 OP) said that men still felt that they had the right to have sex with their wives whenever they felt like it and that women had to try to re-educate them. When Elena (49 L) told Lucía that she could keep this right as a gift, Katy (26 P) asked if she could have that particular right. She explained that she wanted to give it to her husband. Even though when she says 'no' she means 'no', she says she wants to stick it to the head of the bed to refer to when necessary. She then read her right: 'The right to exercise sexuality with autonomy in accordance with the needs, principles and desires of each individual, taking into account the rights of the other.' When Katy (26 P) said that she didn't understand what this meant, Nancy (37 P) suggested that they explain what the word 'autonomy' meant to start with. Lucía (59 P) helped out saying that autonomy was about freedom: 'It is about doing what *you* want to do', she added, 'without anyone telling you what to do.' Elena said that when she desires something, they are her desires, separate from her husband's desires. She said it was important for her to make this distinction to be able to feel pleasure. Katy said that she and her partner respected each other and talked things through, including when they wanted to go to bed to make love. Elena quipped: 'Do you always do it in bed; never in the sink, on the table, in the shower, in the car?' Jana (38 L) added 'on the table's good!' All the women laughed.

Gina (68 L) read out the right that she had picked: 'The right to count on an adequate legislation in relation to abortion, which sees abortion as a public health problem and which prioritises women's lives.' Elena asked Gina what she thought about abortion. She replied that she was against it; she thought that it was bad, and that if a woman gets pregnant she has to resign herself to it and have the baby and bring it up. She herself had had 10 children. Elena asked her what she thought about other women that had had abortions; would she condemn them? Gina said that she would tell them to think about it. Now there were ways of preventing unwanted pregnancies whereas before that was not possible and the *mamitas*, little (young) mothers, were obliged to abort. When I asked about the case of rape, Gina conceded that she agreed with abortion in this case because it was by force and not in the context of a relationship. Elena then asked what she thought about a situation where it was the husband that had raped the woman, because it is sometimes the husband that takes the woman by force? Gina said that she had not thought about that. She said that she herself had experienced this problem and for that reason she had rejected affection from her children and her husband because he made her do things that she didn't want to. Elena pressed her: 'so you don't condemn abortion in women who have been raped?' Gina answered, 'Yes, it is like you are saying, but I don't really know what to answer, but in the other case of rape by force, yes, she can have an abortion, because in that case there is no affection.'

At this point Loreto (40 L) addressed the group as a whole saying that there was a reality behind the demand for this right and that she wanted to draw attention to the 150 000 abortions which took place each year: 'we poor women have abortions in the worst conditions. That is the reality regardless of whether we are in agreement with abortion or not.'

Elena added that because of this fact we needed a law that protected women. The majority of women who died as a result of abortions which were badly carried out in miserable unhygienic conditions were 'like us', poor women and not rich women, who pay to have a safe abortion in an expensive clinic.

Nancy (37 P) said that she accepted that if abortion were to be legalised it would not be *pan de cada día*, something that is just like the bread you eat everyday. She thought that abortion was a matter for the couple, but that if you wanted to have a good time and not get pregnant, you had to take preventive measures. She believed that young women were not as innocent as they were in days gone by: 'they have information'. These days there were not just one or two ways of preventing pregnancy but 'a thousand ways', although the form of prevention chosen should be by mutual agreement and, if the woman gets pregnant, both of them should accept responsibility. She said that, for her, the life of a young being was very important and we did not have the right to prevent it being born; 'I wanted to have children, I had three, I didn't want any more, so I take preventive measures.' She believed that the authorities ought to increase awareness amongst young people, but accepted the need for a limited law in relation to abortion.

Rosario countered Nancy's assertion that there were 'thousands' of methods of contraception'. She pointed out that a 15 or 16 year old girl would be embarrassed to go to the local clinic to find out about contraceptives. She would have to arrive at 6 a.m. like all the other patients to get a number and wait to be seen and if another woman saw her there she would get embarrassed. Jana (38 L) agreed and highlighted the fact that adolescent pregnancies had not decreased; the figures were the same as before even though there was supposedly so much more information available. She said that she also felt that abortion was her right. She said that she respected Nancy's opinion, which may be religious or moral, but what would happen to her if she had a partner, decided to have children, got pregnant and then the relationship failed? She would have to continue a pregnancy which she knew was going to result in the birth of an unwanted child, knowing also that unwanted children were the most likely to become delinquents or drug addicts. Jana asked Nancy to consider those women who decide one way or another to end a pregnancy 'with the ultimate right to decide in conscience what she wants or doesn't want with her body, with her pregnancy and with her future with a child.' Lucía (59 P) asked, what about that 'life that is coming?' Jana responded by saying that she had every respect for the position that you don't have the right to take away anybody's life, but that her perception of the situation was different. Nancy agreed that it should be a question of personal choice.

Jana went on to explain that all the sexual and reproductive rights that they were discussing were about how things *ought* to be, they don't reflect the reality of women's lives at present:

> I too am a part of all these women who live sexually oppressed and I know that I (we) don't live this way (ie. as the rights suggest things should be), because I carry with me a whole history that causes me to repress myself.

There was silence. The women all looked deep in thought. Verónica (55 P) finally broke the silence by reading out the right that she had picked out: 'The right to education policies which promote from infancy onwards the valuing of sexuality as an important aspect of life which needs to be lived in a pleasurable way without fear or guilt.' Verónica said that she agreed that this was very important. She had a daughter who was a nursery school assistant who had tried to explain to the children that babies were not brought from Paris by a goose, or born from bread or a little cabbage, or an egg from the mother, as they had been told at home. But some of the children's mothers came to the school to complain. Elena explained that this was what happened to 'us women' as adults, that 'we are frightened and lie to ourselves because we were frightened of the unknown and we don't realise that our children will learn from our ignorance too unless we start learning something new'. Soraya (26 P) said that in her children's school the children were taught about the development of babies from when the baby began to form and how it was born, showing them normal and caesarian births and forceps deliveries on video. Loreto acknowledged that this represented some progress but 'what about what happens before that?' She also observed that, whilst there was much talk about condoms and other contraceptives, in the AIDS adverts on TV they had censored any mention of condoms and nobody taught young people what kind of condom they should use or how or when they should put it on and remove it. Thus the fact that something is talked about publicly, she said, does not necessarily imply it constitutes 'information'. Not even parents teach their children these things, added Elena. Lola (34 OP) said that they should pressurise the authorities to include sexual education in the school curriculum; the others agreed.

Isabel (29 P) read from her piece of paper: 'The right to be valued as a person and not only on the basis of maternity; that women be recognised as having an identity of their own with capabilities and potential beyond their reproductive capacity.' Isabel said that she thought this meant recognising women with all their rights and not just on the basis of their capacity to reproduce. Loreto expanded on this saying that it meant that women should be recognised and valued as people, not just as 'an incubator', which tends to be the greatest value given to women and the basis on which they are respected. Elena said, 'It meant that you should be valued as Isabel, intelligent, smiling, and recognised with all the qualities that you have, not only as the mother of your children. That your partner values you and tells you that you do nice things and that you are gorgeous, that is what it means.' All agreed on the importance of this right.

Nancy (37 P) read out the next right: 'The right to have education policies in relation to public health that promote sexual and reproductive health on the part of men and their active participation in contraception.' Nancy explained that this referred to men taking responsibility in relation to contraception so that it was no longer just the responsibility of the woman. Elena pointed out that women have to go to the clinic, they have to take contraceptives or have them fitted, they have to go to have PAP tests, while the men are sitting comfortably at home watching television: 'we do it all on our own'. Jana added, 'and then you get pregnant and they (the men) tell you off!' Rosario felt that another problem in relation to public health was the lack of information: 'they don't ask what we want or tell us what they are going to put in place as contraceptives'. Nancy said that the problem was that a lot of women didn't dare to ask things. Loreto made the point that men are fertile all the time and yet it is us women, who are only fertile a few days each month, that take contraceptive pills or have IUDs. She said that we should think about why this might be, why is it that it is not men that are taking the pills? She said that this had to do with society and culture.

The workshop finished an hour later than it was meant to, as no one had wanted to go home. Several women said that while it was one thing to discuss these rights with other women, it was another to make them work in practice in their own relationships. Constanza (39 P) said that they would have to support each other to put these rights into practice. They all expressed a wish to do more work on the theme. As well as taking home with them their 'right', each woman was also presented with a little homemade card as a souvenir of the workshop and the fact that it was 25 November the International Day Against Violence Against Women. With a picture of a large, naked, smiling woman on the front of it, inside the card read:

Woman: Defend your sexual and reproductive rights because they are
the basic elements of justice, dignity and happiness for you as a person

Conclusion

As the links between civil society and the state have begun to be rebuilt
in Chile, women have created spaces in which to reflect and develop. In
this process they make use of and adapt alternative ideas and discourses
and challenge dominant ideas about gender identities that discriminate
against them and inhibit the exercise of their citizenship, in their personal lives, in their local communities and *vis-à-vis* the state: in effect
generating their own ideas about what citizenship should mean. The
new international discourse on women's rights and, in particular, the
extension of the concept of citizen to incorporate new areas of rights
such as reproductive and sexual rights play an important role in this
process. The international discourse on reproductive and sexual rights
may be seen to provide a moral resource that women can draw upon to
assert their citizenship in different contexts. Seen from this perspective,
women's activities can have a bottom-up effect on gender, disrupting
state constructions and cultural stereotypes, and redefining the content
and practice of citizenship.

In this context citizenship and rights discourses may be seen to be of
strategic use, providing alternative conceptions of gender and a basis for
individuals to be able to negotiate and operationalise their rights. Rights
discourses, including human rights, can play a transformative role in
the content and practice of citizenship, just as the concept itself becomes redefined in the process of its strategic use. Reproductive and
sexual rights may be seen to help women to gain control over their
bodies, both a prerequisite to and a defining element in the exercise of
citizenship. In this way women begin to assert the basic right of bodily
integrity, and to challenge and transform discursive ideas that inhibit its
exercise. In effect women are constructing their own notions of citizenship drawing on rights discourse in the process.

Whilst particularising the experience of Chilean *pobladoras*, I argue
that their reality also reveals the pervasive axes in women's experience
that make internationally endorsed rights in respect of reproduction
both necessary and applicable. Women say that these rights are important and they are able to apply the concepts of reproductive and sexual
rights to their own experiences, as well as connect their understanding
of these rights to ideas about citizenship. It is clearly necessary to
understand the cultural specificity of their experience in order to com-

prehend the effect this has on women's ability to operationalise their rights as citizens. In Chile this means understanding a specific and particularly pervasive discursive framework which combines ideas from the Chilean Catholic Church, the Mediterranean honour/shame complex as well as indigenous antecedents. In spite of this particularity, however, universal rights are applicable for two reasons. First, because women are able to interpret them and accommodate them to their own experiences, and second, because whilst women's experience is situational and specific, there are many areas of commonality which serve to form the basis of such rights (such as domination by men, childbearing, sexual degradation and violence). It is these areas of women's lives that define them as different kinds of citizen to men.

Despite the advantages, international rights discourses have limitations. Schild and others are right to point up the danger of the state coopting feminist ideas and strategies. In particular there is a risk that the discourse of citizenship could be adopted by the Chilean state as a 'powerful mechanism of integration' and used to form the basis of an 'economic liberalism' which is reconnecting the fabric of state–civil relations in a different way (Schild 1997: 605–6). Rights discourses can easily be coopted and manipulated. But the idea of cooptation is complicated. Modern processes of policy-making consist in so many actions and counteractions, influences and counter-influences, that it is difficult to identify the initial or the ultimate decision-makers. These factors emphasise the importance of the ongoing project of developing subversive female citizens. Women cannot ever hope to negotiate with the state from a position of equal bargaining power. But, in a situation where dichotomies are increasingly breaking down between state and nonstate, there is a need for women to have the tactical tools to maximise the opportunities open to them to live their lives as fully and as freely as possible at a personal level, in their local communities, in relation to the state and as members of the global community.

Notes

1 The term *jaguar* is used in Latin America as a self-conscious translation of the Asian phenomenon of tiger economies in the late eighties and early nineties denoting the rapid economic growth of countries like Singapore, Malaysia and South Korea during that period.
2 Presently (2001) Chile has one of the most severe abortion laws in the world (United Nations, 1994). There is also no right to divorce in Chile.

3   Diego Portales was the dominant figure in Chilean politics in the 1830s and one of the most influential figures in the founding of the Chilean state. He ended the civil wars and inspired the constitution of 1833, which, with minor changes lasted until 1925.

4   The historical literature suggests that this stability has only been achieved by a pattern of state-sponsored violence and coercion (see, for example, Jocelyn-Holt Letelier 1997).

5   There was a history of Church–state conflict until 1925, when a constitution was passed separating the Church from the state, which in fact enabled a closer relationship between the two. Prior to this politics had been defined by whether you were anti-clerical, and hence liberal or radical, or pro-church and hence a conservative. See Collier and Sater (1996) for a detailed discussion of the history of the relationship between the Church and the state.

6   I had originally hoped to include data on men as well as women. However, whilst participating in women's groups gave me access to many women, my access to men was limited, with some exceptions, to more superficial relationships. I was also concerned that, whilst I could have made greater efforts to build relationships with men, this may have compromised my position in relation to some of the women I was working with. Also, in many cases it would have been difficult to conduct interviews with men once I had begun participating with these groups as it marked me in some men's eyes as feminist and therefore anti-men.

7   For the full study see Willmott (1998).

8   The Chilean state, like all others, is not a unitary structure. Rather it is a differentiated set of institutions, social policies, laws and discourses, which themselves are the product of a particular historical, political and cultural conjecture and which are not reducible to 'the state'. Nevertheless, as Yuval-Davis and Anthias (1989: 6) point out we should not lose sight of the state as a separate sphere, 'a body of institutions which are centrally organised around the intentionality of control within a given apparatus of enforcement at its command or basis' (cf. Yuval-Davis 1997: 13).

9   I have borrowed this term from Stølen (1996: 251) who developed it in relation to her work on Argentina.

10   See Willmott (1998, ch. 3) for a description of these competing discourses.

11   The constitution states '. . . the right to life and physical integrity of the person. The law protects the life of those about to be born [*del que está por nacer*].'

12   There are, of course, limitations with this. It ceases to be about a woman's right to choose to control her body and becomes a technical criterion.

13   *El Mecurio, Cuerpo C*, 17 October 2000.

14   All translations from Spanish by author.

15   Her friend had found her wandering round and round her house with the foetus in her hand.

16   A survey by the Grupo Iniciativa Mujeres found that abortion was seen as permissible by a majority in the cases of malformation of the foetus (69 per cent), danger to the woman's life (78 per cent), and when the pregnancy resulted from rape or incest (59 per cent). Only 20 per cent of women interviewed thought abortion should be legal on economic grounds but conversely 30 per cent thought that abortion should be permitted when

the women asked for it. *Encuesta Nacional: opinión y actitudes de las mujeres chilenas soibre la condición de género.*

17 Women's involvement or non-involvement in women's organisations is indicated by the categories: leader (L), participant (P), occasional participant (OP), and non-participant (NP).

18 A collective of organisations and individuals dedicated to promoting reproductive and sexual rights.

19 Tierra Nuestra ran a school for women leaders, which included classes on patriarchy and the history of the women's movement in Chile, as well as practical courses on planning and administering projects.

20 The studies reviewed by Lamadrid Alvarez and Muñoz Gouet suggest that poverty reinforces these social representations. In addition, as they point out, living in precarious economic conditions is not conducive to the development of sensuality (1996: 80).

21 The theme of sexuality was considered so important to women in the coordination of *pobladoras* in San Joaquín, that as well as presenting their own workshops on the theme they applied for funding from the Ministry of Health to arrange a series of workshops presented by professionals.

Bibliography

Carroll, B. A. (1989) 'Women take action! Women's direct action and social change' *Women's Studies Forum*, 12 (1) 3–24

Craske, N. (2000) *Continuing the Challenge: the Contemporary Latin American Women's Movement(s)*, ILAS research paper #23, Liverpool: ILAS

Collier, S. and W. Sater (1996) *A History of Chile, 1808–1996*, Cambridge: Cambridge University Press

Fraser, N. (1989) *Unruly Practices: Power, Discourse and Gender in Contemporary Social Theory*, Minneapolis: University of Minnesota Press

Goetz, A. M. (1995) 'The politics of integrating gender to state development processes: trends, opportunities and constraints in Bangladesh, Chile, Jamaica, Mali, Morocco and Uganda' UNRISD occasional paper for the Fourth World Conference on Women in Beijing 1995, Geneva: UNRISD

Góngora, M. (1986) *Ensayo Histórico sobre la noción de estado en Chile en los siglos XIX y XX*, Santiago de Chile: Editorial Universitaria

Jelin, E. (1996) 'Citizenship revisited: solidarity, responsibility, and rights' in *Constructing Democracy: Human Rights, Citizenship and Society in Latin America*, E. Jelin and E. Hershberg (eds) Boulder, Colo.: Westview Press

Jelin, E. and E. Hershberg (eds) (1996) *Constructing Democracy: Human Rights, Citizenship and Society in Latin America*, Boulder, Colo.: Westview Press

Jocelyn-Holt Letelier, A. (1997) *El Peso de la Noche: nuestra frágil fortaleza histórica*, Santiago de Chile: Planeta

Lamadrid Alvarez, S. and S. Muñoz Gouet (1996) *La investigación social en sexualidad en Chile, 1984–1994*, Santiago: Universidad de Chile, Facultad de Ciencias Sociales, Programa Interdisciplinario de Estudios de Género

Lowden, P. (1993) 'The ecumenical committee for peace in Chile (1973–1975), the foundation of the moral opposition to authoritarian rule in Chile' in *Bulletin of Latin American Research*, 12 (2) 189–204

Matear, A. (1997) 'Desde la protesta a la propuesta: the institutionalization of the women's movement in Chile' in *Gender Politics in Latin America: Debates in Theory and Practice*, E. Dore (ed.) New York: Monthly Review Press

Montecino, S. (1991). *Madres y Huachos: Alegorías del mestizaje chileno*, Santiago: Editorial Cuarto Propio, CEDEM

Moore, H. L. (1988) *Feminism and Anthropology*, Cambridge: Polity Press

Moore, H. L. (1994) *A Passion for Difference: Essays in Anthropology and Gender*, Cambridge: Polity Press.

Pateman, C. (1985) *The Problem of Political Obligation: a Critical Analysis of Liberal Theory*, Chichester: John Wiley

Peterson, V. S. (1996) 'The politics of identification in the context of globalization' *Women's Studies Forum*, 19 (1/2) 5–15

Schild, V. (1997) 'New subjects of rights? Gendered citizenship and the contradictory legacies of social movements in Latin America' *Organization*, 4 (4) 604–19

Stølen, K. A. (1996) *The Decency of Inequality: Gender, Power and Social Change on the Argentine Prairie*, Oslo: Scandinavian University Press

United Nations (1994) *World Population Policies*, New York: United Nations, Department for Economic and Social Information and Analysis, Population Division

Yuval-Davis, N. (1997) 'Women, citizenship and difference' *Feminist Review*, 57, 4–27

Yuval-Davis, N. and F. Anthias (1989) 'Introduction' in *Woman-Nation-State*, N. Yuval-Davis and F. Anthias (eds) Basingstoke: Macmillan – now Palgrave

Waylen, G. (1996) *Gender in Third World Politics*, Buckingham: Open University Press

Willmott, C. (1998). *Gender Citizenship and Reproductive Rights in the Poblaciones of Santiago, Chile*, unpublished Ph.D. thesis, London School of Economics

7
Indigenous Women, Rights and the Nation-State in the Andes

Sarah A. Radcliffe[1]

Introduction

Through a focus on the Andean region, this chapter argues that the rights granted by states – and those fought for by peasants, by indigenous peoples and by women – have not adequately guaranteed indigenous women's rights. The multifaceted and contested identities of indigenous women have rather been made invisible in the separate rights associated with class, 'race'[2] or gender. Indigenous women's fluid and multifaceted identities remain only contingently and incompletely guaranteed by the legislation and political demands made in Andean countries over recent decades. In other words, indigenous women fall between the edifice of rights constructed by the states and political movements of the region.

In the classic liberal interpretation, rights are universal and inhere in each morally equal citizen. In practice however, the social differentiation of subjects – and, historically, the denial of citizenship to groups of women and illiterates – has resulted in uneven access to rights for particular social subjects (Wilson 1997, Freeman 1995, Mendus 1995, Anthias and Yuval-Davis 1992). Historically, Latin American nation-states have been slow to legislate for women's rights, not least because of the gender hierarchies informing state actions and legal systems throughout the region (Dore and Molyneux 2000). Moreover, even as peasants or as ethnic peoples, indigenous women have not found their rights to autonomy written into state constitutions until recently, and then unevenly, as the recent attempts by indigenous groups to gain collective rights make clear (Hindley 1996, Stavenhagen 1996). Histories of the Andean state and political protest by rural and peasant groups – often indigenous peoples in the highlands – reveal the contested nature of citizenship which has varied over time and place, depending on regime type, organisations and political ideologies (Degregori 1998, also Gledhill 1997, Hindley 1996). Subordinate class and social groups have organised to demand the application of rights that exist only on paper, or to extend the range of individual rights enshrined in the constitution, but have often done so in ways that marginalise indigenous women.

In social, economic and political terms, Andean republican states and societies have not considered indigenous women to be citizens in the full sense of the term, that is as valid claimants of rights, despite their subordination, and their own agency in demanding rights.[3] Although human rights issues are reworked constantly in a national and transnational context, indigenous women remain excluded from the social categories to whom rights are awarded or enforced (cf. Wilson 1997: 11). By examining first the way in which states and societies incorporate indigenous women, this chapter examines the political-economic and social-cultural dimensions of indigenous women's situation; that is their 'first' and 'second' generation rights. The discussion then moves to examine the extent to which indigenous women's rights have been worked into political movements' agendas. Case studies of class-based union movements, ethnic identity movements and the women's movement are discussed to illustrate themes of exclusion, while the conclusion assesses the potential future direction of indigenous women's rights.

Indigenous women in economy and society

Rural and urban labour markets are structured around race and gender, shaping indigenous women's opportunities and keeping them in low-paid and low-status work (Andreas 1985, Bourque and Warren 1981). In rural subsistence-oriented communities, indigenous women often had rights under bilateral forms of inheritance to resources, including livestock and land. They have powers over the use of domestic-related materials, and to some extent joint decision-making with husbands over education, investment and sales (see, among others, Miles and Buechler 1997, Fernández Montenegro 1986, Bourque and Warren 1981). Nevertheless by comparison with men, women's access to economic resources is restricted, due to unequal inheritance practices (exacerbated by agrarian reform as discussed below), limited access to credit and cultural constraints on spatial mobility. With insecurity and poverty, indigenous women's urgent concerns tend to be viewed by com-

munal patriarchies and by development organisations as primarily domestic and therefore not central to livelihood decisions. Throughout
the Andes, Mothers' Clubs for the distribution of food aid confirm this
domestic role, while village decision-making structures (*cabildos* in
Ecuador, *comunidades campesinas* in Peru) have had the added effect of
muting women in the voicing of their demands (Bourque and Warren
1981). Patriarchal discourses and practices that denigrate women's political contributions undermine their confidence to speak out, thereby
restricting their rights to participation in community development.

Although women as a whole make up between 19 per cent, 25 per cent
and 27.5 per cent of the adult labour force in Ecuador, Bolivia and Peru
respectively,[4] their contributions are often under-counted, especially in
agricultural areas where indigenous women have historically been concentrated. Census counts of indigenous women's labour in rural economies systematically underestimate their contribution. For example,
women's participation in the agricultural job market was officially declared to be 42 per cent in Ecuador, a figure revised upwards to 72 per
cent in the 1990s (BID 1995: 59). Gender asymmetry in indigenous
households results in the differential valuing of male and female labour
contributions. Normative definitions of work tend to prioritise male
over female contributions, with negative consequences for women's
rights to household resources, as for example in Peruvian peasant communities where 'female' tasks are consistently deprived of tools, credit or
labour power. In family livelihood strategies, women are allocated the
least prestigious jobs, such as cooking and weeding whether in Ecuador,
Peru or Bolivia (Miles and Buechler 1997: 4). In Peruvian Andean villages, patriarchal calculations make young women's labour invisible,
leading to their migration into domestic service, as older women are
not seen to require help (Radcliffe 1986). In Ecuador where men migrate
to the cities leaving indigenous women with small farms, female responsibilities are associated with the 'backward' subsistence sector, and the
gruelling task of managing impoverished family budgets (McKee 1997).

As many rural women have perceived themselves primarily as unpaid
reproductive workers (Bourque and Warren 1981), the census bias is
exacerbated, resulting in indigenous women's invisibility in agrarian
policy and politics, despite their long working days. Attempts by states
to modernise agriculture have often reinforced the relative invisibility of
indigenous and rural women. In the Peruvian Agrarian Reform of 1969
introduced by a progressive military regime to alleviate rural poverty
defined in *class* terms, indigenous women – the majority of temporary
workers on estates – lost the right to land (Deere 1986). With institutional

and social bias against rural women limiting their insertion into agricultural development and land tenure security, the benefits of reform did not reach temporary female labourers. Rural women's share of the agricultural labour force continues to increase, not least with the development of export production of flowers and fruit (Arriagada 1995) – but wage differentials with men and *mestizo* (mixed race) groups remain.

The devaluation of female labour, together with changing craft production patterns, leads many women into domestic service work. Over a quarter of the urban female economically active population is in domestic service, a feminised sector which employs largely racialised women (black, indigenous and *mulata* (indigenous-black)).[5] Reflecting gender ideologies of domesticity in a class-divided and racialised society, domestic service compounds indigenous women's lack of rights to autonomous work choices and a full wage. By contrast, export flower production in Ecuador attracts many rural women for precisely these reasons, that is, autonomy and work choices. Another urban labour market with many indigenous women is that of street-vending and marketing, where lack of access to capital for business expansion and the *machismo* of market unions tends to undermine women's ability to defend effectively their economic and political rights (Lawson 1999). Petty commodity production can also offer income to indigenous women in the city, although the overcrowded sector and women's invisible home-based work restrict access to a secure income. Additionally, most women in this sector tend to identify themselves neither in class nor feminist terms (Buechler 1986), referring instead to their family-centred interests (McEwan Scott 1994).

Men and women's differential insertion into expanding market economies affects their racial labels, which in turn reflects – and exacerbates – indigenous women's lack of rights within systems of resource distribution. The link between a gendered pattern of racialisation and exclusion from socioeconomic opportunities can be illustrated by a Peruvian example. In the highland rural community of Chitapampa, male migration and semiskilled work in the nearby cities provided inhabitants with social status, and the economic networks that led to their description as *mestizo* (mixed 'race', with connotations of a higher social and national status). By contrast, women from the same village were increasingly engaged in field-based labour and subsistence activities which made them 'more indian' (de la Cadena 1995). In the village, women had no effective relations with the urban sector, thus placing them as 'the last link in the chain of social subordination', articulated through race, class and gender (ibid: 333). As elsewhere in Latin America, the 'reproduction and reinforcement of class inequality [takes] place through the interplay of racial discrimination and gender hierarchy' (Wade 1997: 102). While masculine interpretations of racial hierarchies and definitions of 'proficient urban relations' are applied in Andean Peru, indigenous women's perspectives on these hierarchies are silenced: their rights to income, status and security are denied.

Whereas motherhood is a gendered 'right' that Latin American republics have endorsed enthusiastically in their maternal health programmes and discourses, indigenous women are viewed as problem mothers. In Andean republics, racialisation entails different experiences of maternity for different women.[6] In Ecuador, rural and indigenous women were viewed by policy makers and popular opinion as producing 'too many' children, that is, giving birth to 'indian' children rather than nationalist *mestizo* offspring (see Vargas, Chapter 9 this volume).

Summarising the position of indigenous women illustrates the marginal place accorded them in Andean society, in which their rights as members of a rural community are made invisible by masculine interpretations of value. In urban society, indigenous women as workers are often invisible, labouring in workshops or private homes, and are discriminated against by institutions awarding credit, business contacts or union support. In this context, to what extent have states – in their uneven and contested policies over rights and citizenship – pursued indigenous women's rights?

The Andean nation-state and citizenship rights for indigenous women

If peasant and indigenous groups in the Andes have long remained 'unimagined' by their states, indigenous women are even more invisible although they appear at crucial political moments to do ideological work underpinning the specificity of indigenous cultures (which of course does not grant them rights) (Radcliffe and Westwood 1996). Indigenous women have generally been subsumed into state legislation as class subjects, or as women, but rarely in their own right as complex subjects uniting all facets of their identity. In the application of modernist development policies, Andean states in the post-World War II period conceptualised racialised groups as brakes on development, resistant to the modernising thrust of nationhood and thus not valid claimants of rights (Orlove 1993). Being both indigenous and women meant that *indígenas* were particularly nonmodern and non-national

(Radcliffe 1996). Ongoing notions of 'racialised' and gendered citizen-ship entailed a failure to see indigenous women as legitimate claimants of rights; instead, states have frequently attempted their incorporation into *mestizo* development and masculinist political models.

In terms of suffrage, the female right to vote was granted in 1929 in Ecuador (the first Latin American country to do so) and in 1955 in Peru. Unlike men however, Ecuadorian women were not *required* to vote until 1967, as the political establishment feared the Catholic church's influ-ence over women's vote (Navarro and Bourque 1998: 177). In both these countries, the right to vote was granted only to literate subjects, thereby excluding indigenous women (and men) who made up the bulk of illiterates in their respective countries. Suffrage was extended to the entire adult Peruvian population in 1979, thereby including many indi-genous women for the first time in formal citizenship. Similarly, Ecua-dor granted voting rights to nonliterate populations, comprising largely indigenous women, on the return to democracy at the end of the 1970s.

In other spheres of state action, indigenous women were subsumed within wider categories – whether as peasants, women or as ethnic subjects – rather than as a group with specific, and cross-cutting, inter-ests. While Peru arguably began corporatist modernising development in the late 1960s, Ecuador's development patterns reflected a later in-corporation of 'nonmodern' groups into nationhood. Velasco's modern-ising corporatist regime in Peru (1968–75) proposed to draw women directly into 'development' in a state-run programme of promotion and equal rights, although it did so without questioning the specific structural and cultural bases of *campesina* (broadly rural, peasant) women's situation (Ruiz Bravo 1987, Bourque and Warren 1981). As noted above, the major agrarian reform of land redistribution was un-successful in consolidating rural women's rights, as it excluded them from beneficiary status and from representation within new local polit-ical structures (Radcliffe 1993). Only 2 per cent of beneficiaries of the 1969 Agrarian Reform were women (Deere 1985). As in Chile, indigen-ous (and rural) women were excluded from land tenure rights by the definition of beneficiaries as heads of households, a status that women held without recognition and in smaller numbers than men. Moreover, women were subsequently excluded from membership of agrarian units, as this depended on land-holding status and male cultures of public speaking in meetings (Deere 1986).

Other state institutions attempted to bring women into the workforce as class subjects, defining indigenous women as rural workers. In 1972, the Peruvian Association for Cooperation with Peasant Women (ACO-

MUC, Asociación de Cooperación con la Mujer Campesina) was created as a parallel body to the – by default – 'male' institution of the CNA (Confederación Nacional Agraria, National Agrarian Confederation). Through ACOMUC, the state viewed indigenous and rural women primarily as another workforce and interest group in which the 'double day' of productive and reproductive work was taken for granted, without recognition of the racialised labour market (cf. Andreas 1985: 225). ACOMUC aimed 'to promote the fundamental values of the peasant family through the education of family members, [and to encourage] all women to participate in society through the setting up of daycare centres and training programmes' (quoted in Deere 1985: 27, also Dibos Cauri 1976)

In this way, rural women's rights were linked to (patriarchal) families and in effect, as discussed above, silenced female gender concerns at the community level. Moreover, the state persisted in treating indigenous women as a problem, not as a constituency with its own rights. In terms of *women's* rights, the Plan Inca of 1974 in Peru proposed equality for women in rights and obligations, their promotion to high office, the elimination of discrimination, coeducation and common property rights in marriage. Beyond formal recognition, these rights largely remained unimplemented although rural coeducation was a widely executed measure, which improved rural women's citizenship rights by making them literate (cf. Bourque and Warren 1981: 184). Rights outlined in this ambitious plan remained on paper due to a combination of lack of political will, local resistance to changing gender relations, and indigenous women's lack of support.

Other measures taken by the Peruvian government to increase women's rights largely bypassed indigenous women. In 1974, the military government created a National Commission on the Peruvian Woman (CONAMUP) to analyse legislation, oversee small development projects and initiate a series of planning proposals. While this Commission had only marginal impact on rural (indigenous) women, it may have raised the profile of female leaders at the urban and national levels (Anderson 1985). Both the Plan Inca and the CONAMUP were hampered by lack of personnel, resources and political will, as well as by the change in regime from 1976. While women's rights to work, education and assistance in reproductive labour were partially considered in this legislation, patterns of racism and ethnic discrimination operating in communities, national society and labour markets were not addressed. Racial difference between participants and staff further emphasised the passive role offered to indigenous women. Later Peruvian governments under Belaúnde (1980–85) and García (1985–90) effectively continued with assistentialist programmes in which gendered expectations around maternity and female work (the latter under García, especially with the PAIT programme) outweighed any emphasis on rights (Radcliffe 1993). As indigenous women were viewed as problematic mothers (due to racism) and not-quite workers (due to gender discrimination), their ideological and structural position remained one of marginality. In the interplay of responsibilities and citizenship, women's responsibilities came higher on the agenda than their rights.

In Ecuador, similar rural programmes were put in place and indigenous women were again perceived as non-modern, requiring incorporation into development to overcome poverty and marginalisation. After the Andean Mission had reported that rural women were bearers of tradition, development programmes attempted to bring these largely indigenous women into market-led 'modern' society (Radcliffe 1996). Rural development programmes such as FODERUMA in the 1970s and SEDRI in the 1980s, viewed women as passive beneficiaries of small-scale credit and work creation programmes, rather than as citizens with rights. During the 1990s, government development plans began to distinguish between different groups of women (and their rights), whereby urban *mestizo* women gained rights at work and in society, while indigenous women were increasingly controlled and under surveillance.

In summary, indigenous women's political and social rights have been subsumed within nation-state policies in ways that emphasise their gender or their class position, rather than grant them rights as ethnic, class and female subjects simultaneously. Gender bias in class-defined programmes means women are passed over, while an urban/racial bias in gender programmes means rural, indigenous women are not included. Consequently, indigenous women have failed to gain rights granted to male indigenous (land rights) and to other women (paid work), while receiving other rights as a byproduct of redefinitions of citizenship (full adult suffrage). Indigenous women can thus be pictured as marginal recipients of rights, rather than as fully recognised claimants of rights.

Demanding rights: the contradictions of ethnicity, gender and race

The contradictory and contingent relations of 'race' and gender are particularly evident when we examine three major types of political movement that have – in various ways and with varying success – attempted to address the multifaceted rights of Andean indigenous women. These movements include class organisations, cultural identity movements and feminist movements, all of which have mobilised to fight for political and social rights in Andean countries. Each organisation articulates rights in distinct ways, reflecting their positioning *vis-à-vis* the state and with regard to Marxist or 'indianist'[7] ideologies, or a feminist politics respectively. However, the degree to which these specific movements engage indigenous women's interests is highly variable, as the discussion below illustrates. The class-based union organisation is exemplified by the peasant confederations of 1980s Peru, reflecting the wider saliency of class politics at the time. By contrast, the ethnic politics of the 1990s, found throughout the Latin American region, is illustrated by reference to Ecuador where indigenous organisations brought identity politics into the centre of political debate.[8] As Degregori (1998) makes clear, the trajectory of Andean political organisation and state response varies substantially with, broadly, class politics dominating in Peru, and a more indigenous politics in Bolivia and Ecuador. The feminist movement was, from the start, a more international movement yet the problematic insertion of indigenous women and their rights into the agenda of the movement remains notable.

Class-based organisations in Peru

The class-based articulation of indigenous women's rights can be exemplified by the Peruvian Peasant Confederation (Confederación Campesina del Perú, CCP).[9] Within the political project articulated by CCP male and female leaders, gender was secondary to class, framed within a wider contestation of the state's legitimacy. As the Peruvian ACOMUC declined in the late 1970s, women's demands for community decision-making rights and equal wages increasingly became the issues around which nonstate groups mobilised. As women's demands gained space in the CCP programme, women's rights were written in as a discrete element in the peasant-class organisation. At the First National Meeting of Peasant Women organised by the CCP in 1987, women's rights were summarised:

- [we demand] that the state create a policy of *campesina* promotion free from paternalism and politicking, with rights to access to land and/or a productive job; the option of credits and fair prices for products; [and] the provision of basic support services for productive and domestic work;

- that there be equality of conditions and opportunity with men in communities, cooperatives and agricultural units;
- that the peasant movement be informed of women's recognised rights, and for there to be an educational campaign between men and women to achieve the revaluation of women in work and in the home. (CCP 1987: 14–7, author's translation)

In order to inform and establish women's rights at confederation and local levels, the CCP created Women's Affairs officers, and argued for a new 'combative consciousness' of women. These demands and actions were couched in a socialist notion of equal rights, whereby women's concerns were allocated to a second rank of priorities after class. In practice, women's officers tended to be isolated in regional union offices, and gender concerns were perceived as discrete and minor (if not diversionary from the 'true' goal), rather than as relevant in all union work (fieldnotes 1986, 1988). In one respect, the inclusion of women's rights in CCP policy reflected the struggles of a small number of female union members, whose experience of discrimination began in the 1970s land-invasions. In order to clarify their emerging sense of injustice, these activists drew on a number of ideas about women's rights including the United Nations Declaration against Discrimination against Women. Some *campesinas* also developed the ideas of rights expounded in liberation theology in order to articulate a politics of gender rights (fieldnotes from Peru, 1985, 1988).

However despite these attempts, the prevailing union ideology of struggle – against state and dominant class interests – made women's rights a lower priority in their organisations. The emphasis on consciousness for example reflected the confederation's vanguard Marxist politics and was replicated in discussions about women's rights, as illustrated by the following quote. CCP leader Concepción Quispe elaborates on the importance of indigenous women's right to education, seeing it as the route to class, gender and ethnic consciousness (in that order of priority):

The [indigenous] woman needs contradiction to educate herself and become conscious of her own values and to learn from her own experiences. For this, it is necessary for the country to plan education, not only as a mechanism of instruction, but as a means of ethnic realisation, in her own language, and with meaningful content and its own values. This is to be done in tactical alliance with other cultures in order to lead to a consciousness of class, gender and ethnicity, within a determinate political project. (Zúñiga 1987: 40–1, author's translation)

Within this class-rights agenda, women were increasingly seen as a crucial group of potential supporters by both leadership and the grass-roots. By the late 1980s, indigenous women were ambivalently part of union decision-making structures (such as the CCP Commission for the Organisation of the Peasant Woman that brought together eight female leaders for policy development), yet still faced numerous personal and structural forms of discrimination. Even as class actors, indigenous women were not accorded a full place within the CCP and other organisations. The subordination of gender (and ethnic) interests to the class-based politics of this period served to make it more difficult for peasant-indigenous women to articulate their own agenda, while simultaneously placing gender concerns low down on the list of union priorities. Overall, the class-rights based logic of the CCP was exclusionary of gender issues and marginalised indigenous women's rights.

Cultural identity, politics and gender

In the wake of the collapse of the Soviet Union, and the rise of a new generation of educated indigenous leaders, Andean rural politics was transformed. Throughout the region, the class politics of the 1970s shifted into movements that demanded indigenous rights, in a move that combined elements of a union structure with a predominantly ethnic rights base and cultural politics (see Bengoa 1998, Stavenhagen 1996).[10] Rather than demanding rights as land-poor workers, the indigenous movements claim rights to cultural distinctiveness, bilingual education and administrative autonomy, often on a collective basis. Such a politics takes rights issues from the individual level to the problematic and often unlegislated arena of collective rights (Stavenhagen 1996). Recent constitutions in the Andean republics – as elsewhere in Latin America – have incorporated a mention of some collective rights, thereby placing on paper the right to cultural distinctiveness, bilingual education and in some cases, territory. All of these rights were incorporated into the new Ecuadorian constitution of 1998 for example. How has this emphasis on cultural and collective issues affected indigenous women's rights? As we shall see below, the evidence suggests that indigenous identity politics continues to view women's demands as secondary to a set of primary and largely 'gender-neutral' ethnic demands.

The Ecuadorian indigenous movement comprises diverse 'indigenous nationalities' that mobilised around demands for ethnic recognition, culturally-sensitive bilingual education and territories, as land represents the basis for both social cohesion and production (Bengoa 1998, Santana 1995, Van Cott 1994). During the 1990s, this cultural strategy brought about substantial changes in political procedure and cultures as the ILO Convention 169 on Indigenous Rights was ratified, and the 1998 constitution recognised the country's multiethnic character for the first time. Moreover indigenous representatives, including the influential indigenous lawyer Nina Pacari, were elected to the national Congress and to provincial administrations in the elections of 1996, 1998 and 2000. In the wake of these electoral and legislative gains, what has been done about indigenous women's rights?

The ILO Convention 169 on indigenous rights highlights some of the issues. Dating from 1989, the Convention 169 presses governments to ensure that development actions protect the rights of indigenous peoples, and recognise the rights of indigenous groups to possession and ownership of traditional lands and associated natural resources. Ratified by Ecuador in April 1998 (and by Bolivia and Peru in the same decade), the convention goes a long way to recognising indigenous rights, by extending and amplifying the ideas in the 1992 UN Declaration on Minority Rights. Convention 169 states that indigenous peoples have rights, and that the social inequality under which they live violates citizenship and human rights (see Hindley 1996). Rejecting the status of a 'minority' (the language of the earlier UN Declaration), indigenous groups – and, in principle, the governments who ratified the convention – demand specific collective rights *vis-à-vis* the states in which they find themselves (Stavenhagen 1996). However, thinking about collective human rights entails the twin problems of identifying the subject of these rights (Freeman 1995) while not essentialising the collectivity itself (Gledhill 1997: 95–8). Collectivities can violate the human rights of individual members, as the group may be defending an identity or 'essence' for itself in face of discrimination or injustice (Freeman 1995). This 'double bind' – of essentialism and of violation of human rights within the group – applies to indigenous women, whose rights are made invisible by the very position they hold within indigenous society. The ILO Convention falls into the same trap, by not mentioning indigenous women as a particular oppressed subgroup within indigenous populations.

The cultural and collective demands of the Ecuadorian indigenous movement position women and their rights very differently to the CCP class-based unionism. Central to the main indigenous confederation CONAIE[11] and its component organisations lies a complex symbolic politics. This rests upon an interplay between ethnic difference (encompassed by the term 'indigenous nationality') and the essentialism of a pan-indigenous identity that – crucially for our discussion – reinforces gender difference. Ethnic identity is presented as being of equal validity for all members of the indigenous population, regardless of gender, age or location. Despite differential gender experiences in indigenous villages, as described above, the collective rights demanded by the confederations are presented as gender-neutral. Moreover, gender politics are viewed by many indigenous leaders as a western import unknown in indigenous complementary gender relations. For example, the conclusions to a 1989 indigenous women's meeting in Bogotá summarise the view that:

> The communal life, the harmony and respect between men, women and Nature, the fraternity and solidarity and profound spirit of resistance are values to recuperate and construct in our indigenous peoples, blacks and other mixtures arising from the rich process of Latin American *mestizaje*. Equally, to recuperate and achieve the recognition of our values and identities as women. (Bengoa 1998: 46)

Feminism is seen as 'bourgeois' and western, although gender sensitivity is often incorporated into indigenous organisations' proposals for foreign funding.

The indigenous collectivity, however, defines itself – makes its essence – through female gendered icons. Indigenous women represent the collective, without their specificity within the collectivity being recognised beyond the cultural dimension. Whereas men and women in the indigenous movement are increasingly engaged in a cultural hybridity that combines urban/rural, *mestizo*/Andean, modern/traditional elements, women are positioned as the core of indigenous society. As I have argued elsewhere (Radcliffe 1997), indigenous cultural authenticity rests with women who are expected to retain 'traditional' clothing, remain the guardians of indigenous culture and resist any moves to *mestizo* status (Weismantel 1988: 82). By reflecting a 'true' indigenous identity, women represent the collective to be protected by the movements' demand for rights. Within the cultural politics of the indigenous movement, indian femininity stands as a symbol of indigenous resistance to the urban *mestizo* nation-state.

Nevertheless, formal efforts have been made in recent years to involve women and women's issues to the Ecuadorian indian organisations. In the Levantamientos Indígenas (indigenous uprisings) in Ecuador in

1990, 1994 and 1999, which brought the country to a standstill for days, indigenous women played an active part in road-blocks and market closure (Valdés and Gómariz 1995: 106, fieldnotes 1999). By the early 1990s, several organisations from the provincial to the national level had Women's Secretariats to oversee the inclusion of women's demands. Among them were the national confederation CONAIE (whose Women's Secretariat started in 1986), and regional federations such as the Amazonian group CONFENAIE[12] (from 1986), ECUARUNARI[13] (1985), while the Ecuadorian Federation of Evangelical Indigenous (FEINE) had several female leaders. Building on these developments, meetings were held through the late 1980s and early 1990s to draw upon an ever-increasing number of female leaders from around the country. In 1986, CONAIE held its first Congress of Indigenous Women, following this with the foundation of its 'Dirigencia de la Mujer' (Women's Directorate), through to the Third National Meeting in December 1990 (Valdés and Gómariz 1995: 104–6, 115).

One of the founding federations of CONAIE, the Shuar Federation (Federación de Centros Shuar, FCS) established its Gender Commission (Comisión de Género) in 1997 alongside other commissions on health, land titling, education and economic development projects. While gender issues had previously been promoted sporadically, the appointment of a female director, Ernestina Chuindia, represented a new stage in the evolution of a particular gender politics in the organisation. The director was a veteran of grassroots women's organisation in Amazonian communities, with extensive education qualifications,[14] all experiences that she brought into the Federation.

Despite these developments, gender issues remain secondary to the cultural politics of the indigenous movements, where the persistence of a complementary dual model of gender underpins a traditional and symbolic role for indigenous women. Where women have gained a formal position within indigenous organisations, they are generally not granted the resources, decision-making powers and autonomy necessary to articulate an agenda that reflects their gender, class and racial position. Indeed, critics outside the movement argue that the formation of gender commissions and women's secretariats within federations is primarily driven by international donors' agendas, rather than by indigenous organisations themselves.

In human rights theory, it is argued that collective and individual rights are not adequately combined by the mere 'right to exit' from a collectivity if it violates the rights of individual members (Freeman 1995: 39). In the Andes, indigenous women would not necessarily wish to relinquish their indigenous identity in order to pursue individual rights, even if those gender and class rights had been better guaranteed by existing legislation. What is clear however, is that the construction of women's rights within the indigenous movement reflects the particular interpretation of (collective) rights prevalent in Ecuador.

Feminist politics and indigenous women

Events during the UN Decade for Women (1976–85) raised the profile of women's rights in public debates, and reflected the long history of feminist struggles in the region. Liberal feminism prevalent at the time demanded legal parity with men, primarily focusing on rights to equality in pay, civil status and freedom in reproductive issues, and such issues were variously incorporated into international declarations and national legislation on this basis. Multilateral agencies also encouraged states to include women in development policies under the prevailing 'Women in Development' (WID) paradigm, in which racial and class differentiation were not considered. In feminist debates, the dangers of essentialising women as a homogeneous group increasingly came to the fore. In Latin America and beyond, the dangers of treating all women as if they were the same were raised, as nonessential conceptions of femininity were developed.

Expanding international networks among Latin American feminists began to debate difference, although initially the racial and ethnic diversity of women was not systematically discussed. However, in the Second Regional Latin American Meeting of feminists in 1983, held in Lima, racism in women's everyday lives and in the feminist movement became an ongoing topic for discussion (Sternbach *et al.* 1992: 413, 426). However, tensions between *movimientos de mujeres* (popular women's movements) and veteran feminists over the nature of gender demands and their different priorities also revealed that Latin American feminisms were highly diverse, and that racial difference was difficult to incorporate fully into the spectrum of feminist concerns.

Just as development had long lacked a systematic gender analysis, feminist movements in Latin America lacked a systematic *multicultural* analysis. Symbolic measures – such as the naming of 11 October as Indigenous Women's Day – reflected growing region-wide coordination, but limited space for indigenous women as active social subjects within the feminist movement. Moreover, these measures barely obscured the tensions and contradictions between indigenous women and other strands of the Latin American women's movement over priorities.

Indigenous women remained concerned about their rights to economic security in conditions of crisis and recognition of ethnic distinctiveness, often feeling alienated from feminists' exclusive focus on gender. The complex combination of class, ethnic and gender rights demanded by indigenous women was neither widely formulated by themselves, nor generally acknowledged by other strands in the women's movement. The women's movement collective could not take on board the differential identities – and demands for rights – of indigenous women.

The 1995 Fourth World Conference on Women in Beijing represented a further stage in the contradictory and often conflictual relationship between feminist organisations and female indigenous representatives. Discussions in Beijing arguably placed ethnicity and race more centrally within the international women's movement than ever before.[15] Certainly, the preparatory document for Beijing written by the Ecuadorian women's movement acknowledged racism and articulated a politics around indigenous women. Their document positioned the government's maternal-infant politics and the underprovisioning of the Women's Directorate (DINAMU) within the context of a neoliberal development agenda that was unconcerned with feminist issues and in which rural women were largely invisible (CEIMME/Foro Alternativo 1995: 17). In this document, it was argued that 'indigenous women have gender-related problems arising from their own culture and from their articulation into wider society' (ibid.: 39). According to the document, indigenous women were centrally important in productive and family relations, and had specific demands relating to recognition for themselves and indigenous men, recognition of their domestic work, and to equal participation and decision-making rights at all levels of organisation (ibid.: 40). The document further recognised that women were only a minority within the indigenous leadership.

At meetings in the run-up to Beijing however, indigenous women articulated demands that were at odds with the main thrust of the Ecuadorian NGO preparatory document. In a meeting of indigenous women from 22 Latin American countries held in September 1995, one Ecuadorian indigenous leader, Carmen Tene, demanded a defence of pluriculturalism, as well as indigenous women's own voice. As coordinator of Ecuador's indigenous women's movement, she argued that they faced specific discrimination due to being 'indian, mother and female' (*Hoy*, 6 September 1995). In a further comment, Tene attacked the lack of distribution of funds to indigenous women, which remained with the state bureaucracy or with development agencies.[16] Preparatory documents did not, moreover, overcome exclusions in the conference itself. CONAIE's female representative at Beijing felt marginalised by the meeting. As an NGO forum participant, indigenous woman Carmelina Porate argued that 'we were invited but had neither voice nor vote [ni voz ni voto]' (*Comercio*, 6 July 1996: B6). As a government representative, Blanca Chancoso felt similarly excluded from decision-making (*Comercio*, 27 September 1995).

Despite this lack of a shared agenda and indigenous women's exclusion, the campaign against violence has by contrast united indigenous and nonindigenous women in Ecuador. National organisations and transnational advocacy networks pushed the campaign against violence against women up the political agenda during the 1990s, to such an extent that the state instituted changes in its policing and welfare measures along the lines recommended by feminist organisations (Keck and Sikkink 1998). Indigenous women were involved in the campaign for these gender-specific rights during the national level mobilisation. With public information campaigns, indigenous women became better informed about the issues of domestic and intrafamilial violence. At a meeting in January 1994 involving numerous indigenous representatives (including leaders from women's cooperatives), one woman said, 'We are learning from our experiences and we shall take back ways of helping our *compañeras* [friends] who suffer mistreatment from their husbands' (*El Comercio*, 10 February 1994: B7).

Although campaigns against gender violence appear to have included indigenous women and reflected their demands, there are other dimensions of the feminist agenda that fail to represent indigenous women's concerns. Indigenous women have been reluctant to identify as feminist (seeing it as bourgeois and foreign to their culture), while the women's movement itself has only recently begun to address questions of racism and difference.

Conclusions: reconciling gender, class and ethnic rights

As the above discussion shows, Andean state legislation for peasants (by class), indigenous groups (by 'race'), or women include rights applicable to indigenous women by default or in a gender-neutral capacity. By treating indigenous women as coterminous with a community of peasants or indians, the role of community patriarchal hegemony in denying (economic, social and political) rights to women has not been considered by the state. Similarly, the political movements around class, indigenous rights or women's rights – exemplified here by material from Ecuador and Peru – have incorporated indigenous women into their programmes and agendas, but largely in the margins. Indigenous women's rights are perceived and presented in these movements as 'additional' to the main demands, or as equivalent to men's rights. The unidimensional articulation of rights illustrated by state legislation and political movements fails to capture the multifaceted subjectivities of indigenous women, and their diverse (and unfixed) social, economic and political interests. Rather than being reducible to one facet of identity or another, indigenous women's rights 'fall between several stools'.

Rights and demands for rights are contextualised by the identity attributed to – and assumed by – indigenous women. In other words, for women to identify themselves as indigenous – or for other actors to see them as such – reflects the social forces that constrain or define that identity. Stuart Hall and Paul du Gay (1996: 5–6) understand identity as

> the meeting point, the point of suture, between on the one hand the discourses and practices which attempt to 'interpellate', speak to us or hail us into place as the social subjects of particular discourses, and on the other hand, the processes which produce subjectivities which construct us as subjects that can be spoken.

If identities adhere to the social subject within wider discourses, then indigenous women – with all their multifaceted identities – are not 'hailed' as subjects in citizenship rights or in the place of the nation. Moreover, in the daily interactions that shape their subjectivities and actions, many indigenous women internalise an identity that disavows their particular combination of gender, class and 'race'.

The structuring of nationalism around hierarchies of race, gender and class provides links between gender, ethnicity and class thereby structuring identities and social position. Being perceived as 'nonmodern', indigenous women have been subject to attempts by the nation-state to integrate them into the market and nationhood on terms defined by their class status, disregarding gender and ethnic rights. Indigenous women were thereby represented not as full claimants of rights, but as subjects whose nonmodernity precluded them from complete participation in the nation. Moreover, as noted above, social mobility can be associated with changing racial-national identities with self-identified *mestizo*-'white' migrants and urban dwellers laying claim to the nation and the constructs of rights in national citizenship. Indigenous women are arguably more likely than men to pursue an identity through this claim to *mestizo*-white identity. In research carried out in a lower-middle class neighbourhood of Quito, Ecuador, women were more likely to identify as 'white' than men, and were more ambiguous about a *mestizo* or indigenous identity (Radcliffe 1999). In gendered racial-national identity, rural indigenous women erase their specificity as racialised, discriminated women from rural areas, rather identifying with the top of Ecuadorian racial, gender and class hierarchies. Given this disavowal of their identity, urban indigenous women are unlikely to demand rights associated with being indigenous, poor and female, and neither are they granted them on this basis.

Although in economic, social and political terms, Andean indigenous women are among the most vulnerable and disadvantaged groups in society, the rights legislation has only patchily dealt with their concerns. Rights for indigenous women go to the heart of questions about how to reconcile one identity with others, when each facet of identity requires certain rights that may or may not be compatible with others. In the words of Susan Mendus (1995: 18), the issue of human rights revolves around the question of 'the ways in which one identity or set of identities, may be reconciled with others'. Recent discussions have highlighted how in practice rights are linked to contested and fluid boundaries around communities, individual subjects and even nations (Mendus 1995: 18–21). While the application of collective rights law in Andean Latin America in recent years has seemingly brought what Mendus terms the 'acknowledgement of difference' (ibid. 23) into state legislation, several risks still remain not least for indigenous women.[17] The inscription of racial/cultural difference in legislation fixes such an identity, thereby denying the dynamics of change or the contradictory nature of 'submerged' identities within such difference. Indigenous identity is particularly vulnerable to the fixing of a 'victim' identity (Gledhill 1997, Wilson 1997) that deflects attention away from the communal hegemonies through which indigenous culture is reproduced. Specifically, the collective rights awarded to Andean indigenous populations in the 1990s cannot obscure the issue of communal patriarchies that restrict or deny indigenous women's rights within those collectivities (cf. Stavenhagen 1996, Freeman 1995).

Indigenous women's multiple positions require that the routes to empowerment are equally diverse (Miles and Buechler 1997: 9). It is unlikely that different groups of Ecuadorian, Bolivian and Peruvian indigenous women would fight for the same rights, not least as the states and societies with which they must deal have varied histories and agendas. Gender consciousness is not given in the abstract, as the Latin American feminist movement has discovered, but rather is formed in 'concrete, quotidian situations of women' (Vargas 1991). It is by tying together these multiple strands of identity into an effective politics that Andean indigenous women's rights can be achieved.

Notes

1   The Economic and Social Research Council (grant No. R000234321), the Nuffield Foundation and the American Friends Service Committee generously supported the various research projects on which this chapter is based. A preliminary version of the paper was presented at the 1998 Workshop on 'Gender, rights and justice in Latin America'. I would like to thank Nikki Craske, Maxine Molyneux, an anonymous reviewer and Pilar Larreamendy for helpful suggestions and comments. Any errors or misinterpretations are my own.

2   'Race' is considered here as a social interpretation of bodily difference in historically – and geographically specific ways, in which racism constructs the body for ideological ends and becomes naturalised (on the Latin American context, see Wade 1997, Stepan 1991). Indigenous 'racial' labels depend as much on social markers of success/poverty as they do on appearance, because 'the absence of reliable phenotypical markers places special emphasis on clothing, hairstyles, speech and body language to determine who is Indian and who is not' (Weismantel and Eisenman 1998: 131).

3   The majority of examples discussed here are drawn from fieldwork on the peasant unions and domestic service (Peru) and the indigenous movement and nationalism (Ecuador).

4   Census data do not include information on the racial-ethnic identity of respondents, making it difficult to estimate indigenous women's share of the workforce.

5   For life histories of Peruvian indigenous women entering domestic service, see Valderrama and Escalante (1996), and Sindicato de Trabajadoras del Hogar (1982).

6   In Peru, the recent controversy over fertility control programmes illustrates the sensitivity of the issue. The misapplication of sterilisation measures led to women suing the government, on the basis of the right of the individual to be treated with respect.

7   'Indianist' refers here to a pro-indigenous ideology claiming certain essential features of indigenous life, although increasingly indigenous social movements are expressing a hybrid discourse reflecting a variety of influences (see Bengoa 1998).

8   The choice of case study organisations and countries also reflects my own research trajectory over those decades, as the focus shifted from the problematics of female organising in *campesino* unions during the 1980s in Peru, to questions around ethnicity and nationhood in Ecuador in the 1990s.

9   For a discussion of the class-based Movimiento Nacional Revolucionario (MNR, Revolutionary National Movement) in Bolivia, see Ardaya Salinas, (1986). In the MNR or the later 'Housewives Committees' of miners' wives, class-based politics relegated women to supporting male activists.

10 For the life history of a female indigenous leader in the early identity-based Mapuche movement of Chile, see Bunster (1980).
11 Confederation of Indigenous Nationalities of Ecuador.
12 The Confederation of Nationalities Indigenous to the Ecuadorian Amazonia.
13 'The Awakening of Ecuador's Indians' in Quichua.
14 In this respect, she is similar to the new generation of Latin American indigenous leaders (Bengoa 1998), where the leadership is increasingly well-educated, often to university level. Ernestina Chuindia herself was educated through the EBI bilingual intercultural education programme.
15 Gina Vargas, personal communication, at the Institute of Latin American Studies, University of London, conference on 'Gender and Rights in Latin America', October 1998.
16 In Ecuador, disagreement over the nature of ethnic group representation held up the distribution of international funds to indigenous development initiatives (Fieldnotes, Ecuador, 1999–2000).
17 Gledhill (1997: 98–9) notes that neoliberal states can also grant rights to identity groups in order to appropriate these subjectivities, as in Mexico with its indigenous legislation (also Hindley 1996).

Bibliography

Anderson, J. (1985) 'The UN decade for women in Peru' in *Women's Studies International Forum*, 8 (2) 107–9

Andreas, Carol (1985) *When Women Rebel: The Rise of Popular Feminism in Peru*, Westport, Conn.: Lawrence Hill & Co

Anthias, Floya and Nira Yuval-Davis (1992) *Racialised Boundaries: Race, Nation, Gender, Colour and Class and the Anti-racist Struggle*, London: Routledge

Ardaya Salinas, G. (1986) 'The Barzolas and the Housewives Committee' in J. Nash and H. Safa (eds) *Women and Change in Latin America*, South Hadley, Mass: Bergin & Garvey, 326–43

Arriagada, I. (1995) 'Unequal participation by women in the workforce' in J. Dietz (ed.) *Latin America's Economic Development: Confronting Crisis*, Boulder, Colo.; Lynne Reinner, 333–49

Bengoa, J. (1998) 'La emergencia de la cuestión indígena en América Latina' Cambridge: Seminar presented to Centre of Latin American Studies, University of Cambridge, November

BID (1995) *Women in the Americas: Bridging the Gender Gap*, Washington DC: BID/ Johns Hopkins University Press

Bourque, Susan and Kay Warren (1981) 'Rural women and development planning in Peru' in N. Black and A. Cottrell (eds) *Women and World Change: Equity Issues in Development*, Beverley Hills: Sage, 51–99

Buechler, J. (1986) 'Women in petty commodity production in La Paz, Bolivia' in J. Nash and H. Safa (eds) *Women and Change in Latin America*, South Hadley, Mass: Bergin & Garvey, 165–88

Bunster, Ximena (1980) 'The emergence of a Mapuche leader: Chile' in J. Nash and H. Safa (eds) *Sex and Class in Latin America*, New York: J. F. Bergin Publishers, 302–19

CCP (Confederación Campesina del Perú) (1987) *I Asamblea Nacional de la Mujer Campesina: Acuerdos*, CCP: Lima

CIEMME/Foro Alternativo de ONGs (1995) *Informe del sector no gubernamental; País Ecuador*, Quito: Centro de Estudios de investigaciones sobre el maltrato a la mujer ecuatoriana (CEIMME) Centro de Co-ordinación Nacional – Foro alternativo de ONGs

Deere, C. D. (1985) 'Rural women and state policy: the Latin American agrarian reform experience' *World Development*, 13 (9) 1037–53

Deere, C. D. (1986) 'Rural women and agrarian reform in Peru, Chile and Cuba' in J. Nash and H. Safa (eds) *Women and Change in Latin America*, South Hadley, Mass: Bergin & Garvey, 34–56

Degregori, C. I. (1998) 'Ethnicity and democratic governability in Latin America: reflections from two Central Andean countries' in F. Agüero and J. Stark (eds) *Fault Lines of Democracy in Post-transition Latin America*, Miami: North-South Center Press, University of Miami, 203–36

de la Cadena, M. (1995) ' ''Women are more indian'': ethnicity and gender in a community near Cuzco' in B. Larson and O. Harris (eds) *Ethnicity, Markets and Migration in the Andes*, London: Duke University Press, 329–47

Dibos Cauri, B. (1976) *Experiencia de investigación y promoción con el Comité Femenino de la CC San Pedro de Cajas, Tarma*, Lima: CONAMUP

Dore, E. and M. Molyneux (eds) (2000) *The Hidden Histories of Gender and the State in Latin America*, London: Duke University Press.

Fernández Montenegro, B. (1986) *Mujer campesina: experiencias de investigación y capacitación*, Piura: Centro de Investigación y Promoción del Campesinado

Freeman, M. (1995) 'Are there collective human rights?' *Political Studies*, 43, 25–40

Gledhill, J. (1997) 'Liberalism, socio-economic rights and the politics of identity: from moral economy to indigenous rights' in R. Wilson (ed.) *Human Rights, Culture and Context*, London: Pluto Press, 70–110

Hall, S. and P. du Gay (1996) *Questions of Cultural Identity*, London: Sage

Hindley, J. (1996) 'Towards a pluricultural nation: the limits of indigenismo and Article 4' in R. Aitken, N. Craske, G. Jones and D. Stansfield (eds) *Dismantling the Mexican state?*, London: Macmillan – now Palgrave, 225–43

Keck, M. and K. Sikkink (1998) *Activists Beyond Borders: Advocacy Networks in International Politics*, Ithaca: Cornell University Press

Lawson, V. (1999) 'Tailoring is a profession, seamstressing is work! Resiting work and reworking gender identities among artisanal garment workers in Quito' *Environment and Planning A*, 31 (2) 209–27

McEwan Scott, A. (1994) *Divisions and Solidarities: Gender, Class and Employment in Latin America*, London: Routledge

McKee, L. (1997) 'Women's work in rural Ecuador: multiple resource strategies and the gendered division of labour' in A. Miles and H. Buechler (eds) *Women and Economic Change: Andean Perspectives*, American Anthropological Association, 13–30

Mendus, S. (1995) 'Human rights in political theory' *Political Studies*, 43, 10–24

Miles, A. and H. Buechler (eds) (1997) *Women and Economic Change: Andean Perspectives*, American Anthropological Association

Navarro, M. and S. Bourque (1998) 'Fault lines of democratic governance: a gender perspective' in F. Agüero and J. Stark (eds) *Fault Lines of Democracy in*

Post-transition Latin America, Miami: North-South Center Press, University of Miami, 175–202

Orlove, B. (1993) 'Putting race in its place: order in colonial and postcolonial Peruvian geography' *Social Research*, 60 (2) 301–36

Radcliffe, S. A. (1986) 'Gender relations, peasant livelihood strategies and migration: a case study from Cuzco, Peru' *Bulletin of Latin American Research*, 5 (2) 29–47

Radcliffe, S. A. (1993) ' "People have to rise up, like the great women fighters": the state and peasant women in Peru', in S. A. Radcliffe and S. Westwood (eds) *Viva: Women and Popular Protest in Latin America*, London: Routledge, 197–217

Radcliffe, S. A. (1996) 'Gendered nations: nostalgia, development and territory in Ecuador' *Gender, Place and Culture*, 3 (1) 5–21

Radcliffe, S. A. (1997) 'The geographies of indigenous self-representation in Ecuador: hybridity, gender and resistance' *European Review of Latin American and Caribbean Studies*, 63, 9–27

Radcliffe, S. A. (1999) 'Embodying national identities: *mestizo* men and white women in Ecuadorian racial-national imaginaries' *Transactions of the Institute of British Geographers*, 24, 213–25

Radcliffe, S. A. and S. Westwood (1996) *Re-making the Nation: Place, Politics and Identity in Latin America*, London: Routledge

Ruiz Bravo, P. (1987) 'Programas de promoción y organizaciones de mujeres' in A. Grandón, B. Valdivia, C. Guerrero and P. Ruiz Bravo (eds) *Crisis y Organizaciones populares de mujeres*, Lima: Universidad Católica, 91–124

Santana, R. (1995) *Ciudadanos en la etnicidad: los indios en la política y la política de los indios*, Quito: Abya-Yala

Sindicato de Trabajadoras del Hogar (1982) *Basta: testimonios*, Cuzco, Peru: Centro de Estudios Rurales Andinos, Bartolomé de las Casas

Stavenhagen, R. (1996) 'Indigenous rights: some conceptual problems', in E. Jelin and E. Hershberg (eds) *Constructing Demoracy: Human Rights, Citizenship and Society in Latin America*, Boulder, Colo.: Westview Press, 141–59

Stepan, N. (1991) *'The Hour of Eugenics': Race, Gender and Nation in Latin America*, Cornell: Cornell University Press

Sternbach, N. S., M. Navarro Aranguren, P. Chuchryk and S. Alvarez (1992) 'Feminisms in Latin America: from Bogota to San Bernardo' *Signs*, 17 (2) 393–434

Valderrama, R. and C. Escalante (1996) *Andean Lives: Gregorio Condori Mamani and Asunta Quispe Huamani*, Austin, Texas: University of Texas Press

Valdés, T. and Gómariz, E. (1995) *Latin American Women: Comparative Figures*, Santiago: Instituto de la Mujer-Spain/FLACSO

Van Cott, D. L. (ed.) (1994) *Indigenous Peoples and Democracy in Latin America*, New York: St. Martin's Press – now Palgrave

Vargas, V. (1991) 'Apuntes para una reflexión feminista sobre el movimiento de mujeres' in Lola Luna (ed.) *Género, clase y raza en América Latina: algunas aportaciones*, Barcelona: Universitat de Barcelona, 195–204

Wade, P. (1997) *Race and Ethnicity in Latin America*, London: Pluto Press

Weismantel, M. (1988) *Food, Gender and Poverty in the Ecuadorian Andes*, Pittsburgh, Pa.: University of Pennsylvania Press

Weismantel, M. and S. Eisenman (1998) 'Race in the Andes: global movements and popular ontologies' *Bulletin of Latin American Research*, 17 (2) 121–42

Wilson, R. (ed.) (1997) *Human Rights, Culture and Context: Anthropological Perspectives*, London: Pluto Press

Zúñiga, M. (1987) *En busca de una nueva educación para la mujer indígena en el Perú*, Guatemala: Ministerio de Educación de Guatemala, Instituto Indigenistas Interamericano III, Oficina UNESCO para América Latina y el Caribe

8
Economic and Social Rights: Exploring Gender Differences in a Central American Context

Jasmine Gideon[1]

Introduction

The Universal Declaration of Human Rights (UDHR) recognises two sets of human rights: civil and political rights, and economic, social and cultural rights. Two separate Covenants were adopted by the United Nations (UN) when the Declaration's provisions were transformed into legally binding obligations: The International Covenant on Civil and Political Rights (ICCPR), and the International Covenant on Economic, Social and Cultural Rights (ICESCR). This chapter will focus on the latter.

The main argument of my analysis is that economic and social rights should be central to human rights. At present the only international agreement in this area, the ICESCR, is highly gendered making its usefulness as a mobilising tool extremely difficult. Furthermore, economic and social rights are frequently more difficult to 'pin down' leaving much open to interpreting the spirit and the letter of the law. This creates both opportunities and costs for nongovernmental organisations (NGOs) using rights-based discourses. The combination of the 'slipperiness' of these rights and a gendered interpretation of the economy means that the ICESCR is of little practical use for women since many are excluded from the conceptualisation. This has been the case in Central America where the impact of the Covenant has been negligible.

The ICESCR was drawn up in 1966 and ratified in 1976, and it sets out a formal understanding of economic, social and cultural rights. It is important, however, to consider the context in which it emerged. It was developed in an era in which there was near-universal consensus regarding the Keynesian approach to controlling and maintaining high and stable levels of employment in the economy.[2] Moreover, economic and social rights were added to the UDHR in order to appease the Communist States who stressed the importance of such provisions. This therefore raises the question of the usefulness of the ICESCR and its understanding of economic and social rights today. In particular, how useful are such concepts to women? At the time of ratification of the Covenant there was only a limited understanding of the role of women in economic development and research in the area was still not in the mainstream. By the 1980s there was a reintroduction of ideas regarding optimal qualities of the market and the failure of governments to influence them in ways which were socially improving. The influence of these ideas has continued into the present and therefore generates new questions about economic and social rights. Research into women in development has now grown extensively and the importance of a gender and development perspective is now widely acknowledged. Gender-aware approaches to understanding rights have also emerged since it has become apparent that women are not able to access their rights as easily as men (see for example Whelan 1998, Schuler 1995).

This chapter seeks to explore economic and social rights from a gender perspective. Critics have argued that the ICESCR contains a built-in gender bias since its understanding of economic and social rights is one of rights which are only realisable in the paid economy through access to employment in that sector. Since many women are not employed in the paid economy, they have no access to these rights (Peterson and Parisi 1998). Furthermore, the ICESCR does not take into account women's unpaid work but, at the same time, assumes that households operate as individual units. Consequently, there is a need to consider the ways that intra-household arrangements may hinder women's access to economic and social rights.

In order to have a gender-aware conceptualisation of economic rights, it is first necessary to broaden our notion of the economy. We need to understand it as a set of gendered institutions and also to incorporate the unpaid work of social reproduction. Such an analysis can help us to understand more clearly why men and women do not, in practice, enjoy the same economic rights.

This chapter starts with a review of the existing literature on economic and social rights and considers the limitations of the ICESCR in the context of economic reform. It considers why a gender analysis of the economy is important for the realisation of economic and social rights, and illustrates the argument with reference to how the ICESCR applies to Central America. The analysis is confined to six articles from the ICESCR: the right of all men and women to enjoy their economic, social and cultural rights (article 3); the right to work and the full realisation of this right through access to the necessary training (article 6); the right to fair wages, including equal remuneration for work of equal value, without discrimination of any kind and the right to paid holidays (article 7); the right to an adequate standard of living (article 11) and the right to the highest attainable standard of physical and mental health (article 12). Although all five Central American countries have ratified both CEDAW (Convention on the Elimination of all forms of Discrimination against Women) and the ICESCR, evidence from the region indicates that marked gender differences can be seen in the ability of men and women to articulate and enjoy their economic and social rights. Finally, some conclusions are drawn and proposals put forward for ways in which women's groups can use the ICESCR to claim their economic and social rights.

Giving substance to economic and social rights

While rights theorists have now acknowledged economic and social rights alongside the political and civil as core components of human rights, considerable debate still exists in the literature. This section addresses some of the key questions and paradoxes that are central to this chapter. Firstly I consider the extent to which the ICESCR contains a list of aspirations or rights. If it is agreed that these are in fact rights, how can states guarantee them to all of their citizens? Moreover, in the context of economic restructuring, the ability of states to do so becomes even more complex. Indeed, the introduction of a new economic model alongside shifts in gender theory also raises the question of whether it is now necessary for economic and social rights to be redefined.

Steiner and Alston (1996) maintain that the inclusion of economic rights as core universal human rights settles the argument regarding whether they are 'really' rights, at least with regard to international law. Neoliberal opponents of economic and social rights argue that they can at most be a statement of goals or aspirations, rather than a set of rights, which begs the question of which aspirations might be considered rights. Some rights, such as freedom from torture, are easily agreed upon, but others come about through consensus building. What transforms aspirations into rights is that they are guaranteed by a third party – usually the state. But, they are only effective when they have generalised acceptance.[3] In state-centric terms all contracts give rights. The ICESCR contains both rights and aspirations and is therefore a particularly complex agreement.

It is also necessary to consider the extent to which economic rights should be conceptualised separately from social rights. Marshall (1950: 11) for example considered civil, political and social rights in relation to his understanding of citizenship but excluded economic rights. In his view (ibid.: 28), social rights emerge in a particular historical context and reflect the society in which they operate. Yet there is often universal awareness of economic rights, unlike social rights, especially in an era when particular views on the economy are dominant globally. Economic rights are generally understood as incorporating the right to labour, capital, goods and education. Economic rights can therefore be understood as referring to the right to resources. Yet what does this really mean? Does it refer to the right to use one's own labour or the right to have resources, for example owning property? Does it include the right to access resources, for example through having a job; does it include the right to consume resources, for example through education, and if so, is this in exchange for producing other resources? Seen in these terms, economic rights are therefore reducible to the idea of having, or having access to, resources. So, how do social rights differ? Social rights deal with the use of resources, such as education and social security, and can therefore not be guaranteed without giving people access to resources. The analysis here argues that since both sets of rights are reducible to resources it is not possible to make a clear distinction between economic and social rights. In essence all these rights are concerned with the way in which the economy works and the ways in which people are guaranteed resources. This implies that all people must have a minimum claim on resources and this raises a number of questions regarding the ability of free market economies to guarantee these rights universally. However, as previously stated, this chapter argues for a broader understanding of the economy than that often used by economists. The rights incorporated in the ICESCR refer only to the formal, paid economy and as will be discussed below this is problematic from a gender perspective. Moreover, since these rights are human rights it can also be argued that they are rights of individuals and can not be attached to households. If indeed economic and social rights are human rights they must be applied to *all* citizens, female and male.

Politically, the effective realisation of economic and social rights would require a redistribution of power and resources both within countries and among them, which might explain why governments are far less enthusiastic about their realisation. Beetham (1995) and Steiner and Alston (1996) agree that the greatest challenges are now the identification of effective approaches to the implementation of the rights and development of ways in which states can be held accountable to fulfil their obligations. This too poses a number of problems. Commentators have suggested that the wording of the obligations of states in enabling citizens to realise their economic and social rights is very open-ended, with the effect that this obligation is almost meaningless. Alston (1987: 351) argues that one of the most striking features of the Covenant is the vagueness of the normative implications of the various rights it recognises. In particular, much of the debate has focused around Article 2 (1) of the ICESCR which states that state parties must:

> take steps, individually and through international assistance and cooperations, especially economic and technical, to the maximum of its available resources, with a view to achieving progressively the full realisation of the rights recognised in the present Covenant by all appropriate means, including particularly the adoption of legislative measures.

Critics have commented extensively on the phrases 'to the maximum of available resources' and the 'progressive realisation' benchmark. Rights theorist Audrey Chapman (1996: 31) highlights Article 2 of the International Covenant on Civil and Political Rights. In contrast to the ICESCR, this states that state parties have an immediate obligation to respect and ensure all stipulated rights. Chapman argues that the 'progressive realisation' benchmark assumes that valid expectations and the concomitant obligations of state parties under the Covenant are not uniform or universal, but must be seen instead as relative to the levels of development and available resources. Furthermore, the standard of 'progressive realisation' cannot be used as a measuring tool for evaluating compliance without first clarifying what the phrase 'maximum of available resources' entails in specific circumstances. Steiner and Alston (1996: 274) also comment on these points. On the one hand it is suggested that the nature of the obligation is so onerous that virtually no government would be able to comply. Yet, on the other hand, it is argued that the relative open-endedness of the concept of progressive realisation, particularly in the light of the qualification related to the availability of resources, renders the obligation devoid of any meaningful content. In turn this means that governments can present themselves as defenders of economic and social rights without their policies and behaviour being constrained in any way and this paradoxically undermines the spirit of the Covenant itself.[4]

With more complex rights, where interpretation is central, it is worth considering negative and positive concepts of justice. A negative conception merely requires us not to harm people. A positive conception, on the other hand, requires that we do or provide something in order to comply with the spirit of the law. The ICESCR clearly embodies a concept of the rights which requires redistributive action. It is often argued that poor states can't afford such guarantees and neoliberals argue that to guarantee basic economic and social rights to all citizens would require extensive compulsory taxation and an over-bureaucratic and paternalistic state (Beetham 1995: 42). But the real question is about spending priorities. The 1990 United Nations Human Development Report (cited in Steiner and Alston 1996: 290) states:

> [D]eveloping countries are not too poor to pay for human development and take care of economic growth. The view that human development can be promoted only at the expense of economic growth poses a false trade-off . . . Most budgets can, moreover, accommodate additional spending on human development by reorienting national priorities . . . Governments can also do much to improve the efficiency of social spending by creating a policy and budgetary framework that would achieve a desirable mix between various social expenditures, particularly by reallocating resources . . . Such a restructuring . . . will require tremendous political courage. But the alternatives are limited, and the payoffs can be enormous.

Beetham reaches a similar conclusion arguing that politically, the effective realisation of economic and social rights would require a redistribution of power and resources both within countries and between them. Governments, therefore, are not enthusiastic about their realisation. However, institutions are not solely responsible:

> [B]ehind institutions stand people. If institutions whether Northern or Southern states or IFIs (international finance institutions), are unable to fulfil their responsibilities it is partly because not enough people to whom they are accountable are sufficiently convinced of any obligation to aid those in need.
>
> (Beetham 1995: 58)

In the context of globalisation and neoliberalism in the 1980s and 1990s the realisation of economic and social rights has become even more unsure. Molyneux (1998: 240) argues that 'the double transition to economic and political liberalism has led to a formal restitution of civil and political rights, but the process of economic restructuring has had mixed results. While certain macroeconomic indicators have improved, social inequalities have deepened and poverty levels are expected to rise in many countries.' In this climate how can states guarantee economic and social rights to all their citizens? The impact of structural adjustment programmes on the poor has now been widely acknowledged (Cornia, Jolly and Stewart 1987), and in conjunction with the burden of national debts this millstone can lead to a denial of economic and social rights at the local level (Clarke and French 1995: 111). In addition, the spread of international and regional trade agreements has forced governments to reconsider labour market policies. This may further limit governments' abilities to secure economic and social rights for their citizens, and consequently many states are forced to accept a trade-oriented redefinition of economic and social rights (Lamarche 1995: 100). It is not enough to provide employment or income-earning opportunities if these cannot satisfy the basic needs of the income earners, or if the conditions of employment or income earning violate other basic rights such as the rights to health and the rights of children.

Why a gender-aware respecification of the ICESCR is necessary

The principle of gender equality is recognised by the UN Human Rights Charter and enacted in several fundamental human rights instruments, notably the Convention on the Elimination of all Forms of Discrimination Against Women (CEDAW 1979) and the Vienna Declaration and Plan of Action (1993), which recognise women's rights as human rights. Despite this, the principle of gender equality is not systematically integrated into all parts of these agreements and is generally consigned to particular paragraphs. Furthermore, much of the focus is on antidiscrimination rather than gender equality. For example, article 7 of the ICESCR calls for equal pay and equal opportunities. Neuhold (1998: 7) maintains that such agreements often affirm the principle of nondiscrimination yet simultaneously assert the overriding importance of the family. This is problematic since there is an inbuilt assumption that promoting women's needs is consistent with promoting family welfare.

This raises another contradiction; on the one hand, within the rights instruments, women are positioned in relation to their families, yet neoliberal policies all too often ignore women's role in the family.[5] Human rights instruments also do little to challenge the conditions under which families are maintained by women. Since much of women's time is spent carrying out unpaid reproductive work, this limits their ability to enter the formal labour market and political arenas. In turn this limits women's ability to claim their rights (Lister 1997).

The ICESCR, ratified in 1976, follows this pattern. While explicit reference is made to women in a number of areas – for example, referring to the equal rights of both men and women to enjoy all economic and social rights and supporting equal wages for work of equal value without discrimination of any kind – women are only recognised through their labour market participation (in paid work), without also acknowledging their unpaid productive and reproductive work. Furthermore, the Covenant presumes a male head of household and much of the document is directed to 'him' or 'he' (Williams 1998: 14). Although the ICESCR recognises the right of women to paid maternity leave this right is only applicable to women who are already integrated into the paid economy. The ICESCR fails to recognise that many women are excluded from the paid economy and tend to carry out work in the unpaid economy. Yet since their work here is not recognised, they are not entitled to any economic and social rights.

The problem of a built-in gender bias is one that is applicable to the rhetoric surrounding all human rights. As Peterson and Parisi (1998: 141) argue, in their critique of human rights over the last fifty years,

> existing human rights are in fact men's rights; it is 'citizens' (implicitly male/masculine) who enjoy civil and political rights. As a consequence women may enjoy these rights only to the extent that they become like men. [Most importantly] . . . unlike men (especially, elite men) women are not constructed as agents/subjects/persons in their own right or as full adult/decision-makers.

As a consequence women are marginalised and not treated as 'human' agents in relation to economic and social rights; furthermore these rights are construed as pertaining exclusively to the public sphere and paid work (ibid.: 142). This is of particular concern when looking at gender differences in the realisation of these rights. Since the conceptualisation of human rights is mainly applicable to the public sphere, which encompasses both the public and private sectors of production as understood by economists, the identification of women as mothers, who are dependants of male providers, limits their claims to socioeconomic rights; because male breadwinners are expected to provide for the basic needs of their dependants, women are less able to claim such rights on their own behalf. Peterson and Parisi (1998: 148) conclude that this can contribute further to the marginalisation of women since the public realm of the male is protected while the private realm of women's unpaid work is obscured. Williams (1998: 14), too, argues that this gender bias casts doubt on the ability of the human rights system to respond to the needs of women.

Ruth Lister (2000) suggests that in order to challenge women's exclusion from full citizenship a necessary starting point is the rearticulation of the public/private divide. The value of care as an important contribution towards citizenship needs to be acknowledged. In addition, challenging women's exclusion from these rights necessitates a reconceptualisation of the economic, which requires a broader notion of the economy. This can be done by looking at the economy through women's eyes and understanding it as a gendered structure (Elson, Evers and Gideon 1997).

The economy as a gendered structure

Looking at the economy as a gendered structure means considering both the conventional view of production, which emphasises production for the market, and also what Elson, Evers and Gideon (1997) have called the reproductive economy. This enables us to identify particular economic constraints and vulnerabilities that women experience which differ from those which affect men. It is these gendered constraints and vulnerabilities which limit women's potential relative to men, to realise their economic and social rights.

The productive economy is market-oriented and encompasses informal as well as formal sectors, including all paid work, as well as unpaid work in small family farms and enterprises producing goods and services that are, or easily could be, marketed, either regularly or from time to time when surpluses become available. The reproductive economy is the unpaid economy that supports social reproduction and human development through the provision of care for family and community members – care that is overwhelmingly provided by women and girls. The reproductive economy produces labour, the crucial input into the productive economy, and it maintains the daily well-being of the population through activities such as housework, water collection and food preparation.

The interactions between the sales-oriented productive economy and the needs-oriented reproductive economy are central to this analysis. The System of National Accounts (SNA) counts the productive economy and aggregates it to produce the Gross National Product (GNP). However, the unpaid reproductive economy is excluded, by definition, from the accounts. Since women do most of the work in the reproductive economy, this means much of their work is not counted, and not simply because of the difficulties of collecting information. In principle, the reproductive economy can be measured separately, producing a 'satellite account' for unpaid household and community work (Elson, Evers and Gideon 1997). In practice however, productive and reproductive activities physically overlap, especially in regions such as Central America where much of the productive economy is household-based in family farms and businesses (Elson and Gideon 1997).

Gender-based institutional bias in the economy

Gender-based institutional bias occurs where economic institutions operate in ways that tend to reflect male priorities. Institutions function in accordance with laws and norms that are gendered in a number of ways. They fail to value and recognise reproductive work; they show a preference to men and exclude and discriminate against women as clients, recipients, stakeholders and participants; they 'feminise' women's participation to re-establish their secondary, supportive and dependent roles in public services and markets; they treat the household as a single unit and women as dependants of men within the household; and, finally, they reflect gendered incentive and accountability systems (Acker 1992, Goetz 1995, 1997). The presence of gender differences and inequalities means that gender-blind institutional practices will have different impacts on men and women or boys and girls, which can in turn increase gender inequality. For example, gender-biased norms in the allocation of public expenditure result in patterns of expenditure that reproduce rather than diminish gender inequality. Such patterns will typically result in only small allocations to social infrastructure, such as health and education, and to the kinds of physical infrastructure that are critical for supporting women's activities in production and social reproduction (such as housing, water, sanitation, and small-scale transport). This pattern is not intended to be male-biased: it simply results from gendered norms about priorities and procedures (Elson and Evers 1998).

Since institutions tend to reflect the needs of the paid economy and ignore the unpaid economy, this also means that institutions only recognise the rights of those in the paid economy. The lack of recognition of the unpaid, reproductive economy where women are over-represented results in undermining their economic and social rights. Consequently services remain directed towards the needs of the productive economy and women therefore continue to lack access to the tools which could help them claim their rights. For example, public expenditure could be restructured to take account of the needs of the reproductive economy and switching to expenditure on services that will reduce the number of hours women work. Cuts in public expenditure in areas such as the health sector can result in a transfer of costs to the reproductive economy. Gender-sensitive public expenditure would mean improving public provision of services such as water and sanitation, transport and health, that can directly affect women's workload (Elson and Gideon 1997: 36).

Economic decision-making and rights

Any analysis of economies as gendered structures must also examine the gender balance in economic decision-making. This subject is particularly important because it focuses on women's empowerment in the process of economic growth and development. Raising the question, 'who decides?' highlights the distinction between participation in the production process and control over production. When the gender balance in economic decision-making is examined, we find that, when compared to men, women lack voice in all the key institutions of the economy. These absences enable male-biased norms to prevail. The exclusion of women from, or their subordinate position within key institutions, means that they are hindered from articulating and claiming their economic and social rights.

The Central American context

Central America is a region of small, economically vulnerable and trade-dependent countries, surrounded by larger and more industrialised ones. In an attempt to integrate the economies into the world market, economic reform packages have been introduced across Central America. The reforms have had varying impacts. The first country to undergo adjustment was Costa Rica, where a stabilisation programme was initiated in 1983. Guatemala initiated a programme in 1986, El Salvador in

1989, Honduras and Nicaragua, under the FSLN, in 1987. In each country the package included adjustment and stabilisation measures, especially exchange rate devaluation, a liberalisation of markets, cuts in public expenditure and investment, tightening of credit controls and a reduction of the role of the state.

The uncertain economic situation of the region has clear implications for the population. As the data in Table 8.1 illustrate, with the exception of Costa Rica, the region suffers from severe social inequality with widespread poverty in highly divided societies marked by violence of all kinds. Guatemala and El Salvador have suffered civil wars and Nicaragua underwent a revolution followed by counter-revolution. Ethnic difference is also an important axis of social inequality within Central America society, especially in Guatemala where the indigenous population constitutes around 60 per cent of the total population. In Guatemala, Honduras and Nicaragua around half the population lives below the poverty line, infant mortality rates are high as is the number of under weight children. Fertility levels in Central America are among the highest in Latin America and many women, especially poor women, start to have children at a young age. The figures presented in Table 8.1 hide

Table 8.1   Social imbalances in Central America: key indicators (mid-1990s)

	Costa Rica	El Salvador	Guatemala	Honduras	Nicaragua
Real GDP per capita (PPP$)	5,969	2,610	3,682	1,977	1,837
Real GDP per capita of poorest 20% (PPP$)	1,136	n.a.	357	399	479
Population below national poverty line (%) (1)	11	38	58	53	50
Total fertility rate (1995)	3.1	3.3	5.1	4.6	4.1
Annual population growth rate (%) (2)	2.8	4.8	2.9	3.2	2.8
Infant mortality rate (3)	13	34	43	29	44
Underweight children under 5 (%)	2	11	27	18	12
HDI rank	34	114	111	119	126

Notes:(1) = 1989–94; (2) = 1970–95; (3) = per 1000 live births; n.a. not available.
Source: UNDP 1998.

much of the variation that occurs between social classes and between rural and urban areas.

Despite high fertility rates, women in Central America are active in both the productive and reproductive economies (see below). In line with global trends, the region has seen an increase in women's employment in the paid economy. In general this has been a response to the economic crisis and restructuring in the region. However, women are more likely to be in lower paid, lower status jobs than men. As the indicators in Table 8.2 show, the share of income earned by women is on average around 27 per cent of the share of income earned by men. In addition, women are over-represented in the informal sector (Elson and Gideon 1997: 12). Women also lack access to the necessary inputs for production, and in particular, as a result of both legal and cultural norms, they do not have equal access to land.

Another important consequence of the shifts in economic conditions in the region has been changes in household size, composition and headship and today around one-third of households in Central America are headed by women.[6] It has also been argued that despite changing economic roles of men and women in the region, gender-based roles

Table 8.2   Gender differences in Central America: key indicators (mid-1990s)

	Costa Rica	El Salvador	Guatemala	Honduras	Nicaragua
GDI rank	39	103	113	114	115
GEM rank (1)	22	44	46	39	34
Seats in parliament held by women (%)	15.8	15.5	12.5	n.a.	n.a.
Female share of earned income (%)	26.9	33.6	21.3	24.4	28.3
Male share of earned income (%)	73.1	66.4	78.7	75.6	71.7
Households headed by women (%) (2)	20	26.6	16.9	20.4	24.3
Combined 1st, 2nd, 3rd level gross enrolment ratio – female	68.3	58.1	41.7	61.3	65.7
Combined 1st, 2nd, 3rd level gross enrolment ratio – male	59	52.2	46.5	56.2	59.7

Notes:(1) Figures are for 1995; (2) = 1990–92; n.a. not available. GDI = Gender Development Index; GEM = Gender Empowerment Measure.

Source: UNDP 1998, UNDP 1995, Chant 1999.

and identities have remained strong. Nevertheless, these norms have been challenged across the region and demands have been made for a redefinition of gender roles (Elson *et al.* 1997). The implications of these changes regarding rights are now discussed.

Economic and social rights in Central America

This section draws on the theoretical framework to explore gender differences in economic and social rights in Costa Rica, El Salvador, Guatemala, Honduras and Nicaragua. The analysis focuses on three key issues. Firstly, it assesses the implications of the legal 'fuzziness' of economic and social rights for poor women and men. Secondly, it looks at the way in which difference in time use between men and women has an impact on their ability to enjoy these rights. Finally, it considers the impact economic restructuring in the region has had on access to rights by low-income groups, highlighting the gender differences that have emerged.

Some indication of the status of women's rights in the region is possible through existing measurements such as the UNDP gender empowerment measurement (GEM).[7] However, while such indicators are useful, they do not fully reflect women's enjoyment of their economic and social rights. Moreover, for all the countries except Costa Rica, estimates of labour market data are used which casts some doubt on their validity, especially since these tend to underestimate the size of the informal sector; with particular implications for women who predominate in the sector (UNDP 1995).

Article 3: the right of all men and women to enjoy their economic, social and cultural rights

Despite the commitment made by governments to ensure that all men and women can enjoy their economic and social rights, in many cases legal norms exist which place women in a subordinate position and constitute them as dependants of men. While the constitution of a country may guarantee rights to all citizens, this is often undermined by civil laws. In Guatemala, for example, the Civil Code allows the husband to object to the wife engaging in activities outside the household, and restricts her right to personal fulfilment outside her function as wife and mother (Initial Report of Guatemala 1991, submitted to the CEDAW committee, cited in Steiner and Alston 1996: 890).[8] This is reinforced by social and cultural norms. Male and female identities based on traditional notions of reproduction and sexuality are still dominant and the gendered division of labour in the reproductive economy – in which women are responsible for looking after children and carrying out housework – is still firmly in place. However, women are also expected to undertake income generating activities alongside these responsibilities.

Understanding the economy as a gendered structure helps us to realise how the burden of work in the reproductive economy hinders women's ability to articulate and claim their economic and social rights. Evidence from around the world shows that women work longer hours than men; as a result women are more susceptible to 'time poverty' (Lister 1997: 133). In Central America data show that women work longer hours than men: available time budget studies from each country reveal that poor women work up to seventeen hours a day (paid and unpaid) while poor men work around nine hours a day. A study in rural Guatemala concluded that women's average work-burden was 17 per cent greater than men's (UNDP 1995: 91). One result is that women tend to have less leisure time than men. Women's lack of leisure time is a crucial dimension of gender equity and can impinge on both their mental and physical health. Women are also not able to participate equally in cultural activities; such activities are stressed in the ICESCR. As Lister (1997: 133) argues in another context, time is a resource that either constrains or facilitates choices in a highly gendered way. Since many women have less free time than men they are less able to access many of the rights set out in the ICESCR.

The economic reform programmes introduced across Central America have to some extent brought new opportunities for women. A large number of jobs have been created as a result of the increase in the production of nontraditional agricultural exports (NTAEs). However, economic restructuring can jeopardise economic and social rights and may particularly affect women. Studies suggest that although NTAEs may put limited additional income in women's hands, they do create more work for women. A UNICEF study (1994: 162) in Guatemala highlights the fact that women involved in the production of NTAEs, now work four hours more per day than previously. This may be because increased market-based demands mean that a higher output must be produced. Longer working days may not only risk women's own health and nutrition, but with the continued gender division of labour also affects the education, health and nutrition of their children.

Gender differences in time use may also impede women's ability to participate in decision-making arenas. Their reproductive responsibilities leave them less time for these additional activities. Furthermore, many families continue to function according to patriarchal norms, where men play a dominant role in decision-making processes and women remain marginalised (Fauné 1995: 8). Women therefore continue to lack voice in economic and policy debates and often fail to ensure their needs are met. Economic policy-making is dominated by the Ministries of Finance and the Central Banks, where women remain relatively scarce. Government institutions responsible for women's issues in Central America have only limited decision-making abilities, and none participates in the design and implementation of economic policy reform. These institutions vary in rank: for instance, in El Salvador, the recently created Instituto Salvadoreño de Desarollo de la Mujer is headed by the President of the Family Secretariat and includes representatives from different ministries and women's groups. In Guatemala, however, the National Office for Women is a low ranking body contained within the Ministry of Labour. Women do participate to some extent in the higher echelons of political, judicial and administrative power across the region (although this participation is quite limited in Guatemala); however, they tend to be concentrated in areas associated with women's traditional reproductive role, such as health and education, rather than in macroeconomic policy arenas (cf. Htun and Jones, Chapter 2 this volume).

In Central America, the majority of cooperatives, trade unions, NGOs, and trade and commercial organisations remain male-controlled, even where female membership is high. Active movements of women do exist in the region; however, they tend to focus more on social issues, such as domestic violence and human rights, than on issues of economic policy. Studies from the region illustrate the ways in which men dominate household decision-making, most notably through the control of resources (see for example Rojas and Román (1993) on Costa Rica; Chiriboga, Grynspan and Pérez (1995) on Central America; Renzi and Agurto (1997) on Nicaragua).

Article 6: the right to work and the full realisation of this right through access to the necessary training

Central American women are active in the paid economy yet their work is often unrecognised, especially in statistics. Official statistics suggest that agriculture is a male-intensive activity. Yet this is not consistent with evidence found in case studies from the region (IICA/BID 1993). These suggest that women work between four and five hours daily on family farms, and that their contribution rises at harvest time. Statistical surveys are clearly failing to make visible women's contribution to agriculture, especially their unpaid family work. This calls for the right to work to be reassessed to take account of these gender imbalances.

Incorporating the reproductive economy in our analysis also enables us to see that women suffer more constraints than men in their ability to participate in the productive economy. Unpaid work may limit women's participation in paid work, and may also mean that they are less able to attend training courses, particularly if these are not timetabled at hours that are convenient for women. Although some progress has been made in closing gender gaps in technical training in Central America, in an ILO study in Nicaragua, carried out in a number of training centres and factories with 55 male respondents and 46 female respondents, 33 per cent of the women cited their caring duties as the major factor inhibiting their participation in training programmes (ILO 1992).

Article 7: the right to fair wages, including equal remuneration for work of equal value, without discrimination of any kind

The wording of this article, in particular the right to fair wages, highlights the 'slipperiness' of some of the concepts included in the ICESCR. However, it is worth considering how gendered norms mean that women's work continues to be undervalued. Even where it is recognised in the paid economy women are more likely to be employed in low paid, low status jobs. The operation of markets links household and firms into the national economy. Yet as argued above, gender-based institutional bias means that men and women do not enjoy equal access to markets since they operate according to rules and norms that ignore the reproductive economy. In the labour markets wage gaps persist. An examination of the urban informal sector in Central America has revealed that the male-female wage gap is widest in the informal sector where most women are concentrated (Funkhouser 1996: 1746). In Honduras, the informal sector differential is around 40 per cent, although in the other countries it is around 25 per cent; whereas the formal sector gender differential across the region is generally around 10 per cent. Although there are few studies estimating the extent to which wage gaps are due to discrimination, one study in Nicaragua (Behrman and Wolfe 1991) has demonstrated that gender bias accounted for 70 per cent of the difference in male and female earnings in the period 1977–78.[9]

Labour markets are characterised by a gender imbalance in occupational structure. Women across the region are located in low paid, low status posts, while men dominate the higher ranking positions.

Professional and management sectors are male intensive while women are concentrated in personal services such as domestic workers, cooks and clerical workers (Elson *et al.* 1997). Tzannatos (1992) emphasised that it does not make economic sense to maintain gender discrimination in patterns of occupation and pay. If they were eliminated, not only would women's income increase considerably, but also national output could be increased by up to 5 per cent because of more effective allocation of labour. Furthermore, the expansion of global markets has forced governments to reconsider labour market policies and can limit governments' ability to secure economic and social rights for their citizens. This may have important gender implications since key stages of the production process of many NTAEs are often female intensive. In Central America NTAEs now include shellfish and horticultural products and fruit. Here a fairly rigid gendered division of labour is noticeable, the production phase is generally male intensive, while the processing and packing is a female-intensive activity (Fauné 1997).

In Costa Rica, the production of horticultural goods, pineapples and citrus fruit, is contracted out mainly to female smallscale production units. As contract workers women have little control over income from the sale of these products, since marketing tends to be organised by medium and large-scale enterprises which may be owned and controlled by foreign investors (Fauné 1997). Benefits gained from increased income may not be commensurate with the amount of extra work that is created for women. Equally, when production takes place in smallholder production units, women are often unable to market the product themselves and therefore have no control over any income accrued; whereas if women are working as wage labourers for commercial firms then issues regarding job security and health and safety measures require consideration. Women are therefore likely to have little direct access to export markets, which is of particular concern since NTAEs are likely to provide the basis for future expansion of exports.

Article 11: the right to an adequate standard of living

Gender differences are also apparent in the ability of men and women to claim their right to an adequate standard of living, a concept that is itself difficult to define. Gender norms force women to look for income generating activities that allow them to combine both their productive and reproductive roles, but this tends to confine women to activities which provide for survival, but not for improvements in growth and living standards. Fauné (1997) found that in Costa Rica, 58 per cent of female-headed households had a household-based enterprise compared to 16 per cent of male-headed households; in Nicaragua these figures rise to 87 per cent for female-headed households and 70 per cent for male-headed households (Renzi and Agurto 1994). Similarly, Funkhouser (1996) found that female household heads are more likely to work in the informal sector than women in male-headed households or men.

Given women's status as secondary or complementary workers, they are excluded from the resources necessary to improve their standard of living. Despite women's high involvement in agricultural production across the region, they do not have equal land ownership rights. Legal norms regarding land ownership and access to land have resulted in marked gender differences in all five countries (Chiriboga, Grynspan and Pérez 1995, Fundación Arias 1996). Laws may implicitly prevent women from gaining access to land through failing to recognise them as agricultural workers. In Nicaragua, although women were in principle given access to land during the Sandinista period, the assumption that women were not agricultural producers meant that land was not granted directly to them, either as members of cooperatives or as smallholder farmers. This bias has remained and between 1992 and 1994, as land redistribution continued, only 9.8 per cent was given to women. Furthermore, the average size of land plots given to women has been smaller than that given to men (Asociación de Mujeres Profesionales 1996: 26). If women do not own land they are also excluded from accessing other inputs necessary for production, such as credit and agricultural extension services.

Available data from all five countries highlight the gender barriers women face in access to formal credit market. The rules of participation in financial markets and the structure of loan management tend to favour propertied male producers and to exclude most women (cf. Goetz 1995). Although a number of special credit schemes have been introduced across the region which explicitly target women, the gender imbalance in credit allocation remains extremely wide. At most women receive 22 per cent of formal credit loan in Nicaragua. In addition, loans to women are likely to be smaller and may be between 40 and 70 per cent of the size of loans given to men (Renzi and Agurto 1993).[10] Although it is possible that women ask for smaller loans, institutional bias often means that formal lending services are not set up to administer small loans. Women therefore accrue higher transaction costs as a percentage of their total loan due to the fixed costs associated with lending. Another problem is that collateral is necessary to receive loans from formal sector institutions, again prejudicing women's access.

Article 12: the right to the highest attainable standard of physical and mental health

Another right emphasised in the ICESCR is the right to health and this has a number of important gender dimensions. A central element of the economic reform programmes has been a cutback in public expenditure. Public expenditure on physical and social infrastructure is critical for improving the productivity of women's labour in both the productive and reproductive economy. Yet at a regional level, government expenditure is declining in real terms (Elson and Gideon 1997). This means that the real costs are likely to be transferred to the unpaid reproductive economy, where women's labour is already overutilised. In Guatemala and El Salvador, where health spending is only 1 per cent of GNP, this is of particular concern (Elson *et al.* 1997). Throughout the region the emphasis on health care spending has been on curative rather than preventative care. In addition, the introduction of user charges in Honduras and Nicaragua in the early 1990s suggests further restrictions of access to health services. The current pattern of gender relations means that women are likely to be left to make up the shortfall in health care.

Another concern is the consequence of incomplete sharing of income within households on health and well-being. Evidence from Latin America shows that male household heads do not contribute all their wages to household needs, but keep varying proportions for discretionary personal expenditure on leisure items (Chant 1996: 8, López de Maizier 1997). This type of inequality has important consequences and can increase gender differences in well-being and good health. According to the World Bank, 'evidence from Guatemala has shown it takes fifteen times more spending to achieve a given improvement in child nutrition when income is earned by the father than by the mother' (World Bank 1993: 41). In Nicaragua, one survey found better nutritional status in female-headed households, compared to male-headed households (Renzi and Agurto 1994). With the exception of Costa Rica, there appears to be a considerable lack of large-scale sets of gender-disaggregated household data available. This should be a major priority for improvements of statistics that can contribute to the monitoring of economic and social rights.

Conclusions: strategies for change

To date much of the work in the area of gender and economic and social rights has discussed issues of citizenship, centring on how we must extend the notion of citizenship. Here, the analysis has focused on extending the notion of the economy to include the reproductive economy, to make women's exercise of their economic and social rights more effective.[11] The evidence from Central America clearly shows that if women are to enjoy their full economic and social rights there must be a rearticulation of the productive and reproductive economy so that women are not penalised by their obligations. This means acting to transform all key institutions of the productive economy, whether they are firms, banks, marketing systems or public sector organisations, in order that they should recognise the value of women's unpaid reproductive achievements.

In developing strategies that women's groups can adopt to bring about these changes, it is useful to look at the work around CEDAW. Activists have used their government's commitment to CEDAW as an advocacy tool to campaign for change in the position of women's rights in a number of countries around the world (Landsberg-Lewis 1998). Most recently they have been central to the move for the adoption of the optional protocol to CEDAW. Once approved,

> the protocol will give women the right to complain to the Committee on the Elimination of Discrimination against Women about violations of the Convention by their Governments. It will provide for better enforcement of women's rights and will enable the Committee to conduct inquires into serious or systematic abuses of women's rights in countries that are party to the protocol. It will also provide an avenue for women to obtain remedies for breaches of their human rights. (DAW press release, 12 March 1999)

Similarly women's groups in Central America can draw on this experience to campaign for an optional protocol to be adopted by the ICESCR. This will enable them to demand better enforcement of their economic and social rights. Groups can also use their governments commitment to the ICESCR as an advocacy tool and develop local and regional movements around these issues. Although, as Dairiam, the director of International Women's Rights Action Watch Asia Pacific warns, the existence of a positive legal framework for women's rights does not automatically confer rights on women; it does however legitimise women's claims for rights and make possible women's transformation from passive beneficiaries to active claimants (Landsberg-Lewis 1998: 9). Similar arguments apply to the women's claims for their economic and social rights.

Women's movements exist in all five countries, and they have been involved in ensuring their governments maintain their commitment to CEDAW, reinforced in Beijing. Much of this work could now be further developed to incorporate economic and social rights. Organisations such as FIDEG (Fundación Internacional para el Desafío Económico Global) in Nicaragua have already carried out considerable research that highlight gender imbalances in the economy. In proposing new strategies to overcome this, FIDEG have produced a gendered analysis of the Nicaraguan economy (Renzi and Agurto 1997). This could be the first step in developing a satellite account which would highlight the value of women's unpaid work to national economic productivity and development. Similarly, in Costa Rica the Comité de América Latina y el Caribe para la Defensa de los Derechos de la Mujer (CLADEM) has used the constitutional court to challenge successfully the practice of requiring a husband's consent to carry out medical sterilisation (Landsberg-Lewis 1998: 24). Moreover, in Costa Rica other long-term developments have taken place and the question of gender equality has been addressed at state level. In 1995, for example, the Plan Nacional para la Igualdad de Oportunidades entre Mujeres y Hombres (National Plan for Equal Opportunities between Women and Men) was a high profile government attempt to integrate gender equality into public policy.

Information generated from these types of initiatives can be used to prepare 'shadow reports' for the Committee on Economic, Social and Cultural Rights in the same way that women's groups have prepared shadow reports for the CEDAW Committee (Landsberg-Lewis 1998: 35). Countries are expected to submit reports to the Committee on the status of economic and social rights every five years and input from NGOs is welcomed. This could provide an important entry point for women's groups to begin to hold governments accountable over not only their civil and political rights, but also their economic and social rights.

Notes

1 The author wishes to express her thanks to Diane Elson, Barbara Evers and John Salter for their helpful comments on this chapter. She would also like to thank the editors for their suggestions.
2 Keynes argued that it was the responsibilities of governments to maintain adequate levels of employment and ensure that all those who wished to have a job could do so, furthermore he envisaged that this would require some socialisation of spending.

3 It is necessary to make two additional points here. Firstly, it must be remembered that these decisions were made in a particular cultural context. Rights are only meaningful if people exercise them and recognise their existence for others. Secondly, it is important to note that not all citizens are aware of all of their rights and are therefore not necessarily in positive agreement with them.

4 In light of these problems a project is currently underway to develop a standard formatting for documenting violations of certain economic and social rights. The project has been initiated by the Washington-based Science and Human Rights programme of the American Association for the Advancement of Science and Human Rights Information and Documentation Systems, International (HURIDOCS), an NGO based in Geneva. In 1996 the group began to develop a 'violations approach' to monitoring economic and social rights, based on the ICESCR. The project has developed a resource manual for monitoring the right to education, the right to food, the right to health, the right to housing and the right to work. Although these manuals do not claim to attempt to quantify these rights *per se*, they do provide specific and practical strategies for monitoring rights. While a discussion of this is beyond the scope of this chapter more details of the project can be found at their web address <http://shr.aas.org.escr>. A critique of their work from a gender perspective can also be found in Gideon and Elson (1999).

5 See e.g. Molyneux (1998) for further discussion of this.

6 The calculation of the number of female-headed households has been disputed by some authors (see e.g. Varley 1996).

7 The gender empowerment measurement (GEM) measures the ability of women and men to actively participate in economic and political life and take part in decision-making. It focuses on three variables, reflecting respectively women's participation in political decision-making, their access to professional opportunities and their earning power (UNDP 1995: 72).

8 Certain articles in the Guatemalan Civil Code have recently been challenged by the Inter-American Commission on Human Rights (Case 11.625: María Eugenia Morales de Sierra). The case, initiated in 1995, on the grounds that the Civil Code establishes a legal regime defining the role of spouses within a marriage that creates distinctions between men and women which are discriminatory and violate the American Convention on Human Rights. This points to the need for reform of the Civil Code as well as the ways in which women can use legal means to challenge their subordinate status within society. Full details of the case are available in the 1997 Inter-American Commission on Human Rights annual report, available on the website: <www.cidh.oas.org/annualrep/97eng/97ench3Lan.htm>.

9 While these are old data, a more up-to-date study was not located by the author. This highlights the need for more research in this area.

10 It would be interesting to know whether more women than men are refused loans although the author was unable to locate this information.

11 Feminist consultant Maruja Barrig commented that rights discourse is less used in Central America than other parts of Latin America. Furthermore, many women activists in Latin America are not aware of the ICESCR (cf. Craske 2000).

Bibliography

Acker, J. (1992) 'Gendered institutions: from sex roles to gendered institutions' *Contemporary Sociology*, 21 (5) 565–69

Alston, P. (1987) 'Out of the abyss: the challenges confronting the new UN Committee on Economic, Social and Cultural Rights' *Human Rights Quarterly*, 9, 332–81

Asociación de Mujeres Profesionales (1996) 'El Ejercicio de los Derechos de las Mujeres en Nicaragua: Un análisis de Género' Managua: Consultancy Report for SIDA

Beetham, D. (1995) 'What future for economic and social rights?' *Political Studies*, 43, 41–60

Behrman, J. R. and B. L. Wolfe (1991) 'Earnings and determinants of labor force participation in a developing country: are there gender differentials?' in N. Birdsall and R. Sabot (eds) *Unfair Advantage: Labor Market Discrimination in Developing Countries*, Washington DC: World Bank Regional and Sectoral Studies, 95–120

Chant, S. (1996) *Women-Headed Households: Diversity and Dynamics in the Developing World*, Basingstoke: Macmillan – now Palgrave

Chant, S. (1999) 'Population, migration, employment and gender' in R. Gwynne and C. Kay (eds) *Latin America Transformed. Globalisation and Modernity*, London: Arnold, 226–70.

Chapman, A. (1996) ' "A violations approach" for monitoring the International Covenant on Economic, Social and Cultural Rights' *Human Rights Quarterly*, 18, 23–66

Chiriboga, M., R. Grynspan, and L. Pérez (1995) *Mujeres de Maíz. Programa de análisis de la politica del sector agropecuario frente a la mujer productora de alimentos en Centroamérica y Panamá*, San José: IICA/ BID

Clarke, R. and J. French (1995) 'Issues in the enforceability of human rights: a Caribbean perspective' in Margaret Schuler (ed.) *From Basic Needs to Basic Rights*, Washington, DC: Women, Law and Development International, 103–22

Cornia, G. A., R. Jolly, and F. Stewart (1987) *Adjustment with a Human Face*, Oxford: Clarendon Press

Craske, N. (2000) *Continuing the Challenge: The Contemporary Latin American Women's Movement(s)*, Liverpool: Institute of Latin American Research Paper 23

DAW, press release 12 March 1999, downloaded from internet: <www.un.org. daw/cedaw/protocol/adopted.htm>

Elson, D. and B. Evers (1998) *Sector Programme Support: The Health Sector. A Gender Aware Analysis*, GENECON Unit: University of Manchester

Elson, D. and J. Gideon (1997) *Gender Aware Country Economic Reports: Nicaragua*, working paper no. 4, GENECON Unit: University of Manchester

Elson, D. and J. Gideon (1999) *The International Covenant on Economic, Social and Cultural Rights and the Economic Empowerment of Women*, working paper, UNIFEM, New York

Elson, D., B. Evers, and J. Gideon (1997) *Gender Aware Country Economic Reports: Concepts and Sources*, working paper no. 1, GENECON Unit: University of Manchester

Elson, D., M. A. Fauné, J. Gideon, M. Gutiérrez, A. López de Maizier, and E. Sacayón (1997) *Crecer con la Mujer: Oportunidades para el Desarrollo Económico Centroamericana*, San José: Embajada Real de los Paises Bajos

Fauné, M. A. (1995) *Mujeres y Familias Centroamericanas: Principales Problemas y Tendencias*, Tomo III, San José: PNUD

Fauné, M. A. (1997) 'Costa Rica: gender aware country strategy report' in D. Elson, M. A. Fauné, J. Gideon, M. Gutiérrez, A. López de Maizier and E. Sacayón *Crecer con la Mujer: Oportunidades para el Desarrollo Económico Centroamericana*, San José: Embajada Real de los Paises Bajos

Fundación Arias (1996) *El Acceso de las Mujeres a la Tierra en Centroamerica*, Memoria del Taller Centroamericana, San José: Fundación Arias

Funkhouser, E. (1996) 'The urban informal sector in Central America: household survey evidence' *World Development*, 24 (11) 1737–51

Goetz, A. M. (1995) 'Macro-meso-micro linkages: understanding gendered institutional structures and practices' a contribution to the SAGA workshop on Gender and Economic Reform in Africa, Ottawa, 1–3 October

Goetz, A. M. (1997) *Getting Institutions Right for Women in Development*, London: Zed Books

IICA/BID (1993) *Mujeres Productoras de Alimentos en Centroamérica y Políticas Sectoriales*, Costa Rica: IICA

ILO/OIT 'Consejería Regional para la Mujer Trabajadora (1992) Promoción de la participación de la mujer en la formación técnica y profesional' mimeo, Managua, OIT

Lamarche, L. (1995) 'Women's social and economic rights: a case for real rights' in M. Schuler (ed.) *From Basic Needs to Basic Rights*, Washington, DC: Women, Law and Development International, 77–103

Landsberg-Lewis, I. (1998) *Bringing Equality Home. Implementing the Convention on the Elimination of all Forms of Discrimination against Women*, New York: UNIFEM

Lister, R. (1997) *Citizenship: Feminist Perspectives*, Basingstoke: Macmillan – now Palgrave

Lister, R. (2000) 'Inclusion/exclusion: the Janus face of citizenship' in J. Cook, J. Roberts and G. Waylen (eds) *Towards a Gendered Political Economy*, Basingstoke: Macmillan – now Palgrave

López de Maizier, A. (1997) 'Honduras: gender aware country strategy report' in Diane Elson, M. A. Fauné, J. Gideon, M. Gutiérrez, A. López de Maizier and E. Sacayón *Crecer con la Mujer: Oportunidades para el Desarrollo Económico Centroamericana*, San José: Embajada Real de los Paises Bajos

Marshall, T. H. (1950) *Citizenship and Social Class*, Cambridge: Cambridge University Press

Molyneux, M. (1998) 'Analysing women's movements' *Development and Change*, 29 (2) 219–45

Neuhold, B. (1998) 'Women's economic rights as part of international declarations and conventions' *Women In Development Europe Bulletin*, Feb. 4–11

Peterson, V. S. and L. Parisi (1998) 'Are women human? It's not an academic question' in T. Evans (ed.) *Human Rights Fifty Years On: A Reappraisal*, Manchester: Manchester University Press

Renzi, M. R. and S. Agurto (1993) *Qué Hace la Mujer Nicaragüense Ante la Crisis Económica?* Managua: FIDEG

Renzi, M. R. and S. Agurto (1994) *Impacto de los Proyectos FISE en las Condiciones de Vida de los Nicaragüenses*, Managua: FIDEG

Renzi, M. R. and S. Agurto (1997) *La Esperanza Tiene Nombre de Mujer. La Economía Nicaragüense Desde una Perspectiva de Género*, Managua: FIDEG

Rojas, M. and I. Román (1993) 'Agricultura de exportación y pequeños productores en Costa Rica' *Cuaderno No. 61*, San José: FLACSO

Schuler, M. (1995) *From Basic Needs to Basic Rights*, Washington DC: Women, Law and Development International

Steiner, H. and P. Alston (1996) *International Human Rights in Context. Law, Politics, Morals*, Oxford: Clarendon Press

Tzannatos, Z. (1992) 'Potential gains from the elimination of gender differentials in the labour market' in *Women's Employment and Pay in Latin America Part 1: Overview and Methodology*, Regional Studies Program, Report No.10, Washington DC: World Bank

UNDP (1995) *United Nations Human Development Report*, Oxford: Oxford University Press

UNDP (1998) *United Nations Human Development Report*, Oxford: Oxford University Press

UNICEF/SEGEPLAN (1994) *Realidad Socioeconomica de Guatemala, con Enfasis en la Situación del Niño y la Mujer*, Guatemala City: Editoria Piedra Santa

Varley, A. (1996) 'Women-headed households: some more equal than others?' *World Development*, 24 (3) 505–20

Whelan, D. (1998) 'Recasting WID: a human rights approach' working paper no. 6. Washington DC: International Centre for Research on Women

Williams, M. (1998) 'What are economic and social rights? Women's economic and social rights', *Women in Development Europe Bulletin*, Feb. 12–18

World Bank (1993) *World Development Report*, Oxford: Oxford University Press

9

The Struggle by Latin American Feminisms for Rights and Autonomy

Virginia Vargas[1]

Editors' note

We end this volume with a chapter by Virginia Vargas, a feminist activist of the 'historic' generation who has participated in the struggle for democracy and women's rights at the national (Peru), regional and international levels. She is a founding member of the feminist NGO Centro Flora Tristán in Lima, and was Coordinator of Latin American and Caribbean NGOs for the fourth World Conference of Women. She has participated in debates and discussions in many countries both as activist and academic/researcher. In Peru she has long been engaged in the struggle for democracy and was candidate for Congress in 1985. In recent times she has been an outspoken critic of President Fujimori and was one of the leading activists in a coordinating organisation Women for Democracy (Mujeres por la Democracia). Here Vargas offers a critical evaluation of the emergence and use of the rights-based discourse in Latin America over recent years. In so doing, she highlights many of the issues raised by the other contributors, drawing our attention to a theme we highlighted in Chapter 1: that democratisation and the struggle for women's rights cannot be separated. Furthermore, she also emphasises that rights must be understood in the broadest terms in order to enhance their strategic usefulness. In this respect she sees the state as an important terrain on which to pursue the various struggles around rights, as long as social movements retain their autonomy and work in other 'spaces and places'. So whilst she acknowledges the important advances made by women in their dialogue with the state, regional and international institutions and other women's movements nationally and regionally, she cautions that too much emphasis on the formal

embodiment of rights can detract from more substantive questions and can
undermine certain cultural changes necessary for genuine democratisation.
   This caution in regard to the conditions under which rights are fought for,
reflects the difficult experiences that Peru has undergone over the last quarter of
the twentieth century. It has not only suffered a high degree of civil violence
during the days of the Sendero Luminoso guerrilla movement, but has been
cursed with inefficient administrations, and, latterly, the increasingly authori-
tarian and demagogic government of Fujimori. But, as the other chapters in
this volume indicate, her words have resonance beyond the Peruvian context as
well as offering a testimony to the dramatic political events in Peru.

Continuity and change

Towards the end of the twentieth century, second-wave feminism in
Latin America was confronted by a series of profound transformations
in national, regional and global contexts. These changes affected,
altered and disarticulated the different forms of feminist organising
that had emerged and been consolidated in most countries in the region
in the 1970s and 1980s. The Latin American feminisms that had developed during these decades questioned cultural visions and political
paradigms which concealed the complexity of underlying power relations between men and women in socioeconomic, political, cultural and
sexual life. Different types of feminist organisations were founded, from
action oriented collectives to nongovernmental organisations (NGOs),
coalitions and issue- and identity-based networks, both formal and
informal. From the start, the networks provided a link between national
level issues and experiences, in an empowering exchange which generated regional perspectives and channels for lobbying. The actions of
these various groups were underpinned by sustained work in grassroots
women's movements – a two-way learning process that had a permanent impact on the feminist agenda. During this period feminist campaigns were mainly concerned with revealing the political nature of the
private and promoting the cultural transformation of society's
'common-sense' belief systems, by politicising women's uneasiness
about their subordinate situations in daily life and with antidemocratic
gender arrangements (Tamayo 1998).
   These transformations were initially pursued within the framework of
an approach which prioritised feminist identity and declared the shared
experience of gender subordination to be the keystone in the construction of unity among women, leading to undifferentiated policies of
feminist 'sisterhood'. The movement's vision of autonomy, which

centred on the claim to its own space and discourse, allowed it to establish its limits, build its identity and subsequently 'demand to be heard' (Nun 1989). This claim to a voice and a space of its own translated into collective action, street demonstrations and the introduction of new topics for reflection and public debate. As a result, women became visible as social subjects and the conditions were created for the dissemination of feminist proposals within society.

Early on, a large number of feminist organisations adopted a 'double role' both as work centres and active participants in the feminist movement, which took the form of voluntary work. This parallel development proved to be enriching and empowering. The individual organisations acted as conduits for the broader movement's ideas and encouraged an increasing efficiency in the production of knowledge and proposals.

The transition from the 1980s to the 1990s heralded a series of transformations in political, ideological, economic and cultural spheres. The feminist movement was both influenced by and contributed to these transformations. One of the most important changes was the recovery of democratic government in Latin America. New spaces and debates to do with consensus-building and the acknowledgement of differences were emerging. At the same time, states were prioritising reforms, both institutional (state and judicial reform) and in relation to questions such as governability and decentralisation, which were being promoted by civil society.

These changed circumstances heralded increased possibilities for the consolidation of democracy and greater leeway to pursue women's multiple interests. Women's issues steadily became more visible in society, and governments started to demonstrate an unprecedented concern to tackle gender-based discrimination. In consequence, it appeared more likely that the transformations to the existing order that had been pursued by feminists in the 1980s could be accomplished. Many feminist demands were, in fact, addressed in legislation or through the institutionalisation of women's issues. There was also the introduction of affirmative action and quota policies to ensure a greater female presence in deliberative and decision-making arenas (see Htun and Jones, Chapter 2 this volume). The notion that women 'deserved to have rights' began to be asserted.

These advances were taking place at the same time as the neoliberal economic model was being widely adopted by governments throughout the region (and globally). The neoliberal system aimed to resolve the economic instability of previous decades by attempting to reduce inflation and stimulate economic growth. Such 'amendments' to earlier economic failures were, nevertheless, unable to reduce social inequality and poverty, and existing gaps between social groups widened along the lines of race, ethnicity, age, class and geographical location. As a consequence, women's room to manoeuvre and their autonomy were restricted. However, it appeared that the new feminist transformational discourses were unable to articulate a response to these two contradictory dynamics: namely, the advances in the concept of women as the bearers of rights and the steadily worsening standard of living.

The 1990s also witnessed realignments on the international stage, a result of the ambiguous process of globalisation and the revision of the UN's mandate. Feminists began to establish a presence in spaces that were opening up at regional and global levels. In this way, they aimed to influence an international agenda that was addressing a range of situations of exclusion and subordination (affecting girls, women, the poor) and was redefining the great problems of our era: human rights, the environment, population, development to name but some. A significant number of feminist institutions participated in the 'debates' on the content and future perspectives of each of these issues. Feminists thus started to become fundamental actors in the construction of democratic spaces within regional and global civil society.[2]

These innovative incursions at national and supranational levels were encouraged by the new accent on the multiplicity of possible sites of struggle (Phillips 1993). Without abandoning the micro level of democratising everyday life (democratisation of the intimate), it became apparent that different feminist currents were emerging and consolidating their presence and proposals at the macro level. These new currents focused their attention and energies on the question of women's membership of the political community, exploring – as Anne Phillips might say – issues of inclusion and exclusion and challenging the universalist pretensions of modern political thought.

In line with this evolving approach , the new core concepts of democracy and citizenship began to be discussed. Both notions implied the need for a much closer dialogue between states and civil society than had existed in the previous decade. These questions came to be regarded as fundamentally important following the processes of dialogue, negotiation and political participation that were promoted by a broad-based feminist movement within the framework of the UN world summits and conferences of the 1990s. Feminist approaches to the questions of citizenship and democracy were underpinned by a range of strategies which sought to ensure the continued progression towards gender equality in the future, by defending the advances already achieved and further expanding women's citizenship rights. The rights discourse – both public and private – therefore became essential for consolidating the gains that had been made over the preceding 25 years.

The public sphere of social and political intercourse was also affected by the changes in the nature of feminist organising. Many of the organisations that, in the 1980s, had been able to combine movement activism with the creation of work centres or nongovernmental organisations began to appear more like the 'institutionalised' face of feminism. Institutionalisation did not take place only within feminist NGOs. Another example was the establishment of gender studies departments or courses in universities, which signified a huge step forward in terms of the production of knowledge and the creation of new feminisms. In the case of feminist NGOs, however, it appears that the experiences of institutionalisation and negotiation with states and governments led to a sharper focus on questions that were linked less to women's movements and civil society, and more with the need to develop effective strategies in their dealings with public authorities. This tendency was reinforced by the fact that greater emphasis was placed on the public political sphere, agendas were being pared down and energies were concentrated on developing successful lobbying tactics. As a result, central feminist concerns were marginalised and dialogue with other actors in the public arena was weakened.

In these changed circumstances and in line with the new directions being taken by feminisms, many of the concerns that had first been raised in the 1980s began to enter public debate and institutional agendas, distancing them from their original contexts. The incorporation of some feminist proposals from the 1980s into state programmes undoubtedly implied an advance for a significantly greater number of women. Nevertheless, it also led to increased uncertainty regarding the nature of the transformations that feminists wished to achieve, in contrast to the clarity of objectives that had accompanied the movement's development during the previous decades and its establishment as a political and social actor.[3]

Civil society and government: the 'shared' rights discourse

It is clear that the restoration of democracy in Latin America facilitated the adoption of the rights-based discourse by the main sectors of the feminist movement. In tandem, the recently installed governments consolidated their democratic credentials by employing a similar rhetoric and emphasising the construction of citizenship. In practice, however, these two sets of actors adopted quite different approaches to the rights question. Feminists started from the assumption – at least in theory – that the meaning of rights should be discussed from the standpoint of women. This implied questioning the supposed universality of traditional concepts of democracy and citizenship, and drawing attention to their formal, partial and exclusionary nature. In addition, it meant presenting inclusive and subversive proposals, not only to the state, but also to civil society, for the latter both to implement and promote. Evelina Dagnino (1998) notes that the starting point is not a legal approach to winning formal, abstract rights or the implementation of existing rights, but rather the affirmation of the 'right to have rights'. As well as admitting the possible specification of new rights, this formulation includes equality and the right to be different. The notion of the 'right to have rights' implies acknowledgement of their shifting nature.[4] In other words, it allows for the expansion of rights and the identification of previously unrecognised ones from the viewpoint of social actors, rather than their limitation to those that have already been defined. This perspective can therefore include concepts that until now have been devalued within the formal logic of rights; for instance, the social dimension of citizenship (economic rights) or a broader concept of civic citizenship which incorporates sexual rights. This understanding of the question of rights contributed to the elaboration of clearly differentiated and autonomous feminist agendas, which were used as the basis for action and for negotiating with governments.

A key development of the 1990s was the emphasis that governments placed on the rhetoric of rights and the 'recognition' of women's citizenship. By adopting this position, governments found themselves obliged to respond to the pressure from women's movements to define and grant a set of rights to women (while simultaneously restricting other rights, such as economic ones). This was regarded as part of the unfinished task of modernisation and of the concept of good governance as it had evolved over the preceding decade. At the same time, the widespread application of the neoliberal economic model increased social inequalities and widened the gaps between citizens based on ethnic, gender, class and geographical differences. In practice, the neoliberal viewpoint does not recognise the different dimensions of citizenship (civil, political, socioeconomic, cultural). Instead, it tends to promote the construction of citizenship starting from a minimalist conception of democracy, and equates rights with individual access to the market. As Barrig (1998: 7) points out, the perspective adopted by governments illustrates two problems with current forms of democracy in the region: 'the devaluation of democracy to a simple electoral exercise, denying its participatory dimension, through which the articulation of different social voices could enrich government policy; and a practice embedded in the political system that regularly transforms citizens into clients.'

The fact that the 'consensus' regarding the importance of citizens' rights proceeded from different starting points and perspectives meant that feminists were faced with a contradictory and ambiguous situation. On the one hand, it presented increased scope for negotiation and opened up new possibilities for addressing some of the most extreme aspects of women's subordination. This was evident from the debates held and gains made in the international arena of the UN conferences, and the establishment in most Latin American countries of institutional machineries dealing with women's issues. The objective of these women's offices was to incorporate the question of 'gender equality' into public policy-making and in several cases they successfully promoted affirmative action laws or measures, such as electoral 'quotas'.[5] Moreover, in many countries feminists began working in these new governmental institutions,[6] which meant that there was a greater likelihood of a more flexible understanding of women's rights. These experiences demonstrated that the state is not a homogeneous or unitary structure, but a differentiated set of institutions, agencies and discourses, shaped by specific historical and political contexts, which means that it is also a valid site of struggle for social movements (Waylen 1996). In contrast, the feminist movement's point of departure necessitates the formulation of multiple strategies to seek improved conditions for negotiation. This means making the rigid and exclusionary space of formal politics more flexible and participating in debates on conceptual meanings and the whole range of public issues. Otherwise there is a real danger that the feminist presence and proposals may disappear and long-term transformations may no longer be promoted.[7]

The Gordian knot of autonomy in negotiation

Without doubt, feminist movements have a political and historical responsibility to mediate and consolidate the gains made by and for women. It is also essential to recognise that such interactions take place in a setting of unequal power relations and contrasting perspectives.

These facts bring us to one of the most problematic and inescapable tensions affecting the feminist (and every other social) movement: how to maintain the transformational radicalism of feminist thought and action when entering public, political spaces to negotiate and define agendas that affect women.

For the diverse currents of the feminist movement that had emerged and consolidated their identity in opposition to the state during the 1970s and 1980s, the opportunity to exercise the right to make demands on and draw up agreements with public authorities, and to take advantage of the openings in the system, represented an important step forward. This was because it not only improved women's capacity for negotiation, but also enhanced the democratic nature of society by making women visible in those arenas previously monopolised by men. The multiplication of potential sites and modes of participation increased the possibilities for the wide range of women's interests to develop politically and become part of the public agenda. On the other hand, this process entailed the risky business of negotiating from a subordinate position and dealing with the impenetrable workings of government. The movement also faced the ever-present dangers of losing its identity as an expression of democratic civil society and the depoliticisation of women's agendas.[8]

In order to avoid these pitfalls, the autonomy of feminist agendas must be preserved. The bias of existing views on rights and the 'natural' assumptions regarding women's status as second-class citizens must be challenged. The independent nature of feminist projects is what permanently underpins the 'struggle' over the meanings and contents of existing processes. It is not, however, a question of reasserting a defensive and confrontational autonomy, such as that which characterised the first phase of the movement's evolution.[9] The rights-based discourse that emerged in the 1990s implied the development of a much broader universe of relations for feminist movements, with a wider range of interests, more flexible identities and unprecedented forms of interaction between state and civil society. In this context, the meaning of autonomy became more complex and less rigid.

Autonomy has always been one of the central political issues for second-wave feminisms. Both conceptually and in practice it has proved fundamental for the consolidation of an independent platform. The political dimension of autonomy is expressed in the capacity to define one's own agenda, as an emancipatory strategy which allows interaction with society and the state. Since autonomy is a personal and collective practice that occurs within a specific context, its meaning has altered, becoming open to a wider range of interpretations, in line with the expansion of feminist interventions.

The autonomy of feminist movements in the 1990s tended to be based on a position that promoted dialogue and negotiation, while questioning the limits of existing systems. But this process of challenging boundaries requires that feminists' political autonomy be reaffirmed through the presentation of a radically different project for society, expressed in a language and agenda of its own. From this basis feminist movements can start to build up the necessary support networks and alliances, and at the same time maintain a critical view of the limits of actually existing democracies. The only way to incorporate the needs, knowledge, rights and utopian visions of those who are not part of the mainstream is that they themselves present proposals and exert pressure.

It is important to bear in mind that we are discussing exploratory and open-ended processes, which do not start from a single truth or definition of autonomy. As Paoli and da Silva Telles (1998) point out, the Latin American contexts, as well as being marked by inequalities, growing poverty, discrimination, violence, and the persistence of hierarchies and authoritarian social relations, are characterised by a high degree of uncertainty regarding the potential for change. However, this unpredictability also implies a range of new openings for emergent civil society to investigate. In view of this, the complex implications of the practice of autonomy should be taken less as rigid norms, and more as 'guiding tensions'; particularly in the face of the ambiguities of democracy, the perils involved in entering unfamiliar spaces, and the uncertainties surrounding the end of the millennium. These 'guiding tensions' can therefore serve to point the way towards how and when to negotiate, and how and with whom to make alliances. They can, moreover, demonstrate how advances made with respect to one dimension of autonomy may delegitimise, weaken or negate other aspects, and thus they help to maintain a balance between ethics and compromise. However, for the uncertainty and ambiguity to become 'guiding tensions', it is essential that we analyse the potential dangers of these interventions for feminist strategising today.

The risks of the discourse of rights for feminism today

The most important political recourse employed by feminists in the 1990s was the policy of negotiation with actors in the public political sphere, with the aim of increasing women's participation and improving their legal status.[10] However, it gave rise to a series of tensions and conflicts because it neglected other strategies which could widen women's access to democracy, or promote alternative dimensions of women's autonomy and citizenship. As such, feminism depends upon the support of a broader movement in civil society to bolster its minority position and help create a critical mass, which would help counterbalance the impact of its interaction with institutional logic (Guzmán 1996). This base of support, however, has weakened in recent years.

Many feminists, both in Latin America and elsewhere, have highlighted these problems. For instance, Loes Keyser (1996: 2) states, with reference to the progress made at the World Conference on Population and Development in Cairo (1994), that 'the gains have not been without costs'. In her view, the transformational potential of the feminist project is threatened by an agenda on reproductive rights and health that does not combine the campaign for women's rights to self-determination and well-being with the struggle for socioeconomic and political transformations that will enable women to exercise those rights. Another cost, according to Kayser, is the legitimisation of official discourses that modify government agendas but have no real impact, while feminist projects are neglected. Barrig (1997), in her paper on feminist NGOs in Chile, states that 'the movement is not moving forward and there is little renewal in its ranks'. Moreover, in relations with the state, elements of the feminist movement exercise self-censorship and have lost the motivation and need to define its own agenda, since there is no space to build a critical mass (ibid.). Giulia Tamayo (1997) recently warned against the

> extreme turn being taken by feminist activism it its attempt to influence government policies and mechanisms...which neglects the strengthening of citizenship and is especially problematic in the case of governments that are trying to appear democratic when in fact they are not.

Similarly, in their analysis of the Brazilian case, Shumaher and Vargas (1997: 141) argue that

> if we refer to public policies in a strict sense – in other words, as a series of interlinked measures that represent direct government actions in particular areas which aim to intervene in specific social realities – then we must accept that the agenda of the [governmental Women's]

Councils was limited to targeted interventions and localised actions that did not lead to the implementation of public policies.

Sonia Alvarez (1997), for her part, states that the previously clear division between civil society and governments, and between the approaches taken by each, is being eroded. Increasingly, social actors are adopting an exclusive focus on realisable strategies, without even any mention being made of what is really desirable.

Thus, it would seem that feminist incursions into the sphere of formal politics privileged strategies that aimed at strengthening some of the political dimensions of citizenship, whereas little attention was paid to the contents of what was 'under discussion'. Likewise, less energy was directed towards demanding a greater institutionalisation of democracy, and no new strategies were developed to pursue political and cultural transformations or to construct alternative spaces of opposition within civil society. There are many aggravating factors, which do not only relate to how priorities are set in negotiations or how agendas are defined. Other relevant factors include more global changes, the characteristics of political cultures in Latin America, the new forms of feminism that are taking shape, and the ways in which feminist campaigns interact with other democratic struggles within society.

Feminism has changed, and not simply as a consequence of its expansion and decentralisation in multiple arenas and sites of action. As Alvarez (1998) notes, these processes have been accompanied by the accentuation of imbalances between women who act at distinct levels and occupy different spaces. The field of feminist activism, she concludes, is characterised by unequal power relations, which reveal a growing division between two foundational elements of the transformational project of the 1970s and 1980s: its ethical-cultural and structural-institutional dimensions. As a result, the movement's presence appears greatly weakened and, paradoxically, the priority assigned to debating contents and meanings in formal political spaces has meant that in many cases the movement's visibility as an oppositional force within society has faded.

The advancing process of fragmentation and erosion is partly related to the cycles experienced by social movements and to the negative effects of the dynamics of globalisation and neoliberalism.[11] It is also linked to what several authors (Alvarez, most insistently) have called the 'NGOisation' of the feminist movement. The term refers to the fact that in the 1990s Latin American feminisms expressed themselves basically through the work and agendas of feminist NGOs. These had access to external funding (although this is now drying up) and employed full-time professionals, placing them in a privileged position to define the most visible feminist actions and strategies. The NGOs tended to ascribe particular importance to negotiation with the state, reducing the space for the development of strategies relating to the modification of gender stereotypes, awareness-raising, cultural transformations, the inclusion of social diversity and the construction of alliances with other opposition sectors. The approaches developed in the 1990s changed the original 'double role' and increased the 'institutionalisation' of feminist organisations, thus curtailing the multifaceted expressions of the movement as a whole.

As Guzmán (1996) identifies, the relationship with women's movement and other democratic movements was also undermined, which resulted in a weakening of the connections they had established with women who were even more marginalised from power. Consequently, those networks that were established during the 1980s were isolated and became invisible in analyses and debates. This, in turn, undermined feminisms' openness and responsiveness to issues emerging from other social arenas. Without the alliances and interactions which work to transform political culture, the social base of the feminist movement disappears, thus limiting its chances of 'gaining' recognition and its capacity to influence civil society and the government.[12] The potential value of the rights-based approach is also reduced and its ambiguity becomes fully evident, as many authors have warned. Even while we acknowledge its political and practical usefulness in widening women's frames of reference and in encapsulating the idea – as Fraser and Gordon (1997) might say – of having the right to something rather than receiving it as 'charity', this discourse can be misleading because it reinforces one type of rights, namely, formal, political ones (and one dimension of autonomy) at the expense of others. Birgin (1997) argues that it masks real differences between rights that are being claimed (increasingly by women), recognised rights (always restricted in number) and fully awarded rights (even fewer). Molyneux (1998) points out that there are similar risks entailed in the notion of an active citizenship if it is not linked to strategies that are part of a long-term project covering not only political but also economic and social reforms. The equivocal nature of citizenship therefore becomes clear. It is revealed as a 'true lie', in that it contains the promise of equality in the face of great inequalities, but in practice concedes a purely formal equality to those who are in fact not substantively equal (Franco 1997).[13]

Perhaps the most problematic effect of the rights-based approach is one that has already been mentioned at several points in the chapter: the disappearance of the feminist movement's own agenda. This has reduced the opportunities for building a broad base of support for the feminist struggle within civil society, which could exert the kind of pressure needed to achieve the objectives of political and cultural change. In consequence, feminist movements lack the capacity to influence public policies or to contribute to the re-evaluation of democracy. That is to say, 'experts' or lobbyists alone cannot transform demands into public issues. As Guzmán (1996) points out, the stronger and more visible the actors who make demands and push for negotiation, the greater the chances are that the responses will correspond more closely to their original proposals. Fraser (1993) refers to a similar notion when she speaks of the construction of 'oppositional' or subaltern audiences, who inject new cultural and political meanings into public debates. This is an experience that is already underway; it began with the discussions concerning the weaknesses of existing democratic systems and the development of alternative understandings and visions of democracy. The ability to act as an 'oppositional audience' has been one of the most important characteristics of Latin American feminisms, which has allowed their struggles and proposals to become more visible and has opened up a democratic arena *par excellence* in which to project women's interests and desires.

The Peruvian case

The case of Peru reveals in a paradigmatic way the risks and ambiguities contained in the current feminist discourse of rights. Furthermore, the nature of relations between the feminist movement and the government in this country provides a clear example of the tensions affecting feminisms in the region. The Fujimori government, which was indisputably authoritarian, had an increasingly unsustainable record of violations of human and citizens' rights. There is no room here to recount all the details of this lengthy process, so reference will be made only to some of the most flagrant abuses committed. In 1992 Fujimori organised an executive coup backed by the military and, with the support of a civil–military alliance, dissolved Congress, in order to retain power beyond the limits established in the 1979 Constitution. In 1993, during the breakup of his marriage, Fujimori used all the means at his disposal to isolate and publicly humiliate his wife, which provoked the immediate condemnation of feminists. In 1995 he was re-elected president with a huge majority, partly as a result of the crisis affecting the traditional parties and political class. Another decisive factor was his achievement, during his first term in office, of the 'pacification' of Peru and the ending of the internal war that had terrorised the population. This was accomplished at the cost of blatant human rights abuses and a reduction of the autonomy and the appropriation of resources of local authorities, bringing to a halt the process of decentralisation. In 1996 the Constitutional Court, an autonomous supervisory body, was removed by simple decree because some of its members had declared that Fujimori's bid for re-election in the year 2000 was unconstitutional. In 1997 the public learnt of the assassination of a National Intelligence Service (SIN) agent and of the torture which resulted in the physical disablement of Leonor la Rosa, another SIN agent, who denounced the murder and confirmed what was by then public knowledge: that the armed forces were fully committed to guaranteeing Fujimori's permanence in power. The Channel 2 TV station publicly denounced these events, as well as the massive SIN operation to tap the telephone lines of opposition politicians (among them Pérez de Cuellar, formerly Secretary General of the UN and a presidential candidate in Peru). In reprisal, Baruch Ivcher, a major shareholder in Channel 2, was stripped of his Peruvian nationality and had his shares confiscated. At the beginning of 1998 it became known that the state Family Planning Programme was using sterilisation much more widely than any other contraceptive method, especially among rural and indigenous populations. Finally, in mid-1998 the Congress – controlled by a government majority – rejected an initiative presented to call a referendum on whether the president should be allowed to stand for re-election. The initiative is a constitutional right and, in this case, was supported by one and a-half million signatures; that is, 300 000 more than those required. Still, it was ignored.

At the same time, however, during Fujimori's administration 'women's issues' received more attention than at any other time in Peru's history,[14] and he also appointed a record number of women to both political and technical posts in ministries and the state bureaucracy. By 1998, several new state bodies working with and for women had been created: the Ministry of Women and Human Development (PROMUDEH), which included an office dealing with gender issues; the Parliamentary Women's Commission; and the Women's Defensoría (Ombudsman), a subsection of the People's Defensoría (of these three new institutions, only the latter had a clearly democratic structure). The government also set up an advisory committee at ministerial level, which included feminists among its members. In addition, it signed a series of agreements and 'contracts' for the implementation of specific projects with various feminist NGOs, chosen for their proven track record. Many proposals presented by feminist groups were turned into laws or government programmes targeting women. Significant legislative and policy advances were made, such as the law against violence against women and the family planning programme, which was initially supported by feminists. The implementation of this programme led to a head-on confrontation with the church hierarchy.

Given the authoritarian context in which these measures were implemented, it is not surprising that they tended to originate through clientelistic channels, with no established system of consultation with women's organisations, nor that they were applied in a poverty alleviation framework, rather than as part of an egalitarian approach. Many of these new laws and programmes were opportunistically 'adapted' to suit the government's requirements – such as re-election – and also often represented a double-edged sword for women. For example, the changes introduced were frequently so minimal as to have no real effect; laws passed affirming women's rights to control over their own bodies and fertility, were subsequently violated by policies of forced sterilisation (cf. Radcliffe, Chapter 7 this volume); and the laws against domestic violence and in defence of the family in fact ignored existing power relations and restricted women's physical and emotional autonomy. All of this took place within a wider context of minimal conditions of respect for citizens' rights, and maximum exclusion and isolation of 'women's issues' from the construction of democracy.

In the light of these factors, some features of feminist interaction with the government give cause for concern. A study carried out by Rosa María Alfaro for the Calandria Association shows that relations between feminists and the government were generally contractual, clientelistic and personalised, linked to efficiency and to the logic of both the market and international cooperation. The relations established were unstable, lacked continuity, did not constitute strategic agreements and were not underpinned by the feminist organisations' own agendas. In general, the issues varied widely and the initiative was taken by the government (Alfaro 1997). In this context, feminist discourses and proposals tended to become specialised and fragmented. This frequently contributed to the 'depoliticisation' of demands, the disappearance of the feminist agenda and the weakening of the relationship with other women's groupings and social movements. The potential pitfalls were multiplied because there was no discussion of, or answers to, the questions 'how, in what terms, with what tactics, around what outcomes' the strategies *vis-à-vis* the state had been conceived (Pringle and Watson 1994); a situation made even more problematic by the authoritarian context and prevalence of unequal power relations.

It is true that in order to counteract the government's authoritarian policies, Peruvian feminism developed alternative strategies. These included mobilisations, public denunciations, attempted alliances with other democratic forces and the creation of spaces within civil society for collective negotiation, such as the 'broad women's movement' and Women for Democracy, two clearly feminist spaces that included other democratic actors. But these actions were neither constant nor unanimous in their defence of democracy. Some feminist demands, such as those relating to economic justice and sexual rights (in particular abortion and freedom of sexuality) were relegated in the widening process of the re-evaluation of democracy. The changing nature of the links with a debilitated and dispersed popular women's movement was also a feature of the new reality.

Towards the end of the 1990s these factors highlighted the vulnerability of the development of feminism in Peru, and were threatening the rich and varied character of the movement. If feminism lost its explicit commitment to democratic dynamics, it would not only obstruct the expansion of democracy in Peru, but could also halt the progressive acceptance in official arenas of the principle 'right to have rights'. This is because it might be interpreted as feminists only having an interest in 'women's interests'. Similarly it might be used to promote higher levels of female representation and to introduce new legislation, but in a way which could constrain them. It could limit their ability to adopt an autonomous position or demand transparency in political processes, through the establishment of a democratic institutional setting and democratic relations with civil society. Under these conditions, even limited expert support given to government initiatives and women-friendly legislation could, for instance, be interpreted in much broader terms as implying that feminists support the authoritarian government.

Pointers for the future

Feminism was one of the subversive movements to emerge in the twentieth century. Simply by existing, feminisms contributed to democratisation, because they expressed a radical confrontation with the ways and spaces in which power is distributed and exercised in society. The struggle of the feminist movement, and of many others which fought to put an end to exclusion, discrimination and repressive sexual and moral norms, has been described by José Nun (1989) as the rebellion of the chorus: the rebellion 'of those who, by speaking when they are not supposed to and by escaping from the place assigned to the chorus... violate the ritual of discrimination and acceptable behaviour in order to situate themselves at centre stage and demand to be heard.' This rebellion is epitomised, Nun concludes, by the movement for women's liberation.

The achievements of feminism in terms of advancing democracy are many: women have become visible and empowered as social actors; progress has been made in the complex and unfinished process towards the recognition of diversity; society's traditional belief systems have been modified; laws have been passed and the parameters of citizenship have been expanded. However, the most important advance, which underpins and reinforces the successes so far, as well as pointing the way forward, consists in having revealed the dynamic of inclusion and exclusion as an organising principle of power relations within our society. The shift from a needs-based to a rights-based approach, without doubt, played a fundamental role in making this dynamic evident, in widening women's horizons and increasing their levels of autonomy, and in consolidating the gains already made on the threshold of the new millennium.

Nevertheless, it is essential that the struggle for rights acknowledges and incorporates the full diversity of voices, subjects, identities, ethnic groups and spaces where the dynamic of exclusion is still expressed in hidden ways. Citizenship struggles which do not assimilate the experiences and realities of women's daily lives, including issues such as sexual rights, will be unable to subvert current male-biased conceptualisations of citizenship. Those who campaign for political rights while neglecting or ignoring social or cultural rights (for example, economic justice and recognition of both diversity and the power relations that negate it) sustain and legitimise the exclusionary character of existing democracies and formulations of citizenship. For this reason, feminist agendas should not simply limit their struggle to the recognition of rights, but should expand their focus to include citizenship in a broader sense and its relationship to human rights. In addition, they need to be fully aware of the fact that the expansion of women's citizenship cannot be evaluated in isolation, but only in permanent relation to the quality of democracy in the region.

Historically, feminists have engaged in a radical campaign against the subordination and exclusion of women. However, it is increasingly evident that this endeavour is not, nor can it be, separated from other sectors' and movements' democratic struggles for equality within our societies. Consequently, the construction of a 'democratic and feminist pole' within civil society, to advance these efforts and lay the foundations for negotiations with the public, political sphere, is urgently required. In this way it becomes clear that civil society's autonomy *vis-à-vis* the government is precisely what makes its contribution enriching and ensures the creation of strong political, social and economic institutions to control and balance the way public power is exercised in people's lives.

The pursuit of women's rights must therefore be accompanied by a strategic vision of the future in which the autonomy of feminist agendas does not mean defending a discourse and space of their own. Instead autonomy should be seen as the articulation of these agendas with those of other democratic social forces, and the construction of a civil society that contains multiple spaces for reflection and action, in which to process not only what is possible, but also what is desirable. Finally, it is clear that this arena for coalition-building with other movements also represents a 'site of struggle' in which to incorporate the perspective of women's rights into democratic agendas.

Personal political postscript

On 16 September 2000, less than two months after the inauguration of his third period of government in Peru, following a fraudulent electoral process, President Fujimori found himself obliged to call new elections. The long struggle for democracy, national mobilisation and international pressure, in addition to the dictatorial nature of the regime, had together finally provoked results. It was a victory for democracy and a victory for women. In this process of resistance against dictatorship, women played a significant role through various initiatives. One of these, and one which is the most comprehensive and extensive, is the political movement 'Women for Democracy' (Mujeres por la Democracia, MUDE). This is an inclusive and flexible forum, which combined feminist concerns with the struggle for democracy.

From my own personal political viewpoint, MUDE's attempts to link feminist struggles with the construction of democracy highlighted the possibility of articulating a response to the ambivalence that has been part of the feminist struggle for equality in a country like Peru. That is to say, the attainment of citizen's rights for women, as I discussed in the chapter, responds not only to feminist demands but also to our countries' incomplete process of modernity, a process in which women have played a pivotal role. The semblance of a shared rights discourse between the state and feminism manifested its clearest limitations in Peru. With the government's promotion of women's citizenship, particularly its political dimension, came a fundamental contradiction. On one hand the government seemed to encourage state institutions in favour of women and recognition of their citizenship, and on the other hand this 'equality' was being achieved at the cost of women's dignity: rights changed into gifts and charity, and votes were swapped for food or money. We discovered, to our cost, that democracy and citizenship did not necessarily go hand in hand. Without a democratic space, citizens' rights could not be put into practice.

Concern about democracy is not new to feminisms. It has had a substantial impact on their development. However, it came from a different perspective: in the urgent struggle for women's recognition, feminisms adopted the view early on that 'what isn't good for women, isn't good for democracy'. This position was sustained in many painful experiences of exclusion, not only from state politics, but also from different sectors of civil society including those that proposed alternatives to the existing democracies. Our concern with democracy also came about because we knew that we had much to contribute. Our viewpoint proved to be accurate, but insufficient. Inverting the sentence brought with it a turn-around in direction, in the politics of alliances and in the definition of a new centrality to feminist struggles. '*What isn't good for democracy, isn't good for women*' was the phrase that summed up this turnaround and it is the slogan with which MUDE reclaims that intrinsic link between rights and democracy. And even if they are two sides to the same coin, there are moments when the emphasis on one or other dimension can profoundly modify the meaning of feminist struggles: when, as in Peru, what appears to be good for women is not good for democracy. With this shift, there began a constant revision of how the construction and expansion of women's citizenship is not an isolated process but one which develops in permanent relation to the equality of democratic processes.

For me this is 'Women for Democracy'. It constitutes a gamble, a search and a constant entreaty against the temptations of equality which continue to plague feminisms and which, unwittingly, many times have run the risk of giving modernising legitimacy to a dictatorial government.

Lima, September 2000

Notes

1 The author would like to thank Niki Johnson for assisting with style and Anne-Marie Smith for translating the postscript.

2 The 1993 World Conference on Human Rights in Vienna was, without doubt, the 'touchstone' for the consolidation of an integral perspective on rights: it was there that it was recognised that 'women's rights are human rights'. The 1994 World Conference on Population and Development in Cairo progressed further along the same line with the recognition of reproductive rights, thus leaving the door open for the recognition of sexual rights. The 1995 Fourth UN World Conference on Women in Beijing and the parallel NGO Forum reaffirmed this perspective, by incorporating in the Platform for Action a set of recommendations for governments which included proposals presented by global level women's movements.

3 Beginning in 1981, Latin American and Caribbean feminists organised regional 'encounters' (*encuentros*) to discuss the advances made by and the multiple expressions of feminism, and the diversity of the transformational strategies being pursued. The encounter held in Chile in 1996, a year after the Beijing Conference, was especially conflictual and critical of participation in and negotiation with governments. Within the vast heterogeneity of feminism, this encounter revealed the existence of a polarity between one current that defended an autonomy expressed in terms of a discourse and space of its own, and a range of currents that supported the dynamic of dialogue with governments, although the latter differed among themselves with respect to the strategies for negotiation and the contents of the agenda of transformation.

4 Editors' note: this cultural and psychological shift is discussed in relation to reproductive rights in Willmott's Chapter 6.

5 Editors' note: see Chapter 2 by Htun and Jones, and Chapter 4 by Macaulay for further discussion of these issues.

6 Many feminists who used to work, or continue to do so, with the government – either in Women's Offices or in the elaboration of public policies on women – have analysed the tensions that exist between themselves and feminists outside the government. These relate to the lack of mobilisation of support for certain measures, to the differences between the government's and the movement's approaches, and to the issue of representativeness (see e.g. Montaño 1999, Bonder 1995, Valenzuela 1995). It would appear that the possibility of forming a 'triangle of empowerment' between feminists within the state, feminist members of the bureaucracy (femocrats) and feminists in movements, such as has been achieved in many European countries, is a process still underway in Latin America. Its successful completion depends, among other things, on the advance of democratic institutionalisation. On the triangle of empowerment, see Lycklama à Nijeholt, Vargas and Wieringa (1997).

7 Clearly, it is not to be expected that governments will adopt movements' agendas wholesale, nor that the feared cooptation of movements is inevitable. Alvarez (1997) points out that in the interaction with governments, proposals presented by movements or pressure groups undergo a process of partial and selective 'adaptation', according to their interests and political aspirations.

Nevertheless, this adjustment does not mean that movements cannot generate conditions within civil society to exert pressure, with respect to those aspects of the feminist agenda that governments are unwilling to take on.

8 As Evers (1984) pointed out some years ago, this tension does not affect only feminist movements. It has always been a point of conflict within social movements and still complicates the process of defining strategies: social movements are confronted by a choice between either gaining some spaces of power in dominant structures, with the attendant risk of continued subordination, or maintaining an autonomous identity and refusing to negotiate, which carries the risk of remaining weak and marginalised. The challenge lies precisely in finding the strategies that will allow the movement to find a balance between the two extremes.

9 This 'defensive' autonomy was undoubtedly justified during the difficult process of growing as a movement and as individuals, and learning to exist and develop codes of its own. Gramsci (1975) calls this process the 'moment of political rupture'.

10 Editors' note: this multi-faceted negotiation is particularly evident in Chapter 2 by Htun and Jones, Chapter 3 by Friedman, and Chapter 5 by Johnson.

11 These complexities and limitations cannot be attributed solely to problems inherent to feminism. They also correspond to current conditions in which not only governments, but also civil societies, are undergoing changes. Lechner (1997) illustrates these shifts clearly by pointing out how social movements' room for manoeuvre is restricted by transformations in the public and private spheres. As such, economic reforms restrict the government's field of action, and at the same time promote an irresistible tendency towards the privatisation of social behaviour within consumer society, which holds even in the case of marginalised sectors. Individuals evaluate and calculate the time, energies and financial costs of engaging in public activities in a different way. Calls for solidarity become irrelevant unless they take into account this ego-led culture which is suspicious of collective commitments.

12 Editors' note: whilst these tensions are visible in many of the chapters, the difficulties of changing culture, even at the personal level, are highlighted by Radcliffe in Chapter 7 and Willmott in Chapter 6.

13 Editors' note: Gideon (Chapter 8) addresses the difficulties of getting socioeconomic rights onto the political agenda and the limitations of international agreements in this respect.

14 Fujimori was the only president in the world to attend personally the Beijing Conference, where he publicly defended women's right to control their fertility.

Bibliography

Alfaro, Rosa María (1997) *Mundos de Renovación y Trabas para la Acción Pública de la Mujer*, Lima: Calandria Association

Alvarez, Sonia (1997) 'Estrategias democráticas desde la sociedad civil', paper presented at seminar 'Relations between the feminist movement, democracy and the state', Centro Flora Tristán, Lima

Alvarez, Sonia (1998) 'Latin American feminisms "go global": Trends of the 1990s and challenges for the new millenium' in Sonia E. Alvarez, Evelina Dagnino and Arturo Escobar (eds), *Cultures of Politics/Politics of Cultures: Revisioning Latin American Social Movements*, Boulder, Colo.: Westview Press

Barrig, Maruja (1997) 'De Cal y Arena: Ongs y movimiento de Mujeres en Chile' Informe, mimeo

Barrig, Maruja (1998) *El Malestar del Feminismo Latinoamericano: una nueva lectura*, Tiempos Modernos Consultores, Lima

Birgin, Haydee (1997) Report on the seminar 'Citizenship and democracy', Universidad Católica del Perú/Centro Flora Tristán, Lima

Bonder, Gloria (1995) 'La agenda feminista para una política pública' in *Cuadernos de Beijing* Coordinadora Regional de ONGs de América Latina y El Caribe, Lima, Perú

Dagnino, Evelina (1998), 'Culture, citizenship and democracy. Changing discourses and practices of the Latin American Left' in Sonia E. Alvarez, Evelina Dagnino and Arturo Escobar (eds) *Cultures of Politics/Politics of Cultures: Revisioning Latin American Social Movements*, Boulder, Colo.: Westview Press

Evers, Tilman (1984) 'Identidade: A fase oculta o movimientos sociaes' *Novos Estudios*, 2 (4)

Franco, Carlos (1997) 'Una mentira verdadera', *Cuestión de Estado. Ciudadanía en el Perú y ¿detrás de la moda, qué?* 20 (April) Lima: Instituto de Diálogos y Propuestas

Fraser, Nancy (1993) 'Repensar el Ambito Publico: una contribucion a la critica de la democracia realmente existente' in *Debate Feminista* (Mexico) 4 (7) 23–58

Fraser, Nancy and Linda Gordon (1997) 'Contrato versus Caridad. Una reconsideración de la relación entre ciudadanía civil y ciudadanía social' Con/textos # 2. Programa de Estudios de Genero. Pontificia Universidad Católica del Perú. Facultad de Ciencias Sociales. Año 1, No 2. Lima

Gramsci, Antonio (1975) *Notas sobre Machiavello: El Estado y la Política. Análisis de Situación y Relaciones de Fuerza*, Mexico: Ed. Juan Pablos

Guzmán, Virginia (1996) 'La equidad de género como tema de debate y de políticas públicas', in *Encrucijadas del Saber: Los Estudios de Género en las Ciencias Sociales*, Lima: Ed. Pontificia Universidad Católica

Keyser, Loes (1996) 'The costs of the women and health gains at the UN conferences: new challenges for the women's health movement' paper submitted to the 8th International meeting on Health, in Rio de Janiero, Brasil (8va Reunión Internacional de Salud. Rio de Janeiro)

Lechner, Norberto (1996) 'Los límites de la sociedad civil' *Foro*, 26, Bogotá: Ed. Foro Nacional por Colombia

Lechner, Norbert (1997) 'La reforma del Estado entre modernizacion y democratizacion' in *Un Estado para la Democracia*, Instituto de Estudios para la Transicion Democratica, Fundación Federich Evert, Mexico

Lycklama à Nijeholt, Geertjee, Virginia Vargas, Saskia Wieringa (eds) (1997) *Triángulo de Poder*, Bogotá: Ed. Tercer Mundo

Molyneux, Maxine (1998) 'Analysing women's movements' *Development and Change*, 29 (2)

Montaño, Sonia (1999) *Un Cuarto en el Estado. Revista fempress*, Enero 1999

Nun, José (1989) *La Rebelión del Coro*, Buenos Aires: Ed. Nueva Visión

Paoli, María Celia and Vera da Silva Telles (1998) 'Social rights: conflicts and negotiation in contemporary Brazil' in Sonia E. Alvarez, Evelina Dagnino and Arturo Escobar (eds) *Cultures of Politics/Politics of Cultures: Revisioning Latin American Social Movements*, Boulder, Colo.: Westview Press

Phillips, Anne (1993) 'Must feminists give up on liberal democracy?' in David Held (ed.) *Prospects for Democracy. North, South, East, West*, Stanford: Stanford University Press

Pringle, Rosemary and Sophie Watson (1994) 'Women's interests and the post-structuralist state' in Michèle Barret and Anne Phillips (eds) *Destabilizing Theory: Contemporary Feminist Debates*, Cambridge: Polity Press

Shumaher, Shuma and Elizabeth Vargas (1997) 'Lugar En El Gobierno: Alibí O Conquista?' in *Debate Feminista*, (Mexico) 8 (15) 128–45

Tamayo, Giulia (1997) 'La maquinaria estatal: Puede suscitar cambios a favor de las mujeres?' pull-out section from *Socialismo y Participación*, #79. CEDEP, Lima, Perú

Tamayo, Giulia (1998) 'Re-vuelta sobre lo privado/re-creación de lo publico: La aventura inconclusa del feminismo en América Latina' in Cecilia Olea (ed.) *Encuentros, (des) Encuentros y Búsquedas: El Movimiento Feminista en América Latina*, Ediciones s Flora Tristán, Lima

Valenzuela, María Elena (1995) 'La Legitimidad de la Agenda de las Mujeres' in *El Estado y el Movimiento de Mujeres: Retos y Posibilidades. Foro de ONGs sobre la Mujer Beijing 95*, Coordinadora Regional de ONGs de América Latina y El Caribe

Waylen, Georgina (1996) 'Democratization, feminism and the state in Chile: the establishment of SERNAM' in Shirin M. Rai and Geraldine Lievesley (eds) *Women and the State: International Perspectives*, London: Taylor & Francis

Appendix

Table A.1 Selected data on women's status in Latin America 2000

Country	Human development index(a)	Gini coefficient	Gender-related development index(a)	Gender empowerment index(a)	Female GDP per capita	Male GDP per capita	Female EAP (%)	Women in parliaments (%)
Argentina	0.827 (39)	0.46	0.814 (37)	n/a	4,835	15,976	24.9	26.5
Bolivia	0.652 (112)	0.52	0.641 (94)	n/a	1,589	4,187	30.1	11.5
Brazil	0.739 (79)	0.63	0.733 (67)	0.367 (70)	3,813	9,205	25.9	5.7
Chile	0.844 (34)	0.57	0.832 (33)	0.449 (54)	5,853	19,749	32.1	10.8
Colombia	0.768 (57)	0.58	0.765 (51)	0.515 (31)	4,725	8,945	32.1	11.8
Costa Rica	0.801 (45)	0.46	0.795 (42)	0.550 (23)	3,643	9,575	24.1	19.3
Cuba	0.765 (58)	n/a	0.762 (53)	0.556 (21)	2,013	4,181	37.8	22.6
Dominican Republic	0.726 (88)	0.50	0.716 (75)	0.528 (25)	2,374	7,186	26.1	16.1
Ecuador	0.747 (72)	0.53	0.728 (70)	0.516 (29)	1,925	7,927	20.7	14.6
El Salvador	0.674 (107)	0.50	0.667 (89)	0.491 (41)	1,688	4,120	28.9	9.5
Guatemala	0.624 (117)	0.59	0.608 (101)	0.482 (44)	1,861	6,298	20.1	8.8
Honduras	0.641 (114)	0.59	0.631 (98)	0.450 (53)	1,130	3,293	22.7	9.4
Mexico	0.786 (50)	n/a	0.778 (48)	0.511 (33)	4,594	12,216	25.7	16.0
Nicaragua	0.616 (121)	n/a	0.609 (100)	n/a	1,169	2,835	27.3	9.7
Panama	0.791 (49)	0.57	0.786 (47)	0.467 (47)	4,140	10,135	28.8	9.9
Paraguay	0.730 (84)	0.52	0.717 (74)	0.405 (65)	1,918	6,009	22.0	2.5
Peru	0.739 (80)	0.44	0.726 (71)	0.421 (63)	2,335	7,061	22.1	
Uruguay	0.826 (40)	0.42	0.823 (36)	0.441 (56)	6,305	12,275	36.2	12.1
Venezuela	0.792 (48)	0.44	0.786 (46)	0.484 (48)	5,006	12,661	27.2	

Sources: UNDP report *Globalization with a Human Face* except for Gini coefficient which is from Inter-American Development Bank (http://www.iadb.org/int/sta/ENGLISH/staweb/index.htm#bsed) and Women in Parliaments which is from the Interparliamentary Union (http://www.ipu.org/wmn-e/classif.htm).

Index